A WAR NOBODY WON

THE SINO-VIETNAM WAR 1979

A WAR NOBODY WON

THE SINO-VIETNAM WAR 1979

Col Harjeet Singh (Retd)

PENTAGON PRESS

A War Nobody Won: The Sino-Vietnam War 1979
Col Harjeet Singh (Retd)

First Published in 2015
Reprinted July 2016, April 2017

ISBN 978-81-8274-861-3

Published by
PENTAGON PRESS
206, Peacock Lane, Shahpur Jat,
New Delhi-110049
Phones: 011-64706243, 26491568
Telefax: 011-26490600
email: rajan@pentagonpress.in
website: www.pentagonpress.in

Printed at Aegean Offset Printers Greater Noida (U.P.)

CONTENTS

CHINA
LAO PEOPLE'S DEMOCRATIC REPUBLIC
THAILAND
CAMBODIA
NORTHEASTERN
NORTHWESTERN
RED RIVER DELTA
NORTH CENTRAL COAST
SOUTH CENTRAL COAST
CENTRAL HIGHLANDS
SOUTH EASTERN
MEKONG RIVER DELTA
GULF OF TONGKIN
SOUTH CHINA SEA
GULF OF THAILAND
Hainan Dao
HANOI
VIENTIANE
PHNOM PENH
Ho Chi Minh City (Saigon)
Hue
Da Nang
Hai Phong
Cao Bang
Lao Cai
Sa Pa
Lai Chau
Dien Bien Phu
Thai Nguyen
Ha Long (Hong Gai)
Hai Duong
Phu Ly
Nam Dinh
Thai Binh
Ninh Binh
Thanh Hoa
Sam Son
Vinh
Dong Hoi
Quang Tri
Hoi An
Tam Ky
Quang Ngai
Kon Tum
Pleiku
Qui Nhon
Tuy Hoa
Buon Me Thuot
Nha Trang
Da Lat
Cam Ranh
Phan Rang
Phan Thiet
Vung Tau
Bien Hoa
Tay Ninh
An Loc
Phuoc Binh
Chau Phu
Long Xuyen
Rach Gia
Can Tho
My Tho
Tan An
Go Cong
Truc Giang
Khanh Hung
Vinh Loi
Ha Tien
Kampot
Prey Veng
Svay Rieng
Kracheh
Pouthisat
Moung Roessei
Batdambang
Sisophon
Siem Reap
Pakse
Thakhek
Savannakhet
Nong Khai
Udon Thani
Luang Prabang
Sam Nuea
Nanning
Longzhou
Ningming
Qinzhou
Beihai
Zhanjiang
Haikou
Sanya
0 50 100 150 200 km
0 25 50 75 100 mi
VIET NAM
National capital
Major city
Town, village
International boundary
Regional boundary

LIST OF MAPS

LIST OF ILLUSTRATIONS

ABBREVIATIONS

APC	Armoured Personnel Carrier
ASEAN	Association of South Asian Nations
CEMA	Council for Mutual Economic Assistance
CMAG	Chinese Military Advisory Group
CMC	Central Military Commission
CNP	Comprehensive National Power
COSVN	Central Office for South Vietnam
DMZ	Demilitarized Zone
DRV	Democratic Republic of Vietnam
EEZ	Exclusive Economic Zone
ICC	International Control Commission
ICP	Indochinese Communist Party
MACV	United States Military Assistance Command, Vietnam
MR	Military Region
NDC	National Defence Council
NLF	National Liberation Front
NPC	National People's Congress
PAVN	People's Army of Vietnam
PLA	Chinese People's Liberation Army
PLAAF	Chinese People's Liberation Army Air Force
PLAF	People's Liberation Armed Force
PRC	People's Republic of China
PRG	Provisional Revolutionary Government of the Republic of South Vietnam
PRK	People's Republic of Kampuchea
SAM	Surface-to-Air Missile

SRV	Socialist Republic of Vietnam
VCP	Vietnamese Communist Party
VWP	Vietnam Workers' Party
VNQDD	Viet Nam Quoc Dan Dang (Vietnamese Nationalist Party)
UN	United Nations
US	United States of America
USSR	Union of Soviet Socialist Republics

1

INTRODUCTION

Overview

The most unexpected and striking event in Southeast Asia after the American-led war in Vietnam (1957-1975) was the 1979 Sino-Vietnamese conflict. Unprecedented in scale and casualties, the brief Sino-Vietnamese border war in 1979 was the bloodiest military conflict in the 'fraternal' communist world. According to the Chinese, the attack on Vietnam in 1979 was triggered by illicit Vietnamese land grabs of Chinese territory following a strategy of revanche. Apparently, from 25 August to 15 December 1978, Vietnam sent a total of 2,000 armed personnel to invade more than 100 areas of China's Guangxi region, instigating 200 border incidents. However, the actual catalyst was much more involved. Ancient history and ethnic issues all played a part. Yet, it was the broader geopolitical events that really provoked the Chinese. By 1978, Hanoi had completed several agreements with the Soviets, all of which threatened Chinese hegemony in communist East Asia. In reaction, China attacked Vietnam on 17 February 1979.

The Sino-Vietnamese Alliance

In the first half of the 20th century, Vietnamese communists battled against foreign imperialists as a result of their inspiration from the growing world-wide socialist movement. In 1946, they conquered significant territory above the 17th parallel, which effectively divided Vietnam into northern (communist) and southern (capitalist) partitions. The North established Hanoi as its capital while the South ruled from Saigon. In 1957, communist guerrillas from the North began launching attacks on southern villages. The skirmishes at length coalesced into full-scale civil war. China, of course, backed the communists.

In the 1950s and early 1960s, relations between China and Vietnam were reasonably close. To be sure, on 6 February 1950, the Chinese and North Vietnamese formed the Sino-Vietnamese alliance according to which both peoples would follow two broad principles: encouraging true friendship between themselves, and creating a geopolitical bloc to guard against imperialist threats. The 1950 Sino-Vietnamese alliance was just the first of a number of such agreements that Beijing and Hanoi concluded between 1950 and 1965.

> At the end of 1949 Viêt Minh [i.e. North Vietnam] prospects changed dramatically when the Communists won control in China.... The long Chinese-Vietnamese border allowed the People's Republic of China (PRC) to supply the Viêt Minh with arms and equipment and to provide advisers and technicians as well as sanctuaries where the Viêt Minh could train and replenish its troops. On 18 January 1950, the PRC formally recognised the Democratic Republic of Vietnam (DRV) and agreed to furnish it with military assistance.... By the end of 1952, more than 40,000 [northern] enlisted men and 10,000 officers had been trained in China. Arms were also available from the substantial stocks of weapons, including artillery that the United States of America (US) had supplied to the Chinese Nationalists.

While China and Vietnam certainly had good formal relations until 1965, informal cooperation flourished between them as well. Indeed, Beijing staunchly supported Hanoi in its wars of national liberation far beyond what formal agreements mandated. For instance, during the American-led war in Vietnam (1957-1975), China even went so far as to provide the North Vietnamese with materiel and space to shelter troops on Chinese territory.

Collapse of the Sino-Vietnamese Alliance

The collapse of the Sino-Vietnamese alliance can be attributed to five separate but related conditions: ancient animosity, irredentism, Indochina, ethnic conflict and Soviet-Vietnamese relations. While Hanoi had positively cooperated with Beijing for over a decade, by 1965 it began fabricating a new brand of anti-China unilateral politics. Naturally, the Chinese disliked the new outlook in Vietnam and tried to change it. It was in China's political interests to have Vietnam on its side. However, over the next thirteen years, the Sino-Vietnamese alliance would deteriorate in sentiment from affability to antipathy. So badly would the alliance worsen, both sides ultimately resorted to armed conflict to resolve their differences.

The Sino-Vietnamese War of 1979 has been poorly covered in contemporary examinations of Cold War geopolitics. This is not surprising, given the unimagined complexity of the conflict. It features a staggering array of casus belli, turning two countries that had once been staunch allies into overt adversaries for reasons related to contemporary geopolitics, border tensions, refugees, and shared history. Only near the end of the conflict, on 18 March 1979, did China openly list five reasons for its invasion:

(a) Vietnam's hegemonic ambitions;
(b) The refusal of Vietnam to respect Chinese borders;
(c) The mistreatment of ethnic Chinese residing in Vietnam (called the Hoa by the Vietnamese);
(d) The oppression of the Vietnamese people; and
(e) The Soviet Union's attempts to expand its influence in Southeast Asia. (Although there is some truth in this explanation, the reality is a good deal more complicated).

On 17 February 1979, the Chinese People's Liberation Army (PLA) attacked Vietnam across the entire 700-kilometre Sino-Vietnamese border. Twenty-seven days later, on 15 March, after penetrating between 20 and 50 kilometres into Vietnamese territory and fighting several large-scale battles, which resulted in thousands of casualties on both sides, Beijing unilaterally withdrew its forces from all but a handful of contested points along the border.

The aim of the invasion was, in the words of the Chinese leadership, to "teach Vietnam a lesson" it would not soon forget. Despite Beijing's victory claim, defence analysts generally agree that the war did not proceed as well as China had expected and that the PLA performed poorly in the conflict. It was China, not Vietnam, which actually received the lesson. China's documentation on the war remains classified and the information available is not only fragmentary and biased, but also of questionable truth. There are few English language accounts and much of what does exist is full of speculation and inaccuracies.

The conflict expounded Beijing's approach to warfare, showing a distinctive set of Chinese characteristics. The Beijing leadership did not hesitate to use force after carefully calculating when and how to use military power. The underlying aim of the PLA was to seize and maintain the operational initiative; and the primary basis on which the Chinese evaluated military success was geopolitical rather than operational performance. The PLA was roughly handled by the Vietnamese, but accomplished Beijing's strategic goals, diverting Vietnam's attention to the military pressure on its northern border which undercut Vietnam's adventurism in South-East Asia. Yet the PLA failed to preclude lessons learned from the conflict from outdated military philosophy and tradition.

Since the early 1950s China had been a strong political and military supporter of Hanoi, helping Vietnam in its revolutionary struggle against the French and defeat of the American aggressors. Current studies show that China's policy towards Hanoi during the first two Indo-China wars was guided by manifold considerations ranging from historical tradition to revolutionary ideology and national security. Throughout, however, the Chinese sense of superiority dominated their perception of their relationship with Vietnam. Although Chinese leaders made repeated statements that the Vietnamese should be treated as equal, such rhetoric itself reflected their strong belief that they occupied a position from which to dictate the values and codes of behaviour that would dominate their relations with their neighbours. Beijing claimed that it had never imposed political and economic conditions on its vast military and material aid to Hanoi. It wanted Hanoi to recognise China's leading role in the national liberation movement in the region and the world. This Chinese attitude was irritating for the Vietnamese, who were especially sensitive about their problematic past with China. Despite Beijing and Hanoi calling each other "brotherly comrades" at the time, the undertone was the Vietnamese growing aversion to China's modern version of their relationship.

The invasion, which lasted less than a month, was essentially a demonstration of China's determination to oppose Vietnamese and Soviet expansionism and hegemonism in Southeast Asia. Beijing wanted to make it clear to Moscow, Hanoi and the world that it would not stand by and permit Moscow to expand its sphere of influence in the world. In the minds of Chinese leaders, China's credibility as a world power and its legitimacy as the leader of the Third World were at stake. In an attempt to reinforce its credibility and in the hope of modifying Vietnamese behaviour, China engaged in a manner of diplomacy such as it has employed on several occasions in the past, going back to the Korean War.

Students of Chinese and Vietnamese history point out that there was a long history of conflict between these two countries. At times of internal weakness in China, Vietnam has traditionally tossed off the bonds of a tributary state and expanded its own empire within the region known as Indochina. After consolidating its affairs under a new dynasty, China would respond by sending out expeditionary armies to reassert its suzerainty over its independent-minded southern neighbour. This historical process has led many analysts to adopt a narrative to explain the dynamics of this relationship. Vietnam is seen as an inherently virile, expansionist military state. China is labelled a Confucian "father state" seeking always to re-establish moral harmony between tributary buffer states and the "Middle Kingdom."

The temptation to reduce contemporary Sino-Vietnamese relations to this kind of narrative is strong, but doing so obscures the many complex variables that are actually at work. The historical traditions no doubt colour the perceptions of Chinese and Vietnamese leaders but they are not completely deterministic. In the case of the 1979 invasion of Vietnam by China, the variables which influenced Chinese and Vietnamese decision-makers appear to be more closely related to contemporary international political realities than to traditional trends. Indeed, it can be argued that China and Vietnam have acted in much the same manner that any nation in similar circumstances might have acted.

Never before had a socialist fraternal country launched a war against another as China did against Vietnam in 1979. The Soviet intervention in Hungary of 1956 was executed in the name of the Warsaw Pact forces under the "agreement" of the Pact members of which Hungary was one. The Soviet invasion of Czechoslovakia in 1968 was carried out in a similar fashion. China and Vietnam concluded no military agreement similar to the Warsaw Pact, nor had Vietnam "agreed" to China's military attacks. China's war with Vietnam was truly an unusual development in the Communist world and, for that reason alone bears greater scrutiny.

Ho Chi Minh had repeatedly stated that China and Vietnam were comrades and brothers. As Marxist comrades, both sides were supposed to settle their disputes in a consultative and persuasive attitude along the party line and the Marxist theory. As oriental brothers, they were to resolve their problems in a spirit of brotherhood or in accordance with the principle of reward and punishment for the maintenance of the family's relations. In this context, the "punitive" war against Vietnam was an action based more on traditional Chinese mentality and moral norms than on Marxist doctrine.

The Root Causes of Sino-Vietnamese War, 1979

China and Vietnam has been viewed as allies in the wars that Vietnam fought with France and the United States, in the decades after the end of the Second World War, till the early 1970s. During the war with the United States, China along with Soviet Union was considered the most ardent allies of Vietnam. However, the relationship between China and Vietnam soured over their different relationships with the Soviet Union. In the late 1960s, Vietnam became an ally of the Soviet Union, and was perceived to be much closer to it than with China. This upset China a great deal. Despite the fact that both China and Soviet Union shared a common ideology in Communism, they viewed one another as adversaries. In fact, in 1969, a nuclear confrontation between China and the Soviet Union was almost exercised, marking the worst situation in their relationship.

Relations between Vietnam and China had been steadily declining since 1975:

- In September 1975, China refused to grant Vietnam the amount of aid it had requested.
- In October 1975, Vietnam's Party Secretary Le Duan travelled to

Moscow where he obtained considerable Soviet aid and where he endorsed Soviet foreign policy positions.

- By December 1975, the Soviets were involved in assisting Vietnam with some 40 economic projects.
- Throughout 1977 and much of 1978, border clashes took place between Vietnamese troops and the troops of the Beijing-backed Khmer Rouge government of Democratic Kampuchea—the Pol Pot government.
- In March 1978, the Vietnamese government decided to nationalise private trade throughout the country. This action most affected the Chinese merchant class, resulting in a mass exodus from the country of overseas Chinese.
- In June 1978, Vietnam joined the Council for Mutual Economic Assistance (CEMA), the Soviet-bloc economic and trade association (earlier known as COMECON).
- In November 1978, Vietnam and the USSR signed a treaty of friendship and cooperation.
- In December 1978, Hanoi announced the formation of a "National Front" in Cambodia, signalling an intention to invade that country.

What took place between 1975 and 1978 was a steady withdrawal of Vietnam from China's sphere of influence. To the Chinese, who had firmly supported North Vietnam during its war with the US, this behaviour was an insult, resulting in loss of face and loss of prestige in the region. Also influencing this tense situation was the thawing of relations between the United States and China during the Carter administration. Beijing's new posture was that the Soviet Union—and not the US—was the principal threat to world security. As relations between Hanoi and Beijing worsened, the Chinese could not prevent the Vietnamese from moving into the Soviet sphere, and this was a direct affront to China's foreign policy objectives.

There is reason to believe that both parties would have preferred a resolution of differences to an outright break in relations. This view is supported by Chinese Vice-Premier Deng Xiao Peng's statements to the press in June 1978, when he portrayed Vietnam's actions as a series of "10 steps" against China. According to Deng, only when Hanoi took the "11th step"—the expulsion of overseas Chinese—had the situation reached a turning point. It was at this time that the Chinese leaders began to warn that Hanoi must be, in their words, "punished." Deng further stated that unless Hanoi moderated its policy on ethnic Chinese, Beijing would retaliate. China subsequently ordered three Vietnamese consulates located in South China closed, and began small-scale military manoeuvres near the Vietnamese border.

Following the Vietnamese invasion of Cambodia, which was a close ally of China, on Christmas day of 1978, war between Vietnam and China was recognised to be ineluctable. As predicted, the war broke out after Vietnam occupied Cambodia in January 1979. The causes for the breakout of the Sino-Vietnam war can be seen in three main facets:

(a) Deng Xiaoping was the paramount leader of China at that time. Since the start of his administration, it was generally seen that the foreign policy of China became more assertive than previous Chinese leaders. Lack of trust in the Sino-Vietnamese relation was a striking feature of the prevailing political situation and these two countries were constantly hostile to each other. The aim of Deng was to contain the Vietnamese and Soviet Union's action in Indochina. Moreover, as one of the communist leaders to support Vietnam in the war against France, and later against the US, Deng regarded the Vietnamese act of befriending the Soviet Union as a betrayal of their largesse. This relationship was exacerbated by the Vietnamese invasion of Cambodia. Certainly, the decision to launch an attack on Vietnam was initiated by Deng at a meeting of the Central Military Commission (CMC) that he had convened.

(b) It is widely believed that Deng formally proposed a punitive war against Vietnam at the CMC conference on New Year's Eve. The decision to attack Vietnam was not generally opposed, given the prestige and senior position of Deng in the party as well as in the State Council.

(c) The hatred held by Deng against Vietnam was discernible in his three-country trip to Thailand, Malaysia, and Singapore. During this trip, the paramount Chinese leader kept reiterating that Beijing would attack Vietnam if it invaded Cambodia.

> Importantly, the Association of South Asian Nations (ASEAN) displayed grave opposition towards such a Vietnamese act. Notably, it was on Christmas Day 1978 that Vietnam launched its attack on Cambodia before its occupation in January 1979. Following the invasion, China immediately attacked Vietnam in February 1979.

At the first glance, the escalation of military clash between China and Vietnam seemed to be a territorial dispute. However, this does not adequately explain the relationship if China's actions are examined more deeply. In fact, it was the concern of China over Soviet Union expansion that served as the prime source of motives for China to wage war against Vietnam.

In the wake of the Cold War era, China did not view the world in bipolar fashion, rather the Beijing administration averred that the world was divided into three power blocs, which included China herself leading the third world in another bloc aside from the US and the Soviet Union.

China also claimed that there was possibility of the outbreak of the World War III, citing that the Soviet Union were spoiling for a fight and China herself was also in preparation for war against the Soviet Union. Thereafter, the relationship between the Soviet Union and China increasingly deteriorated. The Chinese, convinced that the Soviet Union was using Vietnam to increase its presence on China's southern flank, refused to accept Vietnamese domination of Cambodia as they viewed it as a threat to the national security and national interest of China. In light of this, Beijing had to support the Khmer Rouge and attack Vietnam to ensure that the latter withdrew from Cambodia.

Also, on 23 March 1978, Chinese business and industry were seized by the Vietnamese authority and nationalised. This fact, coupled with the Vietnamese invasion of Cambodia provided China with a view that Hanoi had decided to confront with China. In response, China regarded Vietnam not just as ungrateful but was behaving in an extremely provocative manner. Beijing needed to do something, to teach Vietnam a lesson, to exhibit her military might, and to show its fraternity with its ally—Cambodia— while also exposing the weakness of Soviet Union. Thus, the path to war was intensified, and escalation was inevitable.

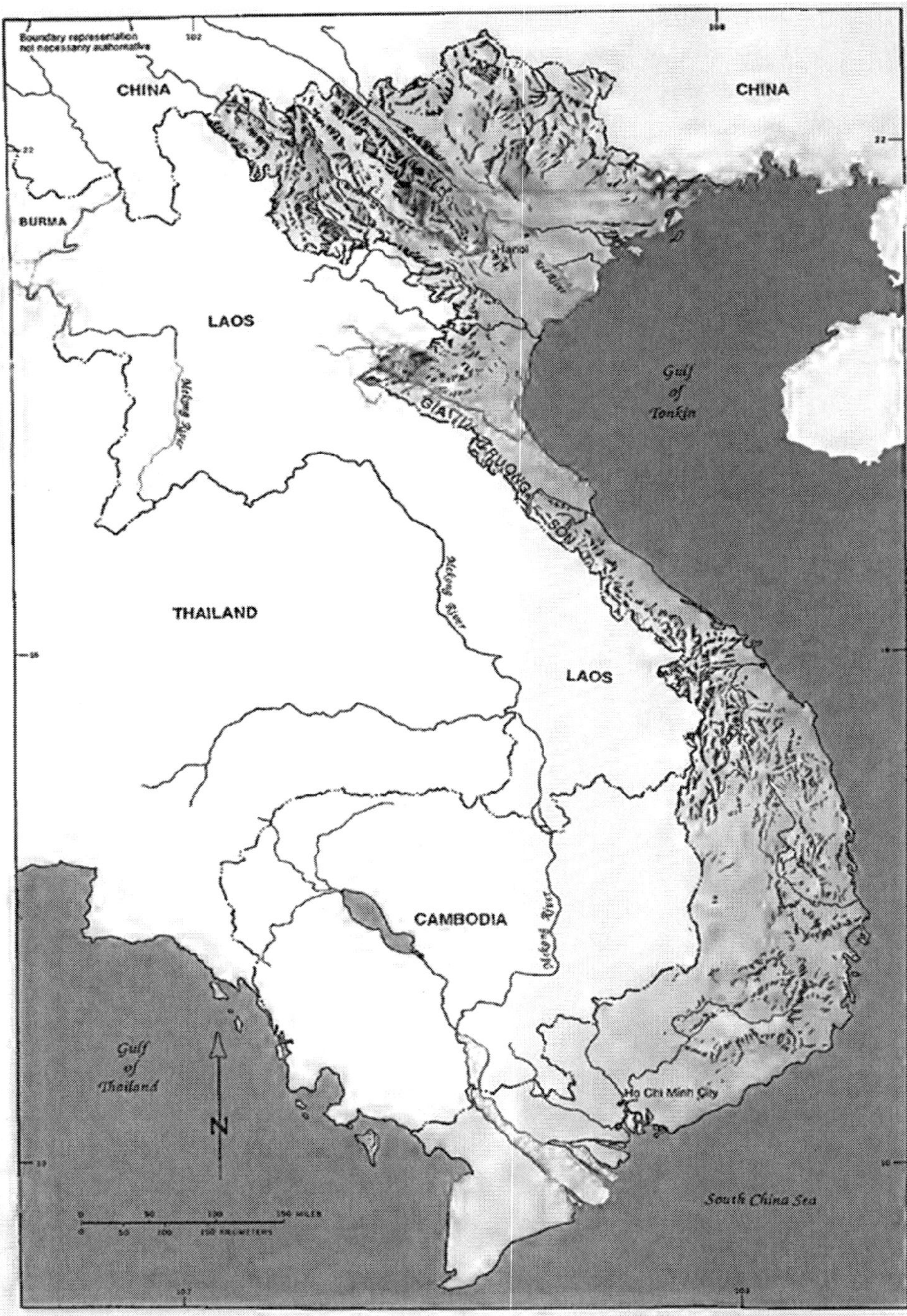

Map 1: Geography of Vietnam

2

GEOGRAPHY OF VIETNAM

Vietnam is located in the south-eastern extremity of the Indochinese peninsula and occupies about 331,688 square kilometres. The S-shaped country has a north-to-south distance of 1,650 kilometres and is about 50 kilometres wide at the narrowest point. Its land boundaries extend 4,639 kilometres with its border countries being Cambodia (1,228 kilometres), China (1,281 kilometres) and Laos (2,130 kilometres).

The boundary with Laos, settled, on an ethnic basis, between the rulers of Vietnam and Laos in the mid-seventeenth century was formally defined by a delimitation treaty signed in 1977 and ratified in 1986. The frontier with Cambodia, defined at the time of French annexation of the western part of the Mekong River Delta in 1867, remained essentially unchanged, according to Hanoi, until some unresolved border issues were finally settled in the 1982-85 period. The land and sea boundary with China, delineated under the France-China treaties of 1887 and 1895, is the frontier line accepted by Hanoi that China agreed in 1957-58 to respect.

Vietnam is a country of tropical lowlands, hills, and densely forested highlands, with level land covering no more than 20 percent of the area. The country is divided into the highlands and the Red River Delta in the north; and the Giai Truong Son (Central mountains), the coastal lowlands, and the Mekong River Delta in the south.

The Red River Delta, a flat, triangular region of 3,000 square kilometres, is smaller but more intensely developed and more densely populated than the Mekong River Delta. Once an inlet of the Gulf of Tonkin, it has been filled in by the enormous alluvial deposits of the rivers, over a period of millennia.

The Red River (*Song Hong* in Vietnamese), rising in China's Yunnan Province, is about 1,200 kilometres long. Its two main tributaries, the Song Lo (Clear River) and the Song Da (Black River), contribute to its high water volume, which averages 500 million cubic metres per second, but may increase by more than 60 times at the peak of the rainy season. The entire delta region, backed by the steep rises of the forested highlands, is no more than three metres above sea level, and much of it is one metre or less. The area is subject to frequent flooding; at some places the high-water mark of floods is 14 metres above the surrounding countryside. For centuries flood control has been an integral part of the delta's culture and economy. An extensive system of dikes and canals has been built to contain the Red River and to irrigate the rich rice-growing delta. Modelled on that of China, this ancient system has sustained a highly concentrated population and has made double-cropping wet-rice cultivation possible throughout about half the region.

The highlands and mountain plateaus in the north and northwest are inhabited mainly by tribal minority groups. The Giai Truong Son originates in the Tibet and Yunnan regions of southwest China and forms Vietnam's border with Laos and Cambodia. It terminates in the Mekong River Delta north of Ho Chi Minh City (formerly Saigon).

These central mountains, which have several high plateaus, are irregular in elevation and form. The northern section is narrow and very rugged; the country's highest peak, Fan Si Pan, rises to 3,142 metres in the extreme northwest. The southern portion has numerous spurs that divide the narrow coastal strip into a series of compartments. For centuries these topographical features not only rendered north-south communication difficult but also formed an effective natural barrier for the containment of the people living in the Mekong basin.

Within the southern portion of Vietnam is a plateau known as the Central Highlands (*Tay Nguyen*), approximately 51,800 square kilometres of rugged mountain peaks, extensive forests, and rich soil. Comprising five relatively flat plateaus of basalt soil spread over the provinces of Dac Lac and Gia Lai-Kon Turn, the highlands account for 16 percent of the country's arable land and 22 percent of its total forested land. Before 1975 North Vietnam had maintained that the Central Highlands and the Giai Truong Son were strategic areas of paramount importance, essential to the domination not only of South Vietnam but also of the southern part of Indochina. Since 1975 the highlands have provided an area in which to relocate people from the densely populated lowlands.

The narrow, flat coastal lowlands extend from south of the Red River Delta to the Mekong River basin. On the landward side, the Giai Truong Son rises precipitously above the coast, its spurs jutting into the sea at several places. Generally the coastal strip is fertile and rice is cultivated intensively.

The Mekong, which is 4,220 kilometres long, is one of the 12 great rivers of the world. From its source in the Tibetan plateau, it flows through the Tibet and Yunnan regions of China, forms the boundary between Laos and Burma as well as between Laos and Thailand, divides into two branches—the Song Han Giang and Song Tien Giang—below Phnom Penh, and continues through Cambodia and the Mekong basin before draining into the South China Sea through nine mouths or *cuu long* (nine dragons). The river is heavily silted and is navigable by seagoing craft of shallow draft as far as Kompong Cham in Cambodia. A tributary entering the river at Phnom Penh drains the Tonle Sap, a shallow freshwater lake that acts as a natural reservoir to stabilise the flow of water through the lower Mekong. When the river is in flood stage, its silted delta outlets are unable to carry off the high volume of water. Floodwaters back up into the Tonle Sap, causing the lake to inundate as much as 10,000 square kilometres. As the floods subside, the flow of water reverses and proceeds from the lake to the sea. The effect is to reduce significantly the danger of devastating floods in the Mekong delta, where the river floods the surrounding fields each year to a level of one to two metres.

The Mekong delta, covering about 40,000 square kilometres, is a low-level plain not more than three metres above sea level at any point and criss-crossed by a maze of canals and rivers. So much sediment is carried by the Mekong's various branches and tributaries that the delta advances sixty to eighty metres into the sea every year. It is estimated that the amount of sediment deposited annually to be about 1 billion cubic metres, or nearly 13 times the amount deposited by the Red River. About 10,000 square kilometres of the delta are under rice cultivation, making the area one of the major rice-growing regions of the world. The southern tip, known as the Ca Mau Peninsula, is covered by dense jungle and mangrove swamps.

Vietnam has a tropical monsoon climate, with humidity averaging 84 percent throughout the year. However, because of differences in latitude and the marked variety of topographical relief, the climate tends to vary considerably from place to place. During the winter or dry season, extending roughly from November to April, the monsoon winds usually blow from the northeast along the China coast and across the Gulf of Tonkin, picking up considerable moisture; consequently the winter season in most parts of the country is dry only by comparison with the rainy or summer season. During the south-westerly summer monsoon, occurring from May to October, the heated air of the Gobi Desert rises, far to the north, inducing moist air to flow inland from the sea and deposit heavy rainfall.

Annual rainfall is substantial in all regions and torrential in some, ranging from 120 centimetres to 300 centimetres. Nearly 90 percent of the precipitation occurs during the summer. The average annual temperature is generally higher in the plains than in the mountains and plateaus. Temperatures range from a low of 5°C in December and January, the coolest months, to more than 37°C in April, the hottest month.

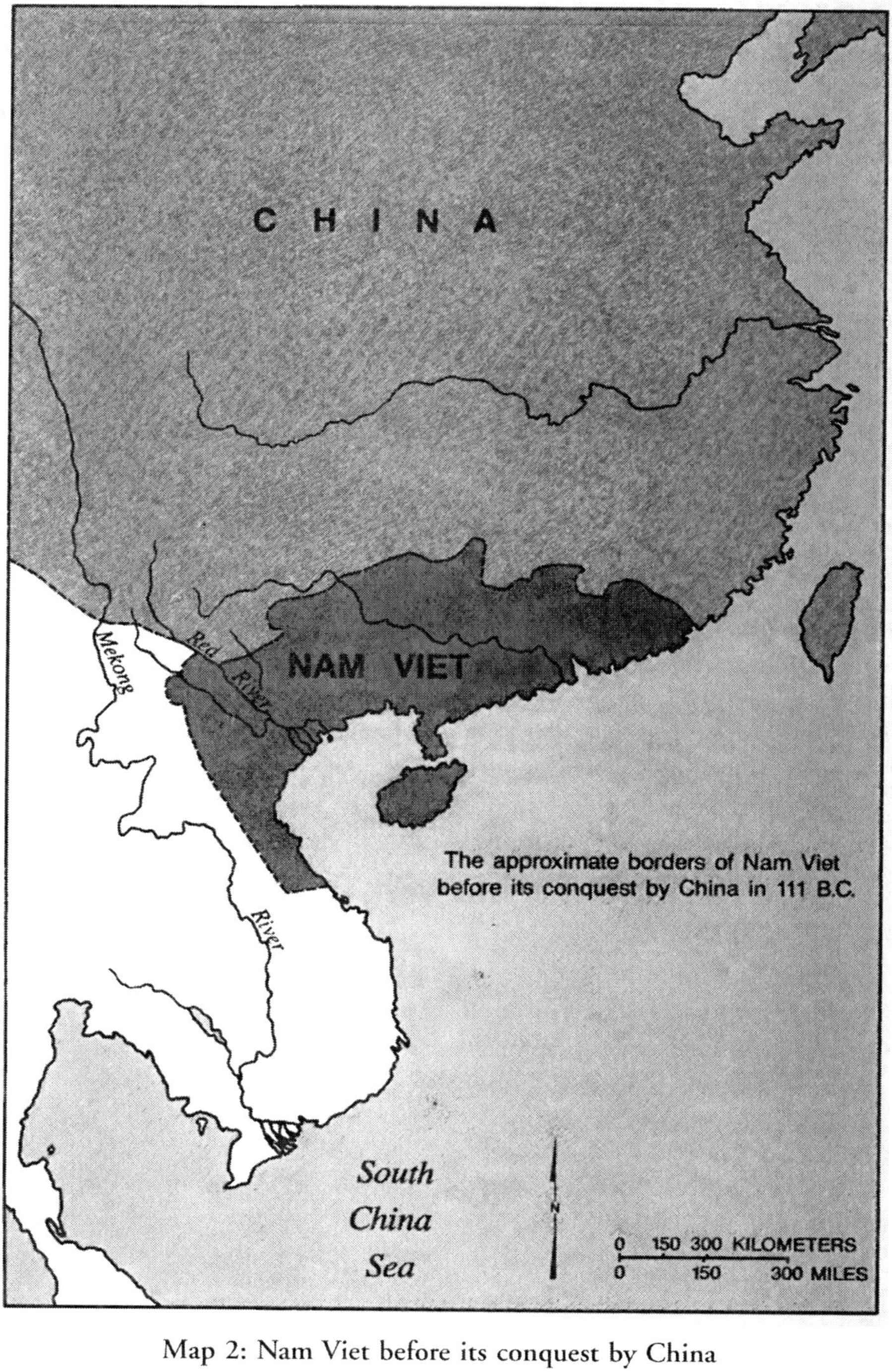

Map 2: Nam Viet before its conquest by China

3

HISTORY OF VIETNAM

Historical Setting

The Vietnamese people represent a fusion of races, languages, and cultures, the elements of which are still being sorted out by ethnologists, linguists, and archaeologists. As was true for most areas of Southeast Asia, the Indochina Peninsula was a crossroads for many migrations of peoples.

The Vietnamese trace the origins of their culture and nation to the fertile plains of the Red River Delta in northern Vietnam. After centuries of developing a civilisation and economy based on the cultivation of irrigated rice, the Vietnamese began expanding southward in search of new rice growing areas. Moving down the narrow coastal plain of the Indochina Peninsula, through conquest and pioneering settlement they eventually reached and occupied the broad Mekong River Delta. Vietnamese history is the story of the struggle to develop a sense of nationhood throughout this narrow 1,500-kilometre stretch of land and to maintain it against internal and external pressures.

The first major threat to Vietnam's existence as a separate people and nation was the conquest of the Red River Delta by the Chinese, under the Han dynasty (206 B.C.-A.D. 220), in the second century B.C. At that time, and in later centuries, the expanding Chinese empire assimilated a number of small bordering nations politically and culturally. Although

Vietnam spent 1,000 years under Chinese rule, it succeeded in throwing off the yoke of its powerful neighbour in the tenth century.

The Chinese Millennium

Vietnamese historians regard Trieu Da as a defender of their homeland against an expanding Han empire. In 111 B.C., however, the Chinese armies of Emperor Wu Di defeated the successors of Trieu Da and incorporated Nam Viet into the Han Empire. The Chinese were anxious to extend their control over the fertile Red River Delta, in part to serve as a convenient supply point for Han ships engaged in the growing maritime trade with India and Indonesia.

During the first century of Chinese rule, Vietnam was governed leniently, and the Lac lords maintained their feudal offices. In the first century A.D., however, China intensified its efforts to assimilate its new territories by raising taxes and instituting marriage reforms aimed at turning Vietnam into a patriarchal society more amenable to political authority. In response to increased Chinese domination, a revolt broke out in Giao Chi, Cuu Chan, and Nhat Nam in A.D. 39, led by Trung Trac, the wife of a Lac lord who had been put to death by the Chinese, and her sister Trung Nhi. The insurrection was put down within two years by the Han general Ma Yuan, and the Trung sisters drowned themselves to avoid capture by the Chinese. Still celebrated as heroines by the Vietnamese, the Trung sisters exemplify the relatively high status of women in Vietnamese society as well as the importance to Vietnamese of resistance to foreign rule.

Following the ill-fated revolt, Chinese rule became more direct. Ma Yuan established a Chinese-style administrative system of three prefectures and fifty six districts ruled by scholar-officials sent by the Han court. Although Chinese administrators replaced most former local officials, some members of the Vietnamese aristocracy were allowed to fill lower positions in the bureaucracy. The Vietnamese elite in particular received a thorough indoctrination in Chinese cultural, religious, and political traditions. One result of Sinicization, however, was the creation of a Confucian bureaucratic, family, and social structure that gave the Vietnamese the strength to resist Chinese political domination in later centuries, unlike most of the other Yue peoples who were sooner or later assimilated into the Chinese cultural and political world. Nor was Sinicization so total as to erase the memory of pre-Han Vietnamese culture, especially among the peasant class, which retained the Vietnamese language and many Southeast Asian customs. Chinese rule had the dual effect of making the Vietnamese aristocracy more receptive to Chinese culture and cultural leadership while at the same time instilling resistance and hostility toward Chinese political domination throughout Vietnamese society.

Chinese Cultural Impact

In order to facilitate administration of their new territories, the Chinese built roads, waterways, and harbours, largely with unpaid labour. Agriculture was improved with better irrigation methods and the use of ploughs and draft animals, innovations which may have already been in use by the Vietnamese on a lesser scale. New lands were opened up for agriculture, and settlers were brought in from China. After a few generations, most of the Chinese settlers probably inter-married with the Vietnamese and identified with their new homeland.

The first and second centuries A.D. saw the rise of a Han-Viet ruling class owning large tracts of rice lands. More than 120 brick Han tombs have been excavated in northern Vietnam, indicating Han families that, rather than returning to China, had become members of their adopted society and were no longer, strictly speaking, Chinese. Although they brought Chinese vocabulary and technical terms into their new culture, after a generation or two, they probably spoke Vietnamese.

The second century A.D. was a time of rebellion in Giao Chi, Cuu Chan, and Nhat Nam, largely due to the declining quality of the Han administrators, who concentrated their energies on making their fortunes and returning north as soon as possible. Revolts against corrupt and repressive Chinese officials were often led by the Han-Viet families. The fall of the Han dynasty in China in 220 A.D. further strengthened the allegiance of the Han-Viet ruling elite to their new society and gave them a sense of their own independent political power. Meanwhile, among the peasant class there was also a heightened sense of identity fostered by the spread of Buddhism by sea from India to Vietnam by the early third century. The new religion was often adapted to blend with indigenous religions. Buddhist temples were sometimes dedicated to the monsoon season, for example, or identified with the guardian spirit of agricultural fertility. Although ruling-class Vietnamese tended to cling to Confucianism, various local rulers patronised the Buddhist religion, thus helping to legitimize their own rule in the eyes of the common people.

After the demise of the Han dynasty, the period of the third to the sixth century was a time of turbulence in China, with six different dynasties in succession coming to power. The periods between dynasties or the periods, when dynasties were weak in China, were usually the most peaceful in Vietnam. When dynasties were strong and interfered with local rule, the Vietnamese aristocracy engaged in a series of violent revolts that weakened China's control over its southern territory. A rebellion led by the noblewoman Trieu Au (Lady Trieu) in A.D. 248 was suppressed after about six months, but its leader earned a place in the hearts and history of the Vietnamese people. Despite pressure to accept Chinese patriarchal values, Vietnamese women continued to play an important role and to enjoy considerably more freedom than their northern counterparts.

Political Resistance to the Chinese

The sixth century was an important stage in the Vietnamese political evolution toward independence. During this period, the Vietnamese aristocracy became increasingly independent of Chinese authority, while retaining Chinese political and cultural forms. At the same time, indigenous leaders arose who claimed power, based on Vietnamese traditions of kingship. A series of failed revolts in the late sixth and early seventh centuries increased the Vietnamese national consciousness. Ly Bi, the leader of a successful revolt in against the Liang dynasty (502-556), was himself descended from a Chinese family that had fled to the Red River Delta during a period of dynastic turbulence in the first century A.D. Ly Bi declared himself emperor of Nam Viet in the tradition of Trieu Da and organised an imperial court at Long Bien (in the vicinity of Hanoi). Ly Bi was killed in 547, but his followers kept the revolt alive for another fifty years, establishing what is sometimes referred to in Vietnamese history as the earlier Ly dynasty.

While the Ly family retreated to the mountains and attempted to rule in the style of their Chinese overlords, a rebel leader who based his rule on an indigenous form of kingship arose in the Red River Delta. Trieu Quang Phuc made his headquarters on an island in a vast swamp. From this refuge, he could strike without warning, seizing supplies from the Liang army and then slipping back into the labyrinthine channels of the swamp. Despite the initial success of such guerrilla tactics, by which he gained control over the Red River Delta, Trieu Quang Phuc was defeated by 570. According to a much later Vietnamese revolutionary, General Vo Nguyen Giap, Vietnamese concepts of protracted warfare were born in the surprise offensives, night attacks, and hit-and-run tactics employed by Trieu Quang Phuc.

The Chinese Tang dynasty (618-907) instituted a series of administrative reforms culminating in 679 in the reorganisation of Vietnamese territory as the Protectorate of Annam (or Pacified South), a name later used by the French to refer to central Vietnam. The Tang dynastic period was a time of heavy Chinese influence, particularly in Giao Chau Province, which included the densely populated Red River plain. The children of ambitious, aristocratic families acquired a classical Confucian education, as increased emphasis was placed on the Chinese examination system for training local administrators. As a result, literary terms dating from the Tang dynasty constitute the largest category of Chinese words in modern Vietnamese. Despite the stress placed on Chinese literature and learning, Vietnamese, enriched with Chinese literary terms, remained the language of the people, while Chinese was used primarily as an administrative language by a small elite. During the Tang era, Giao Chau Province also became the centre of a popular style of Buddhism based on spirit cults, which evolved as the dominant religion of Vietnam after the tenth century. Buddhism, along with an expanding sea trade, linked Vietnam more closely with South and Southeast Asia as Buddhist pilgrims travelled to India, Sumatra, and Java aboard merchant vessels laden with silk, cotton, paper, ivory, pearls, and incense.

As Tang imperial power became more corrupt and oppressive during the latter part of the dynasty, rebellion flared increasingly, particularly among the minority peoples in the mountain and border regions. Although the Viet culture of Giao Chau Province, as it developed under Tang hegemony, depended upon Chinese administration to maintain order, there was growing cultural resistance to the Tang in the border regions. A revolt among the Muong people, who are closely related to the central Vietnamese, broke out in the early eighth century. The rebels occupied the capital at Tong Binh (Hanoi), driving out the Tang governor and garrison, before being defeated by reinforcements from China. Some scholars mark this as the period of final separation of the Muong peoples from the central Vietnamese, which linguistic evidence indicates took place near the end of the Tang dynasty. In the mid-ninth century, Tai minority rebels in the border regions recruited the assistance of Nan-chao, a Tai mountain kingdom in the southern Chinese province of Yunnan, which seized control of Annam in 862. Although the Tang succeeded in defeating the Nan-chao forces and restoring Chinese administration, the dynasty was in decline and no longer able to dominate the increasingly autonomous Vietnamese. The Tang finally collapsed in 907 and by 939 Ngo Quyen, a Vietnamese general, had established himself as king of an independent Vietnam.

Nine Centuries of Independence

The most serious foreign policy problem for the Nguyen rulers, however, was dealing with France through the French traders, missionaries, diplomats, and naval personnel who came in increasing numbers to Vietnam. The influence of missionaries was perceived as the most critical issue by the court and scholar-officials. The French reported 450,000 Christian converts in Vietnam in 1841. The Vietnamese Christians were for the most part organised into villages that included all strata of society, from peasants to landowners. The Christian villages, with their own separate customs, schools, and hierarchy, as well as their disdain for Confucianism, were viewed by the government as breeding grounds for rebellion—and in fact they often were. The French presence did, however, enjoy some support at high levels. There were also members of the Vietnamese court who urged the monarchy to undertake a certain degree of westernisation and reform in order to strengthen itself in the areas of administration, education, and defence. In the southern part of the country, Christians enjoyed the protection of Viceroy Le Van Duyet until his death in 1832. Soon thereafter the Nguyen government began a serious attempt

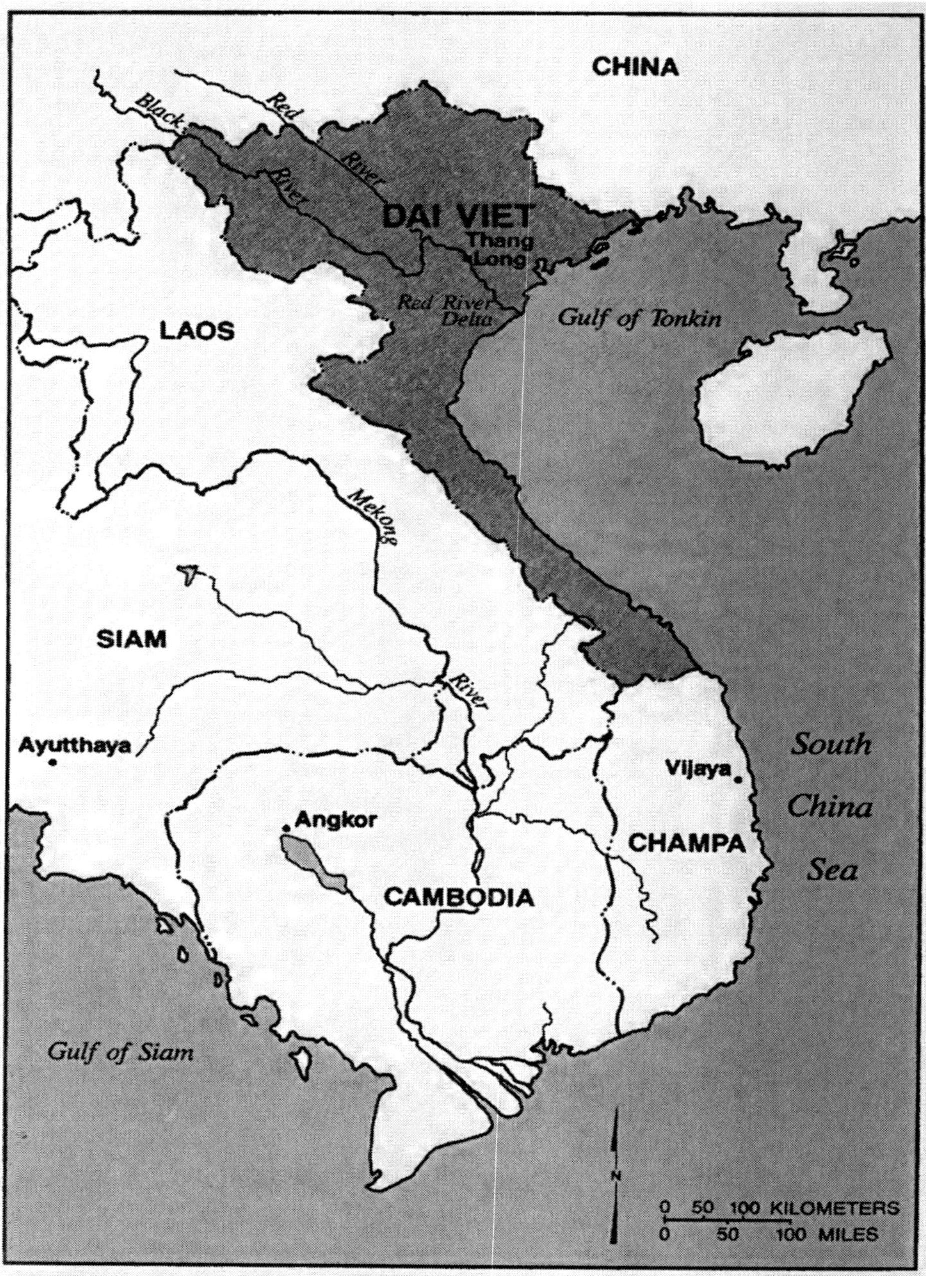

Map 3: Vietnam in 1350 A.D.

to rid itself of French missionaries and their influence. A series of edicts forbade the practice of Christianity, forcing the Christian communities underground. A number of priests and members of the laity were executed by the Vietnamese during the following quarter of a century.

In response, the missionaries stepped up their pressure on the French government to intervene militarily and to establish a French protectorate over Vietnam. During this period, French traders became interested in Vietnam once more, and French diplomats in China began to express the view that France was falling behind the rest of Europe in gaining a foothold in Asia. Commanders of a French naval squadron, permanently deployed in the South China Sea after 1841, also began to agitate for a stronger role in protecting the lives and interests of the missionaries. Given tacit approval by Paris, naval intervention grew steadily. In 1847 two French warships bombarded Tourane (Da Nang), destroying five Vietnamese ships and killing an estimated 10,000 Vietnamese. The purpose of the attack was to gain the release of a missionary, who had, in fact, already been released. In the following decade, persecution of missionaries continued under Emperor Tu Due, who came to the throne in 1848. While the missionaries stepped up pressure on the government of Napoleon III, which was sympathetic to their cause, a Commission on Cochinchina made the convincing argument that France risked becoming a second-class power by not intervening.

Under French Rule

By 1857 Napoleon III had been persuaded that invasion was the best course of action, and French warships were instructed to take Tourane without any further efforts to negotiate with the Vietnamese. Tourane was captured in late 1858 and Gia Dinh (Saigon and later Ho Chi Minh City) in early 1859. In both cases Vietnamese Christian support for the French, predicted by the missionaries, failed to materialise. Vietnamese resistance and outbreaks of cholera and typhoid forced the French to abandon Tourane in early 1860. Meanwhile, fear was growing in Paris that if France withdrew the British would move in. Also current in Paris at that time was the reasoning that France had a civilising mission—a duty to bring the benefits of its superior culture to the less fortunate lands of Asia and Africa. (This was a common justification for the colonial policies of most of the Western countries.) Meanwhile, French business and military interests increased their pressure on the government for decisive action. Thus in early 1861, a French fleet of 70 ships and 3,500 men reinforced Gia Dinh and, in a series of bloody battles, gained control of the surrounding provinces. In June 1862, Emperor Tu Due, signed the Treaty of Saigon agreeing to French demands for the cession of three provinces around Gia Dinh (which the French had renamed Saigon) as well as for the opening of three ports to trade, free passage of French warships up the Mekong to Cambodia, freedom of action for the missionaries, and payment of a large indemnity to France for its losses in attacking Vietnam.

Even the French were surprised by the ease with which the Vietnamese agreed to the humiliating treaty. Why, after successfully resisting invasions by the Chinese for the previous 900 years, did the monarchy give in so readily to French demands? Aside from the seriousness of the loss of Saigon and the possible over-estimation of French strength, it appears that the isolation of the monarchy from the people created by decades of repression prevented Tu Due and his court from attempting to rally the necessary popular support to drive out the French. In fact, by placating the French in the south, Tu Due hoped to free his forces to put down a widespread Christian-supported rebellion in Bac Bo, which he indeed crushed by 1865. French missionaries, who had urged their government to support this rebellion, were disillusioned when it did not, especially after thousands of Christians were slaughtered by Tu Due's forces following the rebellion. The missionaries, however, had served only as an initial excuse for French intervention in Vietnam; military and economic interests soon became the primary reasons for remaining there.

The French navy was in the forefront of the conquest of Indochina. In 1863 Admiral de la Grandiere, the governor of Cochinchina (as the French renamed Nam Bo), forced the Cambodian king to accept a French protectorate over that country, claiming that the Treaty of Saigon had made France heir to Vietnamese claims in Cambodia. In June 1867, the admiral completed the annexation of Cochinchina by seizing the remaining three western provinces. The following month, the Siamese government agreed to recognise a French protectorate over Cambodia in return for the cession of two Cambodian provinces, Angkor and Battambang, to Siam. With Cochinchina secured, French naval and mercantile interests turned to

Tonkin (as the French referred to Bac Bo). The 1873 storming of the citadel of Hanoi, led by French naval officer Francis Gamier, had the desired effect of forcing Tu Due to sign a treaty with France in March 1874 that recognised France's full and entire sovereignty over Cochinchina, and opened the Red River to commerce. In an attempt to secure Tonkin, Gamier was killed and his forces defeated in a battle with Vietnamese regulars and Chinese soldiers, who had fled south following the Taiping Rebellion in that country and had been hired by the Hue court to keep order in Tonkin.

In April 1882, a French force again stormed the citadel of Hanoi, under the leadership of naval officer Henri Riviere. Riviere and part of his forces were wiped out in a battle with a Vietnamese-Chinese army, a reminder of Gamier's fate a decade earlier. While Gamier's defeat had led to a partial French withdrawal from Tonkin, Riviere's loss strengthened the resolve of the French government to establish a protectorate by military force. Accordingly, additional funds were appropriated by the French Parliament to support further military operations, and Hue fell to the French in August 1883, following the death of Tu Due the previous month. A Treaty of Protectorate, signed at the August 1883 Harmand Convention, established a French protectorate over North and Central Vietnam and formally ended Vietnam's independence.

In June 1884, Vietnamese scholar-officials were forced to sign the Treaty of Hue, which confirmed the Harmand Convention agreement. By the end of 1884, there were 16,500 French troops in Vietnam. Resistance to French control, however, continued. A rebellion known as the Can Vuong (Loyalty to the King) movement formed in 1885 around the deposed Emperor Ham Nghi and attracted support from both scholars and peasants. The rebellion was essentially subdued with the capture and exile of Ham Nghi in 1888. Scholar and patriot Phan Dinh Phung continued to lead the resistance until his death in 1895. Although unsuccessful in driving out the French, the Can Vuong movement, with its heroes and patriots, laid important groundwork for future Vietnamese independence movements.

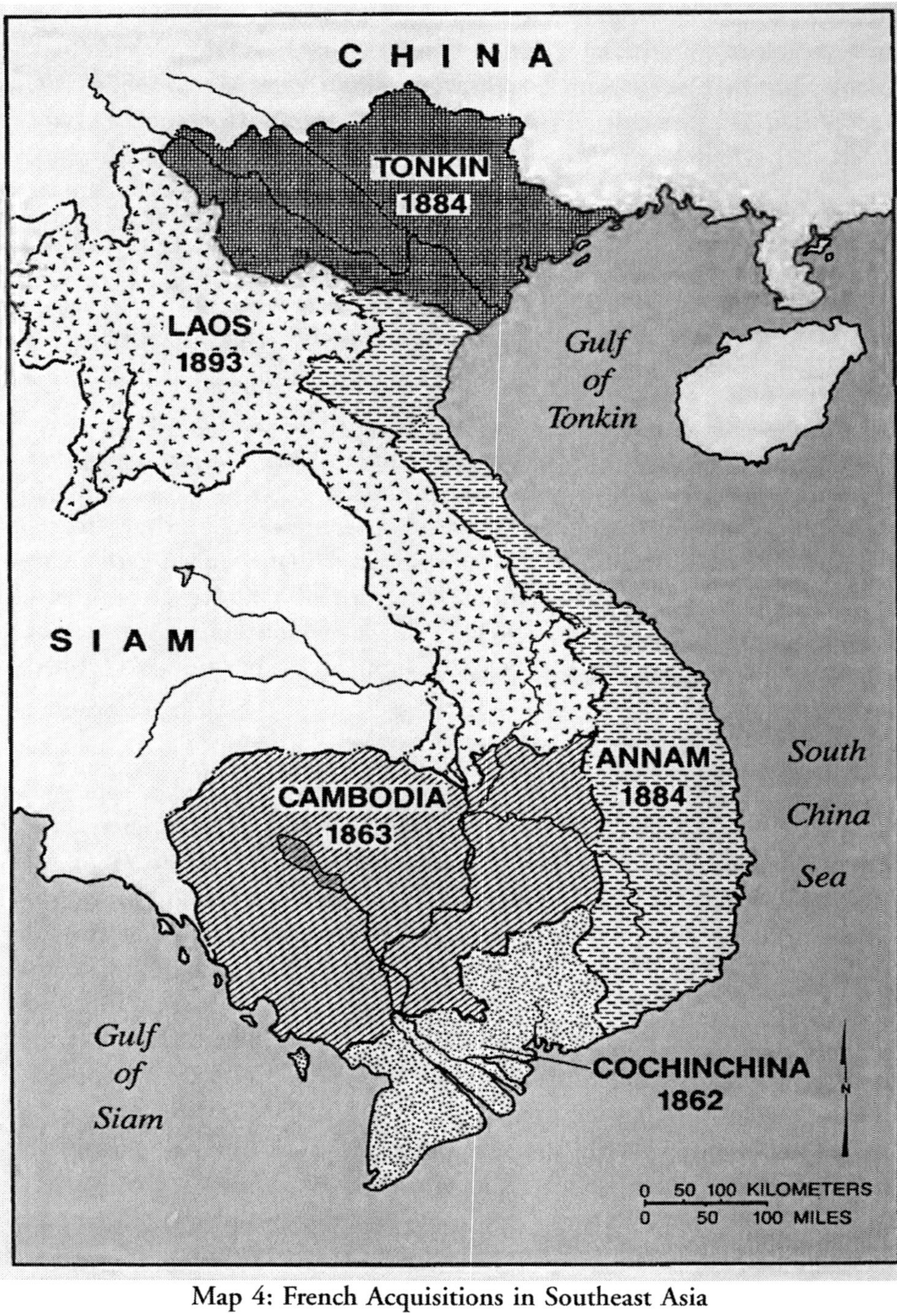

Map 4: French Acquisitions in Southeast Asia

Colonial Administration

Not all Vietnamese resisted the French conquest, and some even welcomed it. The monarchy, through decades of repression, had lost the support of the people; and Tu Due, in the eyes of large segments of the peasantry, had lost his mandate to rule. He had been able to protect his people neither from foreign aggression nor from an unusually high incidence of natural disasters such as floods, famines, locusts, droughts, and a cholera epidemic in 1865 that killed more than one million people. Tu Due's repression of Catholics also created a large opposition group ready to cooperate with the French, and those who did were often rewarded with lands vacated during the French invasion. Much of this land, however, was given to French colonial settlers, often in sizable holdings of 4,000 hectares or more. Gradually a French-Vietnamese landholding class developed in Cochinchina. Vietnamese, however, were appointed only to the lower levels of the bureaucracy established to administer the new colony. Seeking to finance the growing bureaucracy, the early admiral-governors of Vietnam viewed the colony as the source of the necessary revenue. Rice exports, forbidden under the monarchy, reached 229,000 tons annually in 1870. Taxes extracted from Cochinchina increased tenfold in the first decade of French control. State monopolies and excise taxes on opium, salt, and alcohol eventually came to provide 70 percent of the government's operating revenue.

In 1887 France formally established the Indochinese Union, comprising the colony of Cochinchina and the protectorates of Annam, Tonkin, and Cambodia, with Laos being added as a protectorate in 1893. There was a rapid turnover among governors-general of the Indochinese Union, and few served a full five-year term. One who did, Paul Doumer (1897-1902), is considered to have been the architect of a colonial system under which Vietnam was politically dominated and economically exploited. Following the partitioning of Vietnam into three parts, the emperor was stripped of the last vestiges of his authority. In 1897 the powers of the *kinh hoc* (emperor's viceroy) were transferred to the Resident *Superieur* at Hanoi, who governed in the name of the emperor. That same year, the Privy Council in Annam was replaced with a French-controlled Council of Ministers. The following year in Annam, the French took over tax collection and payment of officials. Most of the Vietnamese scholar-officials had refused to cooperate with the French, but those who did were restricted to minor or ceremonial positions. Consequently, Frenchmen were recruited to staff a new, continually expanding bureaucracy.

By 1925 there were 5,000 European administrators ruling an Indochinese population of 30 million, roughly the same number used to administer British India, which had a population more than ten times as large. Under the French laws applicable to individuals, Vietnamese were prohibited from travelling outside their districts without identity papers; and they were not allowed to publish, meet, or organise. They were subject to *corvee* (unpaid labour imposed by the state on certain classes of people, such as peasants, for the performance of work on public projects) and they could be imprisoned at the whim of any French magistrate. The colonial police enforced the law through a network of French and Vietnamese agents.

Land alienation was the cornerstone of economic exploitation under the colonial government. By 1930 more than 80 percent of the rice growing land in Cochinchina was owned by 25 percent of the landowners and 57 percent of the rural population were landless peasants working on large estates. Although the situation was somewhat better in the north, landless peasants in Annam totalled 800,000 and in Tonkin nearly one million. Heavy taxes and usurious interest rates on loans were added burdens on the peasants. More than 90 percent of rubber plantations were French owned. Two-thirds of the coal mined in Vietnam (nearly two million tons in 1927) was exported. Manufacturing was limited to cement and textiles, partly to placate French industrialists who saw Indochina as a market for their own goods. Naval shipyards and armament factories built under the Nguyen dynasty were dismantled under the French. Much of the craft industry survived, however, because it produced affordable consumer goods in contrast to imported French goods, which only the French or wealthy Vietnamese could afford.

French efforts at education in the early decades of colonial rule were negligible. A few government schools were established to train Vietnamese clerks and interpreters. A few Vietnamese from wealthy families, their numbers rising to about ninety by 1870, were sent to France to study. Three *lycees* (secondary schools), located in Hanoi, Hue, and Saigon, were opened in the early 1900s, using French as the language of instruction. The number of *quoc ngu* elementary schools was gradually increased, but even by 1925 it was estimated that no more than one school-age child in ten was receiving schooling. As a result, Vietnam's high degree of literacy declined precipitously during the colonial period. The University of Hanoi, founded in 1907 to provide an alternative for Vietnamese students beginning to flock to Japan, was closed for a decade the following year because of fear of student involvement in a 1908 uprising in Hanoi. In Tonkin and Annam, traditional education based on Chinese classical literature continued to flourish well into the twentieth century despite French efforts to discourage it, but the triennial examinations were abolished in 1915 in Tonkin and in 1918 in Annam. China, which had always served as a source of teaching materials and texts, by the turn of the century was beginning to be a source of reformist literature and revolutionary ideas. Materials filtering in from China included both Chinese texts and translations of Western classics, which were copied and spread from province to province.

Ho Chi Minh and the Communist Movement

The year 1925 also marked the founding of the *Viet Nam Thanh Nien Cach Menh Dong Chi Hoi* (Revolutionary Youth League) in Guangzhou by Ho Chi Minh. Born Nguyen Sinh Cung in Kim Lien village, Nghe An Province in May 1890, Ho was the son of a scholar from a poor peasant family. Following a common custom, His father renamed him Nguyen Tat Thanh at about age ten. Ho was trained in the classical Confucian tradition and was sent to secondary school in Hue. After working for a short time as a teacher, he went to Saigon where he took a course in navigation and in 1911 joined the crew of a French ship. Working as a kitchen hand, Ho travelled to North America, Africa, and Europe. While in Paris from 1919-23, he took the name Nguyen Ai Quoc (Nguyen the Patriot). In 1919 he attempted to meet with United States President Woodrow Wilson at the Versailles Peace Conference in order to present a proposal for Vietnam's independence, but he was turned away and the proposal was never officially acknowledged. During his stay in Paris, Ho was greatly influenced by Marxist-Leninist literature, and in 1920 he became a founding member of the French Communist Party. He read, wrote, and spoke widely on Indochina's problems before moving to Moscow in 1923 and attending the Fifth Congress of the Communist International, also called the Comintern, in 1924.

In late 1924, Ho arrived in Guangzhou, where he spent the next two years training more than 200 Vietnamese cadres in revolutionary techniques. His course of instruction included study of Marxism-Leninism, Vietnamese and Asian revolutionary history, Asian leaders such as Gandhi and Sun Yat-sen, and the problem of organising the masses. As a training manual, Ho used his own publication Duong Cach Menh (The Revolutionary Path), written in 1926 and considered his primer on revolution. Going by the name Ly Thuy, he formed an inner communist group, Thanh Nien Cong San Doan (Communist Youth League), within the larger Thanh Nien (Youth) organisation. The major activity of Thanh Nien was the production of a journal, Thanh Nien, distributed clandestinely in Vietnam, Siam, and Laos, which introduced communist theory into the Vietnamese independence movement. Following Chiang Kai-shek's April 1927 coup and the subsequent suppression of the communists in southern China, Ho fled to Moscow.

In December of that year, a teacher from a Vietnamese peasant family, Nguyen Thai Hoc, founded Viet Nam Quoc Dan Dang (VNQDD, Vietnamese Nationalist Party), in Hanoi. With a membership largely of students, low-ranking government employees, soldiers, and a few landlords and rich peasants, VNQDD was patterned after the Chinese Nationalist Party (Kuomintang), from which it received financial support in the 1930s. Another source of funds for the VNQDD was the Vietnam Hotel in Hanoi, which it opened in 1928 as both a commercial enterprise and the party headquarters. The hotel restaurant, however, provided French agents with an easy means of penetrating the party and monitoring its activities. At various times, the VNQDD attempted, without success, to form a united front with Thanh Nien and other independence organisations. Thanh Nien, being two years older, however, had had a head start over VNQDD in organising in schools, factories, and local government, which it had done with patience and planning. The VNQDD therefore concentrated instead on recruitment of Vietnamese soldiers and the overthrow of French rule.

In Tonkin—the French name for northern Vietnam—the only form of human habitation is the village, wrote the French geographer Pierre Gourou in 1931. One of his assistants in surveying village society in Tonkin was the young historian Vo Nguyen Giap. Later, as the first commander of the People's Army of Vietnam and the strategist behind the victory against the French at Dien Bien Phu in 1954, he made an effort to integrate Vietnamese villages in the larger framework of a struggling nation. Young teachers and poor peasants replaced conservative, elderly landowners as village leaders, so they could mobilise the village communities in active warfare against the city- and garrison-based colonial army.

The wars in Vietnam were decided in the villages. It was said in pre-colonial Vietnam that the power of the emperor stopped at the village gate. Each village was ruled by a self-nominated council of village elders, who negotiated the tax level (money, soldiers and labour) with the emperor's *mandarins* (public officials). The power of the Emperor rested on his army, perhaps also on the need for someone to organise irrigation systems above the village level.

Hanoi was the administrative centre for the northern region of an empire which from 1838 was mainly called Dai Nam, but also carried other names, like Viet Nam. The Chinese and Europeans called it An Nam. Present day *Ha Noi* already existed as a city with a fortress in the period when the Red River Delta was a part of China, and was capital for the independent Viet dynasties from the eleventh century onwards, under the name *Thang Long* (Soaring Dragon). The Nguyen dynasty, who ruled 1802-1945 from the southern city of Hue, chose the name Ha Noi for the former capital.

The words *ha noi* mean "inside the river." The city lies between three rivers, the *To Lich, Kim Nguu* and the big Red River (*Song Hong*). Much of Hanoi is under the water level and is protected by a long dyke.

World War II and Japanese Occupation

The signing of the Nazi-Soviet Non-Aggression pact in August 1939, caused France immediately to ban the French Communist Party and, soon afterwards, to declare illegal all Vietnamese political parties including the Indochinese Communist Party (ICP). The colonial authorities began a crackdown on communists, arresting an estimated 2,000 and closing down all communist and radical journals. The party consequently was forced to shift its activities to the countryside, where French control was weaker—a move that was to benefit the communists in the long run. In November the ICP Central Committee held its Sixth Plenum with the goal of mapping out a new united front strategy, the chief task of which was national liberation. According to the new strategy, support would now be welcomed from the middle class and even the landlord class, although the foundation of the party continued to be the proletarian-peasant alliance.

After the fall of France to the Nazis in June 1940, Japan demanded that the French colonial government close the Hanoi-Kunming railway to shipments of war-related goods to China. In an agreement with the Vichy government in France in August, Japan formally recognised French sovereignty in Indochina in return for access to military facilities, transit rights, and the right to station occupation troops in Tonkin. On 22 September, however, Japanese troops invaded from China, seizing the Vietnamese border towns of Dong Dang and Lang Son. As the French retreated southward, the Japanese encouraged Vietnamese troops to support the invasion.

The communists in the Bac Son district border area moved to take advantage of the situation, organising self-defence units and establishing a revolutionary administration. The French protested to the Japanese, however, and a cease-fire was arranged whereby the French forces returned to their posts and promptly put down all insurrection. Most of the communist forces in Tonkin were able to retreat to the mountains. In similar short-lived uprisings that took place in the area of Cochinchina, however, the communist rebel forces had nowhere to retreat and most were destroyed by the French.

Establishment of the Viet Minh

In early 1940, Ho Chi Minh returned to southern China, after having spent most of the previous seven years studying and teaching at the Lenin Institute in Moscow. In Kunming he re-established contact with the ICP Central Committee and set up a temporary headquarters, which became the focal point for communist policy-making and planning. After thirty years absence, Ho returned to Vietnam in February 1941 and set up headquarters in a cave at Pac Bo, near the Sino-Vietnamese border, where in May the Eighth Plenum of the ICP was held. The major outcome of the meeting was the reiteration that the struggle for national independence took primacy over class war or other concerns of socialist ideology. To support this strategy, the League for the Independence of Vietnam (Viet Nam Doc Lap Dong Minh Hoi, Viet Minh for short) was established. In this new front group, which would be dominated by the party, all patriotic elements were welcomed as potential allies. The party would be forced in the short term to modify some of its goals and soften its rhetoric, supporting, for example, the reduction of land rents rather than demanding land seizures. Social revolution would have to await the defeat of the French and the Japanese. The Eighth Plenum also recognised guerrilla warfare as an integral part of the revolutionary strategy and established local self-defence militias in all villages under Viet Minh control. The cornerstone of the party's strategy, of which Ho appears to have been the chief architect, was the union of the forces of urban nationalism and peasant rebellion into a single independence effort.

In order to implement the new strategy, two tasks were given priority: the establishment of a Viet Minh apparatus throughout the country and the creation of a secure revolutionary base in the Viet Bac border region from which southward expansion could begin. This area had the advantages of being remote from colonial control but accessible to China, which could serve both as a refuge and training ground. Moreover, the Viet Bac population was largely sympathetic to the communists. Viet Minh influence began to permeate the area, and French forces attempted, but failed, to put it down. Ho's efforts during this period were directed primarily at conciliating both the French themselves and the militantly anti-French members of the ICP leadership. The growing frequency of clashes between French and Vietnamese forces in Haiphong led to a French naval bombardment of that port city in November 1946. Estimates of Vietnamese casualties from the action range from 6,000 to 20,000. This incident and the arrival of 1,000 troops of the French Foreign Legion in central and northern Vietnam in early December convinced the communists, including Ho, that they should prepare for war.

On 19 December, the French demanded that the Vietnamese forces in the Hanoi area disarm and transfer responsibility for law and order to French authority. That evening, the Viet Minh responded by attacking the city's electric plant and other French installations around the area. Forewarned, the French seized Gia Lam airfield and took control of the central part of Hanoi, as full-scale war broke out. By late January, the French had retaken most of the provincial capitals in northern and central Vietnam. Hue fell in early February, after a six-week siege. The Viet Minh, which avoided using its main force units against the French at that time, continued to control most of the countryside, where it concentrated on building up its military strength and setting up guerrilla training programmes in liberated areas. Seizing the initiative, however, the French marched north to the Chinese border in the autumn of 1947, inflicting heavy casualties on the Viet Minh and retaking much of the Viet Bac region.

Meanwhile, in April 1947 the Viet Minh in Cochinchina had destroyed all chance for alliance with the religious sects by executing Huynh Phu So, leader of the Hoa Hao. Both the Hoa Hao and the Cao Dai formed alliances soon afterward with the French. The Committee for the South, which had seriously damaged the communist image in Cochinchina by its hard-line approach, was replaced in 1951 by the Central Office for South Vietnam (COSVN, Trung Uong Cue Mien Nam), headed by Le Duan. In the north, however, the political and military situation had begun to improve for the communists by late 1948. The Viet Minh had increased the number of its troops to more than 250,000 and, through guerrilla activities, the communists had managed to retake part of Viet Bac as well as a number of small liberated base areas in the south. ICP political power was also growing, although lack of a land reform programme and the continued moderate policy toward the patriotic landed gentry discouraged peasant support for the communists.

In 1948, the French responded to the growing strength of the Viet Minh by granting nominal independence to all of Vietnam in the guise of "associated statehood" within the French Union. The terms of the agreement made it clear, however, that Vietnam's independence was, in reality, devoid of any practical significance. The new government, established with Bao Dai as chief of state, was viewed critically by nationalists as well as communists. Most prominent nationalists, including Ngo Dinh Diem (president, Republic of Vietnam, South Vietnam, 1955-63), refused positions in the government, and many left the country.

The United States recognised the Associated State of Vietnam in early 1950, but this action was counter-balanced a few days later with the recognition of the DRV by the new People's Republic of China. In March, Ho Chi Minh signed an agreement with Beijing that called for limited assistance to Hanoi. Shortly thereafter, Moscow also formally recognised the DRV, and the Viet Minh became more openly affiliated with the communist camp. Mao Zedong's model of revolution was openly praised in the Vietnamese press; and the ICP, which, on paper, had been temporarily dissolved in 1945 to obscure the Viet Minh's communist roots, surfaced under a new name in 1951 that removed all doubt of its communist nature. More than 200 delegates, representing some 500,000 party members, gathered at the Second National Party Congress of the ICP, held in February 1951 in Tuyen Quang Province. Renaming the ICP the Vietnam Workers' Party (VWP, Dang Lao Dong Viet Nam), the delegates elected Ho as party chairman and Truong Chinh as general secretary.

Dien Bien Phu

With Beijing's promise of limited assistance to Hanoi, the communist military strategy concentrated on the liberation of Tonkin and consigned Cochinchina to a lower priority. The top military priority, as set by Giap, was to free the northern border areas in order to protect the movement of supplies and personnel from China. By autumn of 1950, the Viet Minh had again liberated Viet Bac in decisive battles that forced the French to evacuate the entire border region, leaving behind a large quantity of ammunition. From their liberated zone in the northern border area, the Viet Minh were free to make raids into the Red River Delta. The French military in Vietnam found it increasingly difficult to convince Paris and the French electorate to give them the manpower and materiel needed to defeat the Viet Minh. For the next two years, the Viet Minh, well aware of the growing disillusionment of the French people with Indochina, concentrated its efforts on wearing down the French military by attacking its weakest outposts and by maximising the physical distance between engagements to disperse French forces. Being able to choose the time and place for such engagements gave the guerrillas a decided advantage. Meanwhile, political activity was increased until, by late 1952, more than half the villages of the Red River Delta were under Viet Minh control.

The newly appointed commander of French forces in Vietnam, General Henri Navarre, decided soon after his arrival in Vietnam that it was essential to halt a Viet Minh offensive underway in neighbouring Laos. To do so, Navarre believed it was necessary for the French to capture and hold the town of Dien Bien Phu, sixteen kilometres from the Laotian border. For the Viet Minh, control of Dien Bien Phu was an important link in the supply route from China. In November 1953, the French occupied the town with paratroop battalions and began reinforcing it with units from the French military post at nearby Lai Chau.

During that same month, Ho indicated that the DRV was willing to examine French proposals for a diplomatic settlement announced the month before. In February 1954, a peace conference to settle the Korean and Indochinese conflicts was set for April in Geneva, and negotiations in Indochina were scheduled to begin on 8 May. Viet Minh strategists, led by Giap, concluded that a successful attack on a French fortified camp, timed to coincide with the peace talks, would give Hanoi the necessary leverage for a successful conclusion of the negotiations.

Accordingly, the siege of Dien Bien Phu began on 13 March, by which time the Viet Minh had concentrated nearly 50,000 regular troops, 55,000 support troops, and almost 100,000 transport workers in the area. Chinese aid, consisting mainly of ammunition, petroleum, and some large artillery pieces carried a distance of 350 kilometres from the Chinese border, reached 1,500 tons per month by early 1954. The French garrison of 15,000, which depended on supply by air, was cut off by 27 March, when the Viet Minh artillery succeeded in making the airfield unusable. An elaborate system of tunnels dug in the mountainsides enabled the

Viet Minh to protect its artillery guns, by continually moving them to prevent discovery. Several hundred kilometres of trenches permitted the attackers to move progressively closer to the French encampment. In the final battle, human wave assaults were used to take the perimeter defences, and capture French guns that were then turned on the main encampment. The French garrison surrendered on 7 May, ending the siege that had cost the lives of about 25,000 Vietnamese and more than 1,500 French troops.

The following day, peace talks on Indochina began in Geneva, attended by the DRV, the Associated State of Vietnam, Cambodia, Laos, France, Britain, China, the Soviet Union, and the US. In July a compromise agreement was reached consisting of two documents: a cease-fire and a final declaration. The ceasefire agreement, which was signed only by France and the DRV, established a provisional military demarcation line at about the 17°N parallel and required the regrouping of all French military forces south of that line and of all Viet Minh military forces north of the line. A demilitarised zone (DMZ), no more than five kilometres wide, was established on either side of the demarcation line.

The cease-fire agreement also provided for a 300-day period, during which all civilians were free to move from one zone to the other, and an International Control Commission (ICC), consisting of Canada, India, and Poland, to supervise the cease-fire. The final declaration was endorsed through recorded oral assent by the DRV, France, Britain, China, and the Soviet Union. It provided for the holding of national elections in July 1956, under the supervision of the ICC, and stated that the military demarcation line was provisional and should not in any way be interpreted as constituting a political territorial boundary. Both the US and the Associated State of Vietnam, which France had recognised on 4 June as a fully independent and sovereign state, refused to approve the final declaration and submitted separate declarations stating their reservations.

The Aftermath of Geneva

The Geneva Agreements were viewed with doubt and dissatisfaction on all sides. Concern over possible US intervention, should the Geneva talks fail, was probably a major factor in Hanoi's decision to accept the compromise agreement. The US had dissociated itself from the final declaration, although it had stated that it would refrain from the threat or use of force to disturb the agreements. US President Dwight D. Eisenhower wrote to the new Prime Minister of the Bao Dai government, Ngo Dinh Diem, in September 1954 promising US support for a Non-communist

Vietnam. Direct US aid to South Vietnam began in January 1955, and American advisors began arriving the following month to train South Vietnamese army troops.

By early 1955, Diem had consolidated his control by moving against lawless elements in the Saigon area and by suppressing the religious sects in the Mekong Delta. He also launched a "denounce the communists" campaign, in which, according to communist accounts, 25,000 communist sympathizers were arrested and more than 1,000 killed. In August 1955, Diem issued a statement formally refusing to participate in consultations with the DRV, which had been called for by the Geneva Agreement to prepare for national elections. In October, he easily defeated Bao Dai in a seriously tainted referendum and became president of the new Republic of Vietnam.

Despite the growing likelihood that national elections would not be held, the communist leadership in Hanoi decided for the time being to continue to concentrate its efforts on the political struggle. Several factors led to this decision, including the weakness of the party apparatus in the South, the need to concentrate on strengthening the war-weakened North, and pressure from the communist leadership of the Soviet Union, which, under General Secretary Nikita Khrushchev, had inaugurated its policy of peaceful coexistence with the West. By 1957, however, a shift to a more militant approach to the reunification of the country was apparent. Partly in response to Diem's anticommunist campaign, the Party stepped up terrorist activities in the South, assassinating several hundred officials of the Diem government. This led to the arrest of another 65,000 suspected communists and the killing of more than 2,000 by the Saigon government in 1957. Repression by the Diem regime led to the rise of armed rebel self-defence units in various parts of the South, with the units often operating on their own without any party direction. Observing that a potential revolutionary situation had been created by popular resentment of the Diem government and fearing that the government's anti-communist policy would destroy or weaken party organisation in the South, the VWP leadership determined that the time had come to resort to violent struggle.

Second Indochina War

By 1959 some of the 90,000 Viet Minh troops that had returned to the North following the Geneva Agreements had begun filtering back into the South to take up leadership positions in the insurgency apparatus. Mass demonstrations, punctuated by an occasional raid on an isolated post, were the major activities in the initial stage of this insurgency. Communist-led uprisings launched in 1959 in the lower Mekong Delta and Central Highlands resulted in the establishment of liberated zones, including an area of nearly fifty villages in Quang Ngai Province. In areas under communist control in 1959, the guerrillas established their own government, levied taxes, trained troops, built defence works, and provided education and medical care. In order to direct and coordinate the new policies in the South, it was necessary to revamp the party leadership apparatus and form a new united front group. Accordingly, COSVN, which had been abolished in 1954, was re-established with General Nguyen Chi Thanh, a northerner, as chairman and Pham Hung, a southerner, as deputy chairman. On 20 December 1960, the National Front for the Liberation of South Vietnam, informally called the National Liberation Front (NLF, Mat Tran Dan Toe Giai Phong Mien Nam), was founded, with representatives on its Central Committee from all social classes, political parties, women's organisations, and religious groups, including Hoa Hao, Cao Dai, the Buddhists, and the Catholics. In order to keep the NLF from being obviously linked with the VWP and the DRV, its executive leadership consisted of individuals not publicly identified with the communists, and the number of party members in leadership positions at all levels was strictly limited. Furthermore, in order not to alienate patriotic non-communist elements, the new front was oriented more toward the defeat of the United States-backed Saigon government than toward social revolution.

The Fall of Ngo Dinh Diem

In 1961 the rapid increase of insurgency in the South Vietnamese countryside led US President John F. Kennedy's administration to decide to increase United States support for the Diem regime. Some $US 65 million in military equipment and $US 136 million in economic aid were delivered that year, and by December 3,200 United States military personnel were in Vietnam. The United States Military Assistance Command, Vietnam (MACV) was formed under the command of General Paul D. Harkins in February 1962. The cornerstone of the counterinsurgency effort was the strategic hamlet programme, which called for the consolidation of 14,000 villages of South Vietnam into 11,000 secure hamlets, each with its own houses, schools, wells, and watchtowers. The hamlets were intended to isolate guerrillas from the villages, their source of supplies and information, or, in Maoist terminology, to separate the fish from the sea in which they swim. The programme had its problems, however, aside from the frequent attacks on the hamlets by guerrilla units. The self-defence units for the hamlets were often poorly trained, and support from the Army of the Republic of Vietnam (ARVN) was inadequate. Corruption, favouritism, and the resentment of a growing number of peasants who were forcibly resettled plagued the programme. It was estimated that of the 8,000 hamlets established, only 1,500 were viable.

In response to increased US involvement, all communist armed units in the South were unified into a single People's Liberation Armed Force (PLAF) in 1961. These troops expanded in number from fewer than 3,000 in 1959 to more than 15,000 by 1961, most of whom were assigned to guerrilla units. Southerners trained in the North who infiltrated back into the South composed an important element of this force. Although they accounted numerically for only about 20 percent of the PLAF, they provided a well-trained nucleus for the movement and often served as officers or political cadres. By late 1962, the PLAF had achieved the capability to attack fixed positions with battalion-sized forces. The NLF was also expanded to include 300,000 members and perhaps one million sympathizers by 1962. Land reform programmes were begun in liberated areas, and by 1964 approximately 1.52 million hectares had been distributed to needy peasants, according to communist records. In the early stages, only communal lands, uncultivated lands, or lands of absentee landlords were distributed.

Despite local pressure for more aggressive land reform, the peasantry generally approved of the programme, and it was an important factor in gaining support for the liberation movement in the countryside. In the cities, the Workers' Liberation Association of Vietnam (Hoi Lao Dong

Giai Phong Mien Nam), a labour organisation affiliated with the NLF, was established in 1961. Diem grew steadily more unpopular as his regime became more repressive. His brother and chief adviser, Ngo Dinh Nhu, was identified by regime opponents as the source of many of the government's repressive measures. Harassment of Buddhist groups by ARVN forces in early 1963 led to a crisis situation in Saigon. On 8 May 1963, ARVN troops fired into a crowd of demonstrators protesting the Diem government's discriminatory policies toward Buddhists, killing nine persons. Hundreds of Buddhist monks responded by staging peaceful protest demonstrations and by fasting. In June a monk set himself on fire in Saigon as a protest, and, by the end of the year, six more monks had committed self-immolation.

On 21 August, special forces under the command of Ngo Dinh Nhu raided the pagodas of the major cities, killing many priests and arresting thousands of others. Following demonstrations at Saigon University on 24 August, an estimated 4,000 students were rounded up and jailed, and the universities of Saigon and Hue were closed. Outraged by the Diem regime's repressive policies, the Kennedy administration indicated to South Vietnamese military leaders that Washington would be willing to support a new military government. Diem and Nhu were assassinated in a military coup in early November, and General Duong Van Minh took over the government.

Escalation of the War

Hanoi's response to the fall of the Diem regime was a subject of intense debate at the Ninth Plenum of the VWP Central Committee held in December 1963. It appeared that the new administration of US President Lyndon B. Johnson (who assumed office following the assassination of President Kennedy on 23 November) was not planning to withdraw from Vietnam but, rather, to increase its support for the new Saigon government. The VWP leadership concluded that only armed struggle would lead to success and called for an escalation of the war. The critical issues then became the reactions of the US and the Soviet Union. Hanoi clearly hoped that the US would opt for a compromise solution, as it had in Korea and Laos, and the party leaders believed that a quick and forceful escalation of the war would induce it to do so. Hanoi's decision to escalate the struggle was made in spite of the risk of damage to its relations with Moscow, which opposed the decision. The new policy also became an issue in the developing rift between Beijing and Moscow because China expressed its full support for the Vietnamese war of national liberation. As a result, Moscow's aid began to decrease as Beijing's grew.

Escalation of the war resulted in some immediate success for the struggle in the South. By 1964 a liberated zone had been established from the Central Highlands to the edge of the Mekong Delta, giving the communists control over more than half the total land area and about half the population of the South. PLAF forces totalled between 30 and 40 battalions, including 35,000 guerrillas and 80,000 irregulars. Moreover, with the completion of the Ho Chi Minh Trail through Laos, the number of PAVN troops infiltrated into the South began to increase. ARVN control was limited mainly to the cities and surrounding areas, and in 1964 and 1965 Saigon governments fell repeatedly in a series of military and civilian coups.

The Johnson administration remained hesitant to raise the US commitment to Vietnam. However, in August 1964, following the shelling of US warships in the Gulf of Tonkin off the North Vietnamese coast, Johnson approved air strikes against North Vietnamese naval bases. At President Johnson's urgent request, the US Congress passed the Gulf of Tonkin Resolution, which gave the president the power to take all necessary measures to repel any armed attack against the forces of the United States and to prevent further aggression. This tough US stance was matched in Moscow, in October, when Leonid Brezhnev and Aleksei Kosygin took over control of the government following the fall from power of Nikita Khrushchev.

The new Soviet government pledged increased military support for Hanoi, and the NLF set up a permanent mission in Moscow. US support for South Vietnam, which had begun as an effort to defend Southeast Asia from the communist threat, developed into a matter of preserving US prestige. The Johnson administration, nevertheless, was reluctant to commit combat troops to Vietnam, although the number of US military advisers including their support and defence units had reached 16,000 by July 1964. Instead, in February 1965 the US began a programme of air strikes known as Operation Rolling Thunder against military targets in North Vietnam. Despite the bombing of the North, ARVN losses grew steadily, and the political situation in Saigon became precarious as one unstable government succeeded another. General William C. Westmoreland, commander of MACV from June 1964 to March 1968, urged the use of US combat troops to stop the communist advance, which he predicted could take over the country within a year. The first two battalions of US Marines (3,500 men) arrived in Vietnam in March 1965 to protect the US airbase at Da Nang.

The following month, Westmoreland convinced the administration to commit sufficient combat troops to secure base areas and mount a series of search and destroy missions. By late 1965, the US expeditionary force in South Vietnam numbered 180,000, and the military situation had stabilised somewhat. Infiltration from the north, however, had also increased, although still chiefly by southerners who had gone north in 1954 and received military training. PLAF strength was estimated to be about 220,000, divided almost equally between guerrillas and main force troops, the latter including units of PAVN regulars totalling about 13,000 troops.

The US decision to escalate the war was a surprise and a blow to party strategists in Hanoi. At the Twelfth Plenum of the Central Committee in December 1965, the decision was made to continue the struggle for liberation of the South despite the escalated American commitment. The party leadership concluded that a period of protracted struggle lay ahead in which it would be necessary to exert constant military pressure on the Saigon government and its ally in order to make the war sufficiently unpopular in Washington. Efforts were to be concentrated on the ARVN troops, which had suffered 113,000 desertions in 1965 and were thought to be on the verge of disintegration.

In early 1965, Hanoi had been encouraged by Moscow's decision to increase its economic and military assistance substantially. The resulting several hundred million dollars in Soviet aid, including surface-to-air missiles, had probably been tied to a promise by Hanoi to attend an international conference on Indochina that had been proposed by Soviet premier Kosygin in February. As pre-conditions for these negotiations,

Hanoi and Washington, however, had each presented demands that were unacceptable to the other side. The DRV had called for an immediate and unconditional halt to the bombing of the north, and the US had demanded the removal of PAVN troops from the South. Although both Hanoi and Washington had been interested in a negotiated settlement, each had preferred to postpone negotiations until it had achieved a position of strength on the battlefield.

By mid-1966 US forces, now numbering 350,000, had gained the initiative in several key areas, pushing the communists out of the heavily populated zones of the south into the more remote mountainous regions and into areas along the Cambodian border. Revolutionary forces in the South, under the command of General Nguyen Chi Thanh, responded by launching an aggressive campaign of harassment operations and full-scale attacks by regiment-sized units. This approach proved costly, however, in terms of manpower and resources, and by late 1966 about 5,000 troops, including main force PAVN units, were being infiltrated from the North each month to help implement this strategy. At the same time, North Vietnam placed its economy on a war footing, temporarily shelving non-war-related construction efforts. As a consequence of the heavy US bombing of the North, industries were dismantled and moved to remote areas. Young men were conscripted into the army and their places in fields and factories were filled by women, who also served in home defence and antiaircraft units. Such measures were very effective in countering the impact of the bombing on the North's war effort. The Johnson administration, however, showed no sign of willingness to change its bombing strategy or to lessen its war effort.

During this difficult period, the communists returned to protracted guerrilla warfare and political struggle. The party leadership called for increased efforts to infiltrate moderate political parties and religious organisations. The underground communist leadership in Saigon was instructed to prepare for a general uprising by recruiting youths into guerrilla units and training women to agitate against the city's poor living conditions and the injustices of the Saigon government. Total victory, according to the party leadership, would probably occur when military victories in rural areas were combined with general uprisings in the cities.

In mid-1967, with US troop levels close to the half million mark, Westmoreland requested 80,000 additional troops for immediate needs and indicated that further requests were being contemplated. US forces in Tay Ninh, Binh Dinh, Quang Ngai, and Dinh Tuong provinces had initiated major offensives in late 1966 and in early 1967, and more troops were needed to support these and other planned operations. As a result of these deployments, US forces were scattered from the DMZ to the Mekong Delta by mid-1967. Opposition to the war, meanwhile, was mounting in the US; and among the Vietnamese facing one another in the South, the rising cost of men and resources was beginning to take its toll on both sides. The level of PLAF volunteers declined to less than 50 percent in 1967 and desertions rose, resulting in an even greater increase in northern troop participation.

Morale declined among communist sympathizers and Saigon government supporters alike. In elections held in South Vietnam in September 1967, former generals Nguyen Van Thieu and Nguyen Cao Ky were elected president and vice president, respectively. A number of popular candidates, including Buddhists and peace candidates, were barred from running, and newspapers were largely suppressed during the campaign. Even so, the military candidates received less than 35 percent of the vote, although the election took place only in areas under the Saigon government's control. When proof of widespread election fraud was produced by the defeated candidates, students and Buddhists demonstrated and demanded that the elections be annulled.

The Tet Offensive

In mid-1967 the costs of the war mounted daily with no military victory in sight for either side. Against this background, the party leadership in Hanoi decided that the time was ripe for a general offensive in the rural areas combined with a popular uprising in the cities. The primary goals of this combined major offensive and uprising were to destabilise the Saigon regime and to force the US to opt for a negotiated settlement. In October 1967, the first stage of the offensive began with a series of small attacks in remote and border areas designed to draw the ARVN and US forces away from the cities. The rate of infiltration of troops from the North rose to 20,000 per month by late 1967, and the US command in

Saigon predicted a major communist offensive early the following year. The DMZ area was expected to bear the brunt of the attack. Accordingly, US troops were sent to strengthen northern border posts, and the security of the Saigon area was transferred to ARVN forces. Despite warnings of the impending offensive, in late January more than one-half of the ARVN forces were on leave because of the approaching Tet (Lunar New Year) holiday.

On 31 January 1968, the full-scale offensive began, with simultaneous attacks by the communists on five major cities, thirty-six provincial capitals, sixty-four district capitals, and numerous villages. In Saigon, suicide squads attacked the Independence Palace (the residence of the president), the radio station, the ARVN's joint General Staff Compound, Tan Son Nhut airfield, and the US embassy, causing considerable damage and throwing the city into turmoil. Most of the attacking forces throughout the country collapsed within a few days, often under the pressure of US bombing and artillery attacks, which extensively damaged the urban areas. Hue, which had been seized by an estimated 12,000 communist troops who had previously infiltrated the city, remained in communist hands until late February. A reported 2,000 to 3,000 officials, police, and others were executed in Hue during that time as counter-revolutionaries.

The Tet offensive is widely viewed as a turning point in the war despite the high cost to the communists (approximately 32,000 killed and about 5,800 captured) for what appeared at the time to be small gains. Although they managed to retain control of some of the rural areas, the communists were forced out of all of the towns and cities, except Hue, within a few weeks. Nevertheless, the offensive emphasised to the Johnson administration that victory in Vietnam would require a greater commitment of men and resources than the American people were willing to invest. On 31 March 1968, Johnson announced that he would not seek his party's nomination for another term of office, declared a halt to the bombing of North Vietnam (except for a narrow strip above the DMZ), and urged Hanoi to agree to peace talks. In the meantime, with US troop strength at 525,000, a request by Westmoreland for an additional 200,000 troops was refused by a presidential commission headed by the new US secretary of defence, Clark Clifford.

Following the Tet Offensive, the communists attempted to maintain their momentum through a series of attacks directed mainly at cities in the delta. Near the DMZ, some 15,000 PAVN and PLAF troops were also thrown into a three-month attack on the US base at Khe Sanh. A second assault on Saigon, complete with rocket attacks, was launched in May. Through these and other attacks in the spring and summer of 1968, the communists kept up pressure on the battlefield in order to strengthen their position in a projected series of four-party peace talks scheduled to begin in January 1969 that called for representatives of the US, South Vietnam, North Vietnam, and the National Liberation Front to meet in Paris. In June 1969, the NLF and its allied organisations formed the Provisional Revolutionary Government of the Republic of South Vietnam (PRG), recognised by Hanoi as the legal government of South Vietnam. At that time, communist losses dating from the Tet Offensive numbered 75,000, and morale was faltering, even among the party leadership.

Peace Negotiations

With negotiations making little progress, the US military commander in Saigon, General Creighton W. Abrams, who had held that post since mid-1968, requested and was given permission by President Richard M. Nixon to launch secret bombing attacks, beginning 18 March 1970, on what were described as Vietnamese communist sanctuaries and supply routes inside Cambodia. In late March, Prince Norodom Sihanouk of Cambodia was ousted as chief of state in a military coup led by Premier and Defence Minister, General Lon Nol. Shortly thereafter, the Lon Nol government cancelled an agreement that had allowed North Vietnam to use the port at Sihanoukville. Hanoi reacted by increasing support to the Khmer (Kampuchean) Communist Party, by then under the leadership of the radical Pol Pot. In April, Nixon authorised the invasion of Cambodia by a joint US-ARVN force of 30,000 troops for the purpose of destroying communist bases across the border. Little more than short-term gains were accomplished by the invasion, which resulted in massive protests in the US, leading to the passage of legislation by Congress requiring the removal of US troops from Cambodia by the end of June.

In 1971 and 1972, the communists faced some serious problems unrelated to US offensive operations. The Saigon government began to gain some support in the Mekong Delta because of the implementation of a "land-to-the-tiller" reform programme pressed on the Thieu government by Washington in 1970. Almost 400,000 farmers received a total of 600,000 hectares, and by 1972 tenancy reportedly had declined from about 60 percent to 34 percent in some rural areas. In addition, a People's Self-Defence Force Programme begun about this time had some success in freeing ARVN troops for combat duty, as US forces were gradually withdrawn.

Although it was not clear at the time whether the withdrawal of US troops would cause the ARVN to crumble instantly, as predicted by the communists, the decisive defeat of an ARVN operation mounted against the Ho Chi Minh Trail in Laos in March 1971 was an early indication. At the time of the ARVN defeat, however, the communists were coping with deteriorating morale and with dwindling numbers of troops; a rising desertion rate and falling recruitment levels had reduced PLAF strength from 250,000 in 1968 to less than 200,000 in 1971.

Both on the battlefield and at the conference table, a stalemate of sorts was reached by mid-1971. In negotiations there was some flexibility, as Washington offered a unilateral withdrawal of US forces provided Hanoi stopped its infiltration of the South; and Hanoi countered by agreeing to a coalition government in Saigon along with a US troop withdrawal and to a ceasefire following the formation of a new government. The main point of debate was the retention of President Thieu as head of the South Vietnamese government, which Washington demanded and Hanoi rejected. To break the deadlock, the party leadership in Hanoi turned again to the strategy of a general offensive and uprising.

Accordingly, the Easter offensive was launched beginning on 30 March 1972, with a three-pronged attack across the DMZ through the A Shau Valley. The following day the communists attacked the city of Kontum and the provinces of Binh Dinh and Phuoc Tuy, threatening to cut South Vietnam in two. A few days later, three PAVN divisions attacked Binh Long Province along the Cambodian border, placing the capital, An Loc, under siege. In May the communists captured Quang Tri Province, including the capital, which was not recaptured by the ARVN until September.

By that time, Quang Tri city had been virtually levelled by US air strikes. Although the Easter offensive did not result in the fall of the Saigon government, as the communists had hoped, it did further destabilise the government and reveal the ARVN's weaknesses. The costs were great on both sides, however, and by October both Hanoi and Washington were more inclined to negotiate. By then Hanoi had agreed to accept Thieu as president of a future Saigon government in exchange for the removal of US forces without a corresponding removal of PAVN troops. Thieu's objections to the failure to require the removal of North Vietnamese forces was in the end ignored, and the Agreement on Ending the War and Restoring Peace in Vietnam was signed in Paris on 27 January 1973.

The Final Campaign

Although the terms of the peace agreement were less than the communists had hoped for, the accords did permit them to participate in the new government legally and recognised their right to control certain areas. Most important, the removal of US forces gave the communists a welcome breathing space, allowing them to concentrate on political efforts. In the initial period after the signing of the agreement, the party leadership viewed armed struggle as a last resort only because it was feared that the US might reintroduce its forces. PLAF troops were instructed to limit their use of force to self-defence. Meanwhile, the Thieu government embarked on pacification efforts along the central coast and in the Mekong Delta, which resulted in a reduction of the area under official communist control to about 20 percent of the South.

The Saigon government, however, faced serious difficulties, including the negative effect on the economy of the withdrawal of US forces and a critical refugee problem. During the course of the war, several million Vietnamese had been evacuated or had fled from their villages to find safety and jobs in urban areas. Most of these remained unemployed and, together with militant Buddhist groups, the Cao Dai, and the Hoa Hao, represented a sizable wellspring of discontent with the Thieu government.

In early 1974, the communists launched a campaign to regain the territory they had lost since the cease-fire. Raids were conducted on roads, airfields, and economic installations; the flow of supplies and equipment from the North was stepped up; and a 19,000-kilometre network of roads leading from the DMZ in Quang Tri Province to Loc Ninh, northwest of Saigon, was completed. By summer the communists were moving cautiously forward, seizing vulnerable areas in the Central Highlands and in the provinces around Saigon. There was no direct response from the US, and the resignation of Nixon in August convinced the party leadership that further US intervention was unlikely.

ARVN forces continued to deteriorate, suffering high casualties and facing a lack of ammunition and spare parts. The party leadership met in October to plan a 1975 military offensive concentrating on the Cambodian border area and the Central Highlands. The taking of the Phuoc Long province capital, Phuoc Binh (now Ba Ra in Song Be Province), in early January was followed by a surprise attack in March on Ban Me Thuot, the largest city in the Central Highlands. President Thieu ordered ARVN units at Pleiku and Kontum to leave the highlands and withdraw to the coast to regroup for a counterattack on Ban Me Thuot. The ARVN strategic withdrawal became a rout, however, because PAVN units had already cut the main roads to the coast and fleeing civilians clogged the secondary roads as panic ensued. By the end of March, eight northern provinces had fallen to the communist forces, including the cities of Hue and Da Nang. Buoyed by this stunning victory, the party leadership directed the commander of revolutionary forces in the South, General Van Tien Dung to prepare for an offensive against Saigon. In early April, PAVN and PLAF troops moved south and began an encirclement of the capital. On 20 April, after ten days of stiff resistance, the ARVN Eighteenth Division, stationed thirty kilometres north of Saigon, finally crumbled under the attack of three PAVN divisions. With Saigon in a state of panic, President Thieu resigned the following day and was replaced by Vice President Tran Van Huong. Duong Van Minh, thought to be more acceptable to the communists, took over the presidency on 28 April. The communists refused to negotiate, however, and fifteen PAVN battalions began to move toward Saigon. On 30 April, communist forces entered the capital, and Duong Van Minh ordered ARVN troops to lay down their arms.

Nearly thirty years had passed since Ho Chi Minh first declared Vietnam's independence as a unified nation in September 1945. In the interim, an entire generation of Vietnamese had endured a divided

Vietnam, knowing only continuous warfare. The events of April 1975 not only abruptly concluded the war but also prepared the way for the official reunification of the country the following year, when the Vietnamese people were brought together under one independent government for the first time in more than a century.

4

THE VIETNAMESE ARMED FORCES

The People's Army of Vietnam (PAVN) is a singular military establishment. Its singularity of purpose, as well as form, is a function of its Vietnamese cultural heritage, a centuries-old martial spirit, a history of messianic military leadership possessing extraordinary insight, and decades of combat experience.

As a consequence of the First and Second Indo-China wars, the PAVN was characterised by a sense of newly-acquired destiny, a feeling of international prowess, along with the real limitations imposed by economic stagnation, diplomatic isolation, and uncertainty regarding its closest ally, the Soviet Union. It was in the middle of a debate over the proper use of force (whether it should be applied brazenly as in Cambodia or in the more traditional manner prescribed by "revolutionary force" doctrine) and was determined to modernise its organisation, including reforming the officer corps and renewing the never-ending internal battle against inefficiency and corruption. Finally, the PAVN was faced with the prospect of an inevitable generational change of military leadership. In 1978, the PAVN numbered about three million personnel, including its Paramilitary Force. Nevertheless, it was well integrated into Vietnamese society and enjoyed a good working relationship with both the government and the VCP. It was tightly controlled, chiefly by various mechanisms in the hands of the VCP apparatus within it.

At the same time, the PAVN was limited by critical weaknesses: it was technologically underdeveloped because it lacked modern equipment, weapons, and training; its officer and non-commissioned officer corps were over-aged; and it was highly dependent on outside military sources because there were no indigenous arms factories of any importance in Vietnam. The purpose to which the PAVN has been dedicated over the years has varied greatly and has turned chiefly on the demands of the party. Its basic functions are similar to those of armed forces everywhere: to defend Vietnam's territorial integrity, to support its foreign policy and strategic goals where appropriate, to contribute to the maintenance of its internal security, and to assist in its economic development.

In the first few years after the end of the Second Indochina War, the PAVN's performance was tested twice—in Cambodia and along Vietnam's northern border with China. Its ability to maintain internal security has been tested continuously, although to a lesser degree.

History

The PAVN's progenitor was a collection of guerrilla bands, many of them composed of ethnic minority highlanders, assembled in Indochina during World War II and armed and encouraged by the Allied Forces as opposition to the Japanese army, which had occupied much of Southeast Asia. A few of these guerrilla bands were organised by the ICP, as the VCP was known at the time.

Near the end of the war, the ICP began to experiment with a new kind of military force, called Armed Propaganda units. The first of these units was created in the mountains of northern Vietnam near the China border. The armed propaganda team was the brainchild of Ho Chi Minh (known then as Nguyen Ai Quoc) and a 32-year-old Hanoi history teacher named Vo Nguyen Giap. It was designed both to engage in combat and to do organisational and mobilisation work in the villages. Armed propaganda teams shaped the character of the subsequently formed PAVN.

On 2 September 1945, when Ho Chi Minh officially proclaimed the independence of the nation and announced the formation of the Democratic Republic of Vietnam (DRV), a Ministry of National Defence was created and the ministerial portfolio was given to a non-communist, a measure that reflected the apparently broadly nationalistic composition of the new government. Giap, at the time the second most powerful communist figure, became minister of the interior. A year later the National Defence Council (NDC) was created, and Giap was made chairman, giving him more direct control of the Viet Minh armed force, the precursor to PAVN. When the French returned to Indochina, the newly-formed Viet Minh—consisting of approximately 1,000 men in 13 infantry companies—was driven into the hills behind Hanoi.

The Viet Minh's military force, which fought the French for eight years, was a united-front army, meaning it was communist-influenced but was not entirely communist. For much of the First Indochina War, it was essentially an irregular force, growing to about 60,000 at the end of the first year of the war and to about 380,000 in 1954. Only about a third of these were considered regulars; the remainder were "regional" or "local" forces. This system was the forerunner of the 'three-elements' concept of the armed forces—regulars, regionals (or territorials), and locals—which has been retained in PAVN. The regular force was organised into about 30 infantry battalions of 600 men each and 8 heavy-weapons battalions. Many of the early units were organised along ethnic lines. A preponderance of the day-to-day battles in the First Indochina War was fought by PAVN regional forces and local militia units. Regulars were used sparingly and were committed only to battles of strategic importance, such as the 1950 campaign to push French forces back from the China border region, the attempted capture of Hanoi in 1951, and the battle of Dien Bien Phu in 1954.

In 1954, at the end of the First Indochina War, the PAVN was still a united-front military force. It remained for the party to "regularise" it. Control mechanisms were introduced gradually and perfected, reorganisation was undertaken, military elements were enlarged, support units were added, and formal regulations on military service were developed. A tight system of party controls was introduced, military schools were opened and military assistance was solicited from abroad, chiefly from China. A directive of the Twelfth Plenum of the Central Committee (Second National Party Congress), issued in March 1957, established universal military conscription. By 1965, PAVN numbered 400,000; by 1975, 650,000. Of the approximately three million in uniform in 1978, about one million served in the PAVN Regular Force and two million served in the Paramilitary Force.

In 1959 the VCP (known at the time as the Vietnam Workers' Party—VWP, or Dang Lao Dong Viet Nam) decided to launch an armed struggle in the South in the name of unification of the fatherland. Part of the effort involved creation of a united-front organisation, the National Front for the Liberation of South Vietnam and a united-front armed force, initially called the People's Liberation Army (PLA) and later renamed the People's Liberation Armed Force (PLAF). The mission of the PLAF was to liberate the South in order to permit its unification with North Vietnam, and Hanoi began supplying this force with doctrinal know-how and key personnel. In keeping with a principle of people's war that called on combatants to be self-sustaining,

North Vietnamese leaders also counselled the PLAF to be self-supporting and self-contained and not to rely on, or make requests of, Hanoi. Then and later, however, authorities always stood ready to meet any critical need of their southern brethren. Until 1965 the war in the South was on the shoulders of the PLAF. Its rapid escalation in 1965, however, introduced PAVN troops to the South in ever-increasing numbers, and the burden of the war shifted to them. In 1972, in the so-called Easter offensive, about 90 percent of the combat was carried out by northern regulars. The final campaign in April 1975 was fought almost entirely by PAVN troops. At the time, almost all PAVN infantry divisions were outside North Vietnam in Laos, in Cambodia, or, overwhelmingly, in South Vietnam. After the war, the remnant PLAF force was disbanded, and its members were either demobilised or transferred to PAVN units.

Throughout its developmental period, from the earliest military organisations of the 1930s until the late 1970s, PAVN was heavily influenced by China and by Chinese military thought and doctrine. The original party-led armed force, the Viet Minh army, was created by the Chinese Nationalist Party (Kuomintang) and fielded from China. Later, it was nurtured and funded largely by the Chinese Communist Party. Military manuals were of Chinese origin, first Nationalist then Communist, and in the early years nearly all imported logistic assistance came either directly from China or—if from the Soviet Union—through

China and with Chinese cooperation. During the Second Indochina War, Chinese anti-aircraft troops and Chinese railroad and warehousing personnel served in Vietnam.

Post-Second Indochina War Development

The chief changes in the PAVN, after April 1975, were enormous growth, augmented by increased war-making capability and fire power, and development away from a guerrilla-oriented infantry toward a more orthodox modern armed force. Hanoi's public statements indicated there would be a significant demobilisation of the PAVN immediately after the war and that many PAVN units would be converted into economic development teams. Within a few weeks, however, PAVN units were engaged in a border war in Cambodia with one-time ally, the Khmer Rouge, and were preparing to defend Vietnam's northern border against China.

Following the end of the Second Indochina War, the PAVN was in worse condition than was generally realised. Having been decimated by ten years of combat, it was in organisational disarray, with a logistics system that was nearly worn out. Both, the PAVN and the country were suffering from war weariness, and restructuring and rebuilding were hampered in part because the war's sudden ending had precluded planning for the post-war world. Vietnamese military journals acknowledged at the time that the new situation required the transformation of the PAVN from an army of revolutionary soldiers fighting with guerrilla tactics into an orthodox armed force that could defend existing institutions and fixed installations from internal and external threats. It was a new and broader task, and Ho Chi Minh's observation made at the end of the First Indochina War was frequently quoted: "*Before we had only the night and the jungle. Now we have the sky and the water.*"

Several problems had to be addressed. These included the dual-control system, i.e., the ill-defined division of authority between the military command structure and the party leadership within the armed forces, or between the military commander and the political commissar; the lack of esprit de corps among the rank and file, a general malaise termed "post-war mentality"; and the officer corps' inadequate military knowledge and insufficient military technological skills for the kind of war that had emerged in the 1970s.

There were also policy conflicts over the conduct of large-scale combined or joint military operations and the nature of future military training, a lack of standardisation of equipment, materiel shortages, administrative breakdowns, general inefficiency and lack of performance by basic military units, and an anachronistic party structure within PAVN stemming from an outmoded organisational structure and inappropriate or out-of-touch political commissars.

By 1978 the effort to restore the PAVN had developed into the Great Campaign. This was a five-year programme with five objectives: to increase the individual soldier's sense of responsibility, discipline, dedication, attitude toward solidarity, and mastery of weapons, equipment, and vehicles; to encourage more frugal expenditure of fuel, supplies, and materiel; to improve the PAVN's officer corps, particularly at the basic unit level; to improve military-civilian relations and heighten international solidarity; and to improve the material-spiritual life of soldiers.

The reorganisation was a deliberate effort to professionalise the PAVN officer corps, in part by codifying the military hierarchy within the PAVN, which had never been officially approved. Previous emphasis on egalitarianism had led to virtual denial of even the concept of rank. There were no officers, only cadres; no enlisted personnel; only combatants. Uniforms were devoid of insignia, and references to rank or title were avoided in conversation. With professionalisation, distinctions emerged between officers and enlisted troops. Accompanying the basic law were directives from the Council of Ministers that dealt with PAVN ranks, uniforms, and insignia. A thirteen-rank officer system with appropriate titles was instituted.

Under the new regulations, PAVN officers were distinguished as line commanders, staff officers, political officers, administrative officers, or military-police officers. The new regulations additionally stipulated the use of unit insignia—bright red for infantry, sky blue for air force and air defence force, dark blue for navy, green for border defence, and light gray for specialist technicians—in all twenty five separate services, each of which had its own emblem.

Technological improvements for the PAVN were instituted chiefly under the Great Campaign. Intensive technical training programmes were begun. Heavy emphasis was placed on the training of surface-to-air missile (SAM) battery commanders, advanced air defence technicians, fighter pilots, radar technicians, communications systems operators, and naval officers. The programme was fully supported by the Soviet Union, which provided military aid and technical advisers and trainers. A costly developmental effort, it had not been long under way before events began to conspire against it.

Shortly after the Great Campaign was launched in 1978, Vietnam's disputes with Cambodia and China sharply intensified. On 5 March 1979, the government issued a General Mobilisation Order that established three "great tasks" for Vietnam: to enlarge the national defence structure, meaning to increase substantially the size of the PAVN; to increase agricultural and industrial production in support of the war; and to develop better administrative systems in the party, the PAVN, and the economic sector. The emphasis was on young Vietnamese, who were called to perform separate "great tasks," i.e., annihilate the enemy, develop the paramilitary system, do productive labour, insure internal security, and performs necessary ideological tasks. The order required all able-bodied persons to work ten hours a day—eight hours in productive labour and two hours in military training. It also required universal participation in civil-defence exercises.

During peaceful periods, the VPA has actively been involved in Vietnam's workforce to develop the economy of Vietnam, to coordinate national defence and the economy. The VPA has regularly sent troops to aid with natural disasters such as flooding, landslides etc. The VPA is also involved in such areas as industry, agriculture, forestry, fishery and telecommunications. The VPA has numerous small firms which have become quite profitable in recent years. However, recent decrees have effectively prohibited the commercialisation of the military. Conscription is in place for every male, age 18 to 25 years old, though females can volunteer to join.

The PAVN might be considered as the strongest army in Southeast Asia and one of top ten armies in Asia.

5

THE TRADITION OF MILITANCY IN VIETNAM

Vietnam's past is characterised by a strongly martial spirit tempered by war, invasion, rebellion, insurgency, dissidence, and social sabotage. In their view, the Vietnamese have always lived in an armed camp. The first "deities" of Vietnam, before the time of recorded history, were not gods but generals. Vietnam's naval fleet in the ninth century supposedly was the largest in the world. In the tenth century, when its population could not have numbered more than two million, its army purportedly stood at one million. Asia's first military academy was founded in Hanoi in the thirteenth century.

The fourteenth century produced Tran Hung Dao (1230-1300), the greatest of all Vietnam's many military geniuses, who was consistently able to win battles against vastly superior forces. According to tradition Nguyen Hue (also known as Emperor Quan Trung, 1742-92), another great military leader, fielded an army so disciplined that for the battle of Dong Da in 1789 he force-marched his troops 600 kilometres to fight an uninterrupted five-day battle that left mountains of enemy dead. The Vietnamese take pride in these figures from antiquity and seem particularly adulatory of those most clever in combat, such as the general who persuaded his opponent that he had two armies when the second was only a phantom. Those who sacrificed themselves on the battlefield are reverently remembered. For example, the Hai Ba Trung legend originated early in the first century A.D. It tells of the two Trung sisters, who led their army in a futile effort against a vastly superior Chinese force. Defeated, they drowned themselves in a Hanoi lake. Vietnam's histories depict the nineteenth and early twentieth century's as times of continual rebellion predating the rise of post-World War II Asian nationalism. The century of French colonialism is described as one long, unbroken battle involving virtually all Vietnamese.

Vietnam's national tradition is one in which every Vietnamese is a soldier. This tradition is said to arise not from militarism, but rather from a spirit of *chink nghia* (just cause), which connotes highly moral behaviour rooted in rationality, compassion, and responsibility. Historians assert that the spirit of *chink nghia* sustained the Vietnamese in their long struggle against the Sinicization (*Han-hwa*) efforts of the Han Chinese, and later against French colonialism and American neo-colonialism. Drawn from this, then, is a special kind of martial spirit, both ferocious and virtuous. It is because of *chink nghia* that the Vietnamese have been victorious, while usually outnumbered and outgunned. *Chink nghia* is the mystique that imparts unique fighting capabilities to the Vietnamese: first, it mobilises the people and turns every inhabitant into a soldier; second, it applies the principles of knowing how to fight the strong by the weak, the great numbers by the small numbers, the large by the small.

Vietnam is Asia's most fought-over ground. For centuries the Vietnamese battled the Chinese, the French, the Americans, the Khmer, and again the Chinese. In between they battled the Thai, the Burmans, the Lao, the Cham, the Montagnards, and each other in regional and dynastic combat. In the view of Vietnam's neighbours, Vietnamese campaigns since the fifteenth century have been offensive rather than defensive. But Vietnamese school children are taught that in these wars the Vietnamese always were the victim, never the aggressor. With respect to Vietnam's national security, the point is not whether Vietnamese perceptions are factually correct, but that the Vietnamese act on them.

In the light of threat perceptions, the ruling Political Bureau and the PAVN High Command developed several firm policies to ensure that the country remains more or less permanently mobilised for war; that it must maintain as large a standing army as the system can support; that, as far as it is able, it must be self-sufficient in protecting itself and not rely on outside assistance or alliance; and that internally it must maintain a tightly organised, highly disciplined society capable of maintaining a high level of militant spirit among the general population.

Strategic Thinking

The central factor in Hanoi's strategic thinking, applicable to both external and internal threats, is the concept of *dau tranh* (struggle). Briefly stated, *dau tranh* strategy is the sustained application of total military and non-military force over long periods of time in pursuit of an objective. Its chief characteristic is its conceptual breadth, for it is of greater scope than ordinary warfare and requires the total mobilisation of a society's resources and energies. The strategy is unique to Vietnam because of its close association with the sources of Vietnamese national security strengths. These strengths are the heritage of unity and patriotism, the supportive collectivist state system, the technologically and spiritually developed armed forces, a superior strategy (the *dau tranh* strategy), the undeviating justice of Vietnam's cause.

The aim of the *dau tranh* concept is to put warfare into a new conceptual framework. Its essence is the idea of people not merely as combatants or supporters but as weapons of war to be designed, forged, and launched into battle—hence the term people's war. All people, even children, are regarded as instruments of *dau tranh*. Operationally the strategy has two arms or pincers—armed *dau tranh* and political *dau tranh*. The two always work together to close on and crush the enemy. Political *dau tranh* is not politics but a mobilising and motivating programme operating in a grey area between war and politics. Specifically, it consists of three *van* (action) programmes: the all-important *dich van* (action among the enemy) includes activities directed against the foreign enemy in his home country, the *dan van* (action among the people) includes activities conducted in a liberated area, and the *binh van* (action among the military) includes non-military activities against the enemy's military forces.

Of the three, the *dich van* programme is particularly novel because it seeks to shape outside perception and, beyond this, to persuade outsiders not only that the Vietnamese will be successful in their struggle but that they deserve to be. Strategically, it seeks to undercut the enemy's war effort at home and its diplomacy worldwide. Tactically, it attempts to limit the enemy's military response by inhibiting the full use of his military potential.

Dau tranh strategy defines the enemy narrowly—imperialists, militarists, landlords—but does not denigrate all in the enemy camp. Some are considered merely to have been misled, while others are regarded as foreign patriots who nevertheless support Hanoi's cause. In this way, *dau tranh* not only changes the definition of a combatant but also revises the rules of warfare. It asserts that the final test need not be military, and that the decisive action may take place away from the battlefield.

The strategy requires the support of tremendous organisational resources as it seeks always to realise the ideal of total mobilisation and motivation. It also requires meticulous attention to the mundane details of war and politics, such as logistics and administration. The great utility of *dau tranh* strategy, as evidenced by forty years of use against the French, the Americans, and the Chinese, is two-fold: it can cloud the enemy's perceptions and it can nullify his power. In the judgment of the Vietnamese leadership, it has proved to be highly effective in confounding the enemy's strategic response because it engenders misperception in the enemy camp. Vietnam's leaders have said that the nature of the Second Indochina War was never seen clearly either by the South Vietnamese or by the Americans.

Dau tranh strategy, in effect, dictates the enemy's counterstrategy, even to the extent of forcing him to fight under unfavourable conditions. In circumscribing the enemy's military response by altering his perception of the war, the guiding principle is that military force must always be politically clothed. Every battle must be cast in terms of a political act. When this is not possible—as in a purely tactical engagement, such as that with US forces at Khe Sanh in early 1968—the attack must be made to seem a military action for a political purpose.

After the Second Indochina War, the *dau tranh* concept served the Vietnamese less well. It was employed, more by accident than by design, against the invading Chinese during the brief border war in 1979 and worked fairly well. It did not prove workable in Cambodia, however, and was for the most part abandoned there.

Hanoi regards itself as a major force in Asia. Vietnam's population of about 90 million makes it the thirteenth largest of the world. It is strategically located at a crossroads of Asia and has considerable natural wealth and economic potential. It also has a large, battle-hardened, and well-equipped army.

However, security-wise Vietnam suffers from other remediable liabilities, in addition to inexperienced strategic planners. These included an army still oriented toward guerrilla infantry; an inability to project air and naval forces over long distances; the lack of logistics and transport systems required by a modern armed force (particularly, lack of air transport); a low level of technical competence in the officer corps; and a shortage of good, reliable equipment and weapons. Hanoi's strategic planners, and their Soviet advisers, clearly recognised that new weapons systems were required for the vastly changed security conditions facing Vietnam. Hanoi's vaunted military strongpoint, its divisions of light infantry, however, required conversion to a more orthodox high-technology force in order to become militarily credible in the region.

6

RELATIONS WITH NEIGHBOURS

Overview

Vietnam remained a nation fully mobilised for war. The fact that the PAVN continued to grow, in fact to double in size, after 1975, was a government concession to entrenched PAVN interests as well as to internal and external security fears, many of them brought on by the fact that Vietnam had not renounced warfare as a foreign policy option. In any event, hard decisions lay ahead for the Hanoi leadership concerning the armed forces' share of the annual governmental budget, the ultimate size and deployment of the PAVN, the kind of air and naval power to be developed, the levels of military spending, and the development of indigenous sources of military hardware. Vietnam in 1978 faced only one truly credible external threat —China.

The complex Sino-Vietnamese relationship, dating back two thousand years, is deeply rooted in the Confucian concept of pupil-teacher. Thus, any issues under contention or problems that exist between the two on the surface normally are transcended by this basic relationship. Much of the behaviour demonstrated by the two since 1975—including Vietnam's invasion of Cambodia and China's subsequent "lesson" to Vietnam—is, in fact, traceable to the workings of this deep-rooted historic association. Victory in the Indochina War left Hanoi leaders determined to change the centuries-old relationship.

The Vietnamese sought to end the notion of the rimland barbarian's obligation to pay deference to the Middle Kingdom. They felt the tutelary relationship should give way to one of greater equality. The Chinese, however, considered that nothing significant had changed and that the original condition of mutual obligation should continue. For the Chinese, the touchstone would always be the Sino-Soviet dispute and the need to reduce Soviet influence in Hanoi. Most important for China was the nature of the Soviet presence in Indochina and its future portents. Beijing tried several approaches to induce Hanoi to maintain its distance from Moscow. However, none was successful. China pursued what might be called a campaign of protracted intimidation—military, diplomatic, and psychological pressure—on the Vietnamese, calculating that eventually Hanoi would seek some accommodation.

Cambodia

In the minds of Hanoi's strategic planners, Vietnam's two Indochina neighbours posed nearly as large an external security threat as did China. Strategically, Cambodia and Laos represented weak flanks where internal anti-communist forces could challenge the local regimes and threaten Vietnam itself. Geography increased this threat. Vietnam is an extraordinarily narrow country—at its "waist" near Dong Hoi it is only forty kilometres across—and could be cut in half militarily with relative ease either through an amphibious landing on its coast or through an invasion from Laos. It is also a long country, with some 8,000 kilometres of border and coastline to defend. For these reasons Hanoi was prepared to do whatever was necessary to achieve a secure, cooperative, non-threatening Laos and Cambodia.

During the nineteenth century weaker monarchs in Laos and Cambodia had paid tribute to the Vietnamese court in a system modelled on Vietnam's own relationship to China. After the Second Vietnam War, Laos, with a communist party long nurtured by the Vietnamese, once again entered the client relationship with docility. Cambodia, however, under a ruthless, but anti-Vietnamese dictatorship, resisted being drawn into the Vietnamese orbit. Tension between the two states escalated into open warfare and, in 1978, Hanoi launched an invasion that toppled the Pol Pot regime in Phnom Penh.

The communist victory in Vietnam in 1975 was accompanied by similar communist successes in Laos and Cambodia. The impression of the non-communist world at the time was that the three Indochinese communist parties, having seized control in their respective countries, would logically work together, through the fraternal bond of a single ideology, to achieve common objectives. What appeared to be a surprising deterioration in relations, however, was actually the resurfacing of historical conflict that ideological commonality could not override.

The victories of the Vietnamese communists and the Cambodian communist Khmer Rouge in 1975 did not bring peace. Relations between the two parties had been strained since the close of the First Indochina War. The Geneva Agreements had failed to secure for the Khmer communists, as part of the first Cambodian national liberation organisation, the United Issarak Front, a legitimate place in Cambodian politics. Some Khmer Communist and Issarak leaders subsequently went to Hanoi, but among those who stayed behind, Pol Pot and his faction, who later gained control of the Khmer (Kampuchean) Communist Party, blamed Vietnam for having betrayed their party at Geneva. Pol Pot never lost his antipathy for Vietnam. Under his leadership, the Khmer Rouge adhered for years to a radical, chauvinistic, and bitterly anti-Vietnamese political line. Skirmishes broke out on the Cambodian-Vietnamese border almost immediately following the communist victories in Saigon and Phnom Penh, and in less than four years Vietnam was again at war, this time with Cambodia. Vietnam's offensive forces crossing the Cambodia border in December 1978 took less than a month to occupy Phnom Penh and most of the country.

When tensions between Cambodia and Vietnam broke into the open, the reason was ostensibly Cambodian demands that Hanoi return territory conquered by the Vietnamese centuries earlier. Vietnam's offers to negotiate the territorial issue were rejected, however, because of more urgent Khmer concerns that Hanoi intended to dominate Cambodia by forming an Indochina Federation or "special relationship." In any event, Vietnamese interest in resolving the situation peacefully clearly came to an end once the decision was made to invade Cambodia. The invasion and the subsequent establishment of a puppet regime in Phnom Penh were costly to Hanoi, further isolating it from the international community. Vietnam's relations with a number of countries and with the United Nations (UN) deteriorated.

The UN General Assembly refused to recognise the Vietnamese-supported government in Phnom Penh and demanded a total Vietnamese withdrawal followed by internationally supervised free elections. The ASEAN nations were unified in opposing Vietnam's action. Urged by Thailand's example, they provided support for the anti-Phnom Penh resistance.

The ensuing conflict in Cambodia pitted Vietnamese troops, assisted by forces of the new Phnom Penh government—the People's Republic of Kampuchea (PRK)—against a coalition of communist and non-communist resistance elements. Of these elements, the government displaced from Phnom Penh by the Vietnamese, Pol Pot's communist Khmer Rouge (which had established the government known as Democratic Kampuchea in Cambodia, in 1975), was the strongest and most effective military force, mainly because of support from the Chinese. The extremism and brutality of the Khmer Rouge's brief reign in Phnom Penh, where it may have been responsible for as many as two million deaths, made it infamous.

Serious trouble between Hanoi and the Khmer Rouge under Pol Pot began at the end of the Second Indochina War, when both PAVN troops and the Khmer Rouge engaged in "island grabbing" and seizures of each other's territory, chiefly small areas in dispute between Vietnam and Cambodia for decades. What goaded Hanoi to take decisive action was Pol Pot's determination to indoctrinate all Khmer with hatred for Vietnam, thus making Hanoi's goal of eventual Indochinese federation even more difficult to accomplish. Vietnam's Political Bureau had several options in solving the Pol Pot problem, as it was officially termed. Vietnam's wartime relationship with the Khmer Rouge had been one of domination, in which control had been maintained through the intercession of native Khmers, numbering approximately five thousand, who had lived and trained in North Vietnam. The Political Bureau reasoned that by controlling the Khmer Rouge "five thousand" faction it could control the Khmer (Kampuchean) Communist Party, which in turn would control the Cambodian state and society. This strategy broke down when most of the Khmer communist cadres trained in Vietnam were executed by Pol Pot.

In another effort, the Political Bureau dispatched Le Duan, General Secretary of the Central Committee of the Communist Party of Vietnam, to Phnom Penh soon after the end of the war for a stern meeting with Pol Pot, but his efforts to persuade or intimidate failed. A series of punitive military strikes followed with the objective of triggering the overthrow of Pol Pot. Some of these assaults, such as the one in the Parrot's Beak region in 1977, involved as many as 90,000 PAVN troops, but they came to nothing. There also were covert Vietnamese attempts to eliminate Pol Pot by bribing his bodyguards to assassinate him.

Finally, in early 1978, Hanoi returned to tested methods of revolutionary guerrilla warfare. Special PAVN teams recruited volunteers for a future Khmer liberation army from Khmer refugee camps in southern Vietnam. About 300 of the most promising were taken to Ho Chi Minh City (formerly Saigon), installed in the former Cambodian embassy building, and organised into armed propaganda teams, with Khmer Rouge defector Heng Samrin in charge of training. The plan, according to programme defectors, was to send armed propaganda teams, like the Kampuchea Liberation Front, into Cambodian provinces along the Vietnamese border to infiltrate Khmer villages and begin organisation and mobilisation work. A Radio Liberation broadcast unit would be established, a liberated area would be proclaimed, and eventually a Provisional Revolutionary Government of Kampuchea would be formed that would then dispatch emissaries abroad in search of support. In late 1978, however, this revolutionary guerrilla war strategy was suddenly abandoned in favour of a full-scale, blitzkrieg-style attack on Cambodia. Later it became evident that the idea for the attack had come from young PAVN officers, many of whom had been trained in Moscow, who had assured the Political Bureau that the matter could be resolved in a maximum of six months. The Political Bureau's decision to attempt a military solution in Cambodia was taken against the advice of General Giap and probably most of the other older PAVN generals.

PAVN struck across the Cambodian border from the Parrot's Beak area of Vietnam on Christmas Day 1978. The drive was characterised by a highly visible Soviet-style offensive with tank-led infantry that plunged suddenly across the border, drove to the Thai border, and then fanned out to occupy Cambodia within days. Heng Samrin and his 300 Khmer cadres proceeded to form a new government, called the People's Republic of Kampuchea, in Phnom Penh, and began building an army to take over from the occupying PAVN. The first indication to the PAVN high command in Hanoi that it was in fact trapped in a protracted conflict came in the summer of 1979, when a major pacification drive, launched by PAVN forces using some 170,000 troops, proved to be inconclusive. It was only in the wake of that drive that PAVN settled down to the slow task of pacifying Cambodia.

In retrospect, Vietnam's invasion of Cambodia appears to have been a serious mistake. Apparently it was a decision hastily taken in the belief that a quick, successful takeover would force the Chinese to accept the new situation as a fait accompli. The undertaking was also based on the estimate that Pol Pot had neither the political base nor the military power to resist a traumatic assault, which would shatter his capability to govern and cause the Khmer people to rally overwhelmingly to the new government. Assumptions proved wrong, and the strategy failed. The invasion did not solve the Pol Pot problem, but rather bogged Vietnam down in a costly war that tarnished its image abroad and undermined relations with China that might otherwise have been salvaged. The war drained the economy and continued to be one of Vietnam's unsolved national security problems.

Laos

In contrast to its relationship with Cambodia, Vietnam's relations with communist Laos have been fairly stable. Historically, the ethnic tribes comprising present-day Laos had been less resistant to Vietnamese subjugation, and relations had never reached the level of animosity characteristic of the Vietnam-Cambodia relationship. Although Hanoi was a signatory to the Geneva Agreement of 1962 that upheld the neutrality of Laos, it failed to observe the agreement in practice. During the Second Indochina War (for example, the North Vietnamese obtained the cooperation of the Lao People's Revolutionary Party (Pathet Lao) in constructing and maintaining the Ho Chi Minh Trail, a road communications network that passed through the length of Laos. Thousands of Vietnamese troops were stationed in Laos to maintain the road network and provide for its security.

Vietnamese military personnel also fought beside the Pathet Lao in its struggle to overthrow Laos' neutralist government. Cooperation persisted after the war and the Lao communist victory. In 1976, agreements on cooperation in cultural, economic, scientific, and technical fields were signed between the two countries, followed in 1977 by a twenty-five-year Treaty of Friendship and Cooperation. The treaty was intended to strengthen ties as well as sanction Vietnam's military presence in, and military assistance to, Laos. Following Vietnam's invasion of Cambodia, Laos established links with the Vietnamese-supported PRK in Phnom Penh.

China

The deterioration of Sino-Vietnamese relations was gradual, commencing perhaps most dramatically with Richard M. Nixon's 1972 visit to China (which Hanoi later called the beginning of China's betrayal of Vietnam), but in the mid-1970s the signs of an impending breakdown were barely discernible. Until 1977 the Vietnam-Cambodia dispute appeared to the outside world to be purely bilateral, and China's strategic considerations seemed only distantly connected to the skirmishes taking place on the Vietnamese-Cambodian border. The Chinese in the 1976-77 period were preoccupied with internal affairs, including the deaths of Mao Zedong and Zhou Enlai, the arrest of Mao's widow, and the return to power of Deng Xiaoping. As the situation between Vietnam and Cambodia deteriorated, Cambodia's strategic importance to both China and Vietnam became more evident, and signs of a potential Sino-Vietnamese rift became clearer. Aside from risking the return of the Khmer Rouge, Vietnam viewed disengagement from Cambodia as tantamount to inviting China to establish a foothold on a second Vietnamese frontier. In China's view, Vietnam's sustained presence in Cambodia precluded such a development, but, more importantly, it placed Cambodia under the authority of an historic Asian adversary now closely allied with a superpower rival, the Soviet Union.

Vietnam's and China's shared modern experiences, namely their common exploitation by colonial powers and adaptations to communist ideology, did little to alter Vietnam's historical view of China, which was coloured by lengthy periods of Chinese conquest and domination. During the Second Indochina War, China acted as North Vietnam's closest ally, but, according to later Vietnamese statements, the Chinese tried to dominate the relationship from the beginning. Vietnam's desperate need for Chinese assistance forced it to maintain good relations with Beijing for the duration of the war, despite Vietnamese suspicions that China's ultimate purpose was to weaken Vietnam.

After the end of the Second Indochina War, underlying tensions between the two countries surfaced, and in 1978 a number of issues converged to bring the relationship to the breaking point. In addition to the growing dispute in Cambodia, these issues included territorial disagreements and Vietnam's treatment of its own largest minority group, the *Hoa* or ethnic Chinese, who numbered nearly two million.

The territorial dispute between China and Vietnam involves primarily delineation of territorial waters in the Gulf of Tonkin and sovereignty over two archipelagos in the South China Sea, the Paracel and the Spratly Islands (the Xisha and the Nansha in Chinese; the Hoang Sa and Truong Sa in Vietnamese). A border dispute on land (less than sixty square kilometres) was responsible for the relatively steady occurrence of low-level border clashes involving cross-border violations and the exchange of small-arms fire. In 1958 the two governments decided to defer settling their border differences until after victory had been achieved in the South.

Disagreement over territorial waters in the Gulf of Tonkin stemmed from agreements reached between China and France in 1887, stipulating a territorial limit of no more than three nautical miles. These agreements had been adequate until 1973, when Hanoi announced to Beijing its intention to negotiate contracts with foreign firms for the exploration of oil in the Gulf of Tonkin. The disputed islands in the South China Sea assumed importance only after it was disclosed that they were near the potential sites of substantial offshore oil deposits. In January 1974, Chinese military units seized islands in the Paracels occupied by South Vietnamese armed forces, and Beijing claimed sovereignty over the Spratlys.

Following their conquest of South Vietnam in the spring of 1975, units of the PAVN nevertheless moved to occupy the Spratly Islands previously held by the Saigon regime. Vietnam's treatment of the Hoa became an issue in 1978, when Hanoi instituted a crackdown on the Chinese community because of its pervasive role in domestic commerce in the South and its alleged subversive activities in the North. The government action forced an unprecedented exodus of thousands of Hoa across the border into China, prompting Beijing to accuse Vietnam of persecuting its Chinese community and of breaking a 1955 agreement that called for the gradual and voluntary integration of the Hoa into Vietnamese society. The situation was aggravated when Vietnam denied landing privileges to three Chinese ships dispatched to evacuate Hoa seeking voluntary repatriation to China. Beijing threatened Hanoi with unspecified retaliation, and Chinese activities on the Sino-Vietnamese border escalated.

The deterioration in bilateral relations became evident when China reduced, in May 1978, and then cancelled, on 3 July, its remaining aid projects in Vietnam. The official announcement followed by only a few days Hanoi's admission on 29 June to the Soviet-dominated Council for Mutual Economic Assistance. A few months later, in November 1978, a new era in Soviet-Vietnamese relations began with the signing of a Treaty of Friendship and Cooperation that called for mutual assistance and consultation in the event of a security threat to either country. The document facilitated Soviet use of Vietnamese airports and port facilities, particularly the former United States military complex at Cam Ranh Bay. In return, it assured Vietnam of economic and military aid for the anticipated invasion of Cambodia and established the Soviet Union as a deterrent to possible Chinese intervention in Cambodia.

Vietnam's decision to align with the Soviets, together with its invasion of Cambodia and mistreatment of the Hoa, provoked Beijing to "teach Hanoi a lesson." A "self-defence counterattack," mounted by China along the Sino-Vietnamese border on 17 February 1979, ended less than a month later, on 5 March, when Chinese leaders announced that their objectives had been met and proceeded to withdraw their forces. Despite the Chinese boast of having shattered the myth of Vietnam's invincibility, the invasion effected little more than the diversion of some Vietnamese troops from

Cambodia. The bulk of the resistance reportedly was offered by local Vietnamese border units and regional forces. Outnumbered, they performed well, exposing significant weaknesses in Chinese tactics, strategy, logistics, equipment, and communications. In the final analysis, the results were far from conclusive. Peace negotiations were initiated following the disengagement of forces, but broke down several times before being discontinued in December 1979.

The Soviet Union

Since the earliest days of the Vietnamese Communist Party (VCP), when the party's primary mentor was the Comintern, the Soviet Union has played a complex role in VCP affairs. Many of Vietnam's leaders had trained in the Soviet Union and had formed personal ties with their Soviet contemporaries. Historically, however, the relationship between the two nations has been characterised by strain, particularly on the Vietnamese side, and the record suggests several instances of Soviet neglect or betrayal of Vietnamese interests. These included Moscow's indifference to the founding of the VCP in 1930; failure to support materially or otherwise the Vietnamese resistance war against the French in the 1930s and early 1940s; failure to recognise North Vietnam until five years after its founding; failure to support Vietnam's application for membership in the UN in 1948 and 1951; support for the partitioning of Vietnam at the Geneva Conference in 1954; and sponsorship of a proposal to admit both North and South Vietnam to the UN in 1956. These examples of Soviet policy reminded the Vietnamese of the peril inherent in placing too much trust in a foreign ally.

The Sino-Soviet split in the late 1950s favourably altered the Soviet attitude toward Vietnam. Beginning in 1965, the Soviets initiated a programme of military assistance to Hanoi that proved invaluable in carrying on the Second Indochina War. Hanoi, however, continued to suspect Soviet motives and perceived that Soviet aid, when offered, was insufficient and given only grudgingly after repeated appeals.

Following the conquest of South Vietnam in 1975, Hanoi sought to retain the equilibrium of its wartime relations with both China and the Soviet Union, but mounting tensions with Beijing, culminating in the loss of Chinese aid in 1978, compelled Hanoi to look increasingly to Moscow for economic and military assistance. Beginning in late 1975, a number of significant agreements were signed between the two countries. One coordinated the national economic development plans of the two countries, and another called for the Soviet Union to underwrite Vietnam's first post-reunification Five-Year Plan. The first formal alliance was achieved in June 1978 when Vietnam joined Comecon. That organisation, which facilitated the economic integration of the Soviet Union, six East European countries, Cuba, and Mongolia, was able to offer economic assistance for some of the projects abandoned by China.

Vietnam's decision to invade Cambodia, which the leadership apparently made shortly after joining Comecon, required more than economic assistance from the Soviets. The possibility of a formal alliance between Hanoi and Moscow had apparently been discussed since 1975, but the Vietnamese had rejected the idea in order to protect their relationship with China. In 1978 that relationship had deteriorated to the point where protecting it was no longer a consideration, and circumstances in Cambodia confirmed the need for Vietnamese-Soviet military cooperation. In spite of Vietnam's needs, it is likely that the November 1978 Treaty of Friendship and Cooperation was imposed by the Soviets as a condition for military assistance. As a result of the treaty, the Vietnamese granted the Soviets access to the facilities at Da Nang and Cam Ranh Bay. Use of the bases represented a substantial regional strategic gain for Moscow, whose naval bases in the Pacific Ocean, until then, had been limited to the Soviet Far East.

Soviet support sustained Vietnamese operations in Cambodia. Military aid in 1978 approached US$800 million annually, but after the Vietnamese invasion of Cambodia and the Chinese attack on Vietnam in February 1979, the figure rose to almost US$1.4 billion. The sharp increase, reflecting the Soviet effort to replace quickly Vietnamese equipment losses on the Sino-Vietnamese border, was subsequently reduced.

Chinese Prime Minister Zhao Ziyang, Chairman Deng Xiaoping and Chinese Party General Secretary

Chinese officer briefing artillery crew

Chinese militiamen mustered from Guangxi province line up in teams of stretcher bearers bound to support the ground campaign

Chinese troops advancing

Chinese troops attacking a village

Vietnamese artillery

Vietnamese militia

Vietnamese militia resisting the Chinese offensive

Vietnamese refugees flee approaching Chinese forces in the strategic border province of Lang Son

Vietnamese soldiers returning from duty on the Chinese border

Lang Son following the 1979 Chinese invasion

Vietnamese in Lang Son province ford the Ky Cuong River on makeshift pontoon rafts, as the existing bridge has collapsed

Vietnamese official briefing the press

Chinese prisoners of war

Aerial view of Lang Son

Vietnamese prisoners of war

7

THE PATH TO WAR

The Chinese decision to launch a punitive war on Vietnam occurred within a complex geopolitical game. There was not a sole reason for China to invade Vietnam. Instead, Beijing sought multiple goals from launching a limited war and not all of them depended on a successful military operation.

The Emergence of Deng Xiaoping

In many respects, the year 1975 is the benchmark for most of the decisions that led to the Sino-Vietnamese war. Zhou Enlai, the architect of China's foreign policy for decades, lay on his deathbed slowly succumbing to cancer. He appeared briefly in January at the Fourth National People's Congress (NPC), to oversee the election of his chosen successor, Deng Xiaoping, to the post of First Deputy Premier of the People's Republic of China (PRC) and the Chief of Staff of the PLA. Throughout 1975 Deng would attempt to carry forward the policies which Zhou had formulated in the post-Cultural Revolution period. The previous year Deng had expounded the most important of these at the United Nations. The "Three Worlds" thesis, proclaiming that China no longer acknowledged the existence of the socialist camp, was a declaration that China would take upon itself the leadership of the Third World in its struggle against the hegemony of the imperialists (the United States) and the social imperialists (the Soviet

Union). This policy was another manifestation of Beijing's efforts to marshal the widest possible united front against its main enemy—Moscow.

The expectation that the reunification of North and South Vietnam and the overthrow of the Lon Nol government in Phnom Penh in April 1975 would mean an end to more than 30 years of war in Indochina was quickly shattered. Hanoi soon became involved in a series of escalating crises with its socialist neighbour, the Democratic Republic of Kampuchea (Cambodia). The sudden collapse of the Lon Nol and Thieu regimes in Cambodia and South Vietnam caught China somewhat unprepared. Beijing had been urging Hanoi to proceed more gradually with its major offensives, since 1972, citing the need for greater development of the Maoist "people's war" movement in South Vietnam. Furthermore, the Chinese, now on much better terms with the US, were in no hurry to see North and South Vietnam reunited. Since the early 1970's, China had grown increasingly apprehensive about the role that an independent, unified, and resurgent Vietnam would play in a Southeast Asia where American influence was dwindling.

By the end of 1975, Sino-Vietnamese relations were cool but not antagonistic. The state bureaucracy under Zhou and Deng appeared to have decided on a carrot-and-stick policy, intended to maintain a strong stance against closer Hanoi-Moscow relations while holding out the promise of assistance, which Hanoi needed to rebuild its war-torn economy. The events of the following year, however, made it extremely difficult for Beijing to implement this policy successfully. In 1976 China entered a period of great internal turbulence. Zhou died in January. Deng was formally purged from his posts in April. After a brief ascendancy of the radicals under the Gang of Four, Mao Zedong died in September and a coup led by the moderate faction under Acting Premier Hua Guofeng and aging Marshal Ye Jianying (Yeb Chien-ying) took control in October. Although not as disrupted as it had been during the Cultural Revolution, Chinese foreign policy in 1976 was concerned only with the most pressing and immediate issues. Southeast Asia was not yet in this category.

With Zhou's death and Deng's purge in early 1976, the decision-making structure in Beijing fragmented. Even with the death of Mao in September and the purge of the Gang of Four in October, the new leadership under Hua Guofeng failed to establish an effective political base. By early 1977 the economy was in chaos, food was scarce in parts of the country, the railroad system had all but come to a stop, and the campaign to purge supporters of the Gang of Four had become bloody without approaching a conclusion. As a result, very little national-level attention was being paid to any but the most critical external problems.

The decision to rehabilitate Deng at the Third Plenum of the 10th Central Committee of the Chinese Communist Party (CCP) (16-22 July 1977), came as a result of two factors:

(a) strong lobbying on his behalf by Wei Guoquing and Xu Shiyou, leaders in southern China, and
(b) recognition in the Politburo that only Deng had a strong enough political base to restore order.

His rehabilitation had been bitterly argued all spring because many members of the Politburo and the Central Committee, including Chairman Hua, had participated in Mao's "deepen the criticism of Deng" campaign in 1976. Deng's re-emergence marked the beginning of a slow but steady centralisation of authority and decision-making.

After his re-emergence, first on Deng's list of priorities was to reintroduce the "four modernisations" policy that Zhou Enlai had first introduced at the Fourth National People's Congress (NPC) in 1975. The primary objective of the four modernisations (agriculture, industry, national defence, and science and technology) was to make China a modern industrial nation by the turn of the century. The magnitude of the task was enormous. Not only would China have to make up for long years of isolation, during which its general level of technology had fallen 20 years behind the West, but China would have to heal the deep scars left over from the bitter years of the Cultural Revolution and the manoeuvrings of the Gang of Four. Virtually no sector of the economy or the society had been untouched. The memories of these years were still fresh in the minds of every Chinese. Deng had to overcome psychological as well as visible obstacles. Furthermore, radicals and supporters of the "gang" were still a force to be dealt with.

As 1977 came to a close, Deng made significant strides in consolidating his power. With his close political ally, Wei Guoquing, installed as head of the Political Department of the PLA in October, a new Central Committee behind him, and another round of purges and executions in progress through the provinces to eliminate non-supportive officials and radicals, he had the power centres sufficiently in hand to look outside China's borders. In September he sent a high-level military delegation to France, the highest ever to leave China for the West since 1949, to shop for modern weapons. The same month he announced to the world that China had successfully tested missiles with nuclear warheads. For the first time since Mao's death, China began to move forward under an effective leader.

At the same time, however, the border conflict between Cambodia and Vietnam was escalating and tensions were mounting on the Sino-Vietnamese border. The Chinese leadership at first had been slow to react to the oncoming crisis, but as Deng consolidated his position and initiated economic and administrative reforms to support the new modernisation programme, he viewed the hostility of the Vietnamese and the spectre of Soviet involvement in Southeast Asia increasingly as serious threats to his four-fold modernisation drive.

The Situation in Vietnam

By early 1977 Vietnam found itself enmeshed in a growing crisis with its intractable neighbour to the west. From March to May Cambodian forces staged several serious border incidents, shelling border towns and accelerating the flood of refugees. In June, Hanoi proposed high-level talks to de-escalate the tensions. When Phnom Penh turned the proposal down, Hanoi sent its defence minister, General Giap, to Beijing in an attempt to seek Chinese assistance to resolve the difficulties. In Beijing, Giap emphasised Sino-Vietnamese friendship but his overtures, lacking any commitment to an anti-Soviet stance, did not win any promises from the Chinese, who were neither inclined nor able to exert leverage on Hanoi's behalf. On his return from Beijing, Giap personally inspected Vietnamese defences along the Cambodian front.

In May 1977, Hanoi reasserted its independence by promulgating a 200-mile territorial zone in the South China Sea that encompassed the

Paracels and the Spratlys, laying claim to their oil-rich sea beds, which until 1975 Hanoi had acknowledged to be Chinese. (This at least has been Beijing's consistent contention.) Along the Sino-Vietnamese border, Vietnamese and Chinese troops were engaged in frequent rock-throwing incidents, harassment of border guards, and the movement of the 300-odd border markers back and forth 50 to 100 metres during the night. It is unclear, at this point, to what extent the deteriorating situation between Cambodia and Vietnam contributed to the deterioration of relations between China and Vietnam, but in the summer of 1977 Hanoi found itself increasingly at odds with both Beijing and Phnom Penh.

Chinese leaders were particularly disturbed with Hanoi in July when Hanoi signed a long-term peace and friendship treaty with Laos, which sanctioned a 40,000 man Vietnamese occupation army on Laotian territory. These forces served as a blocking force which could prevent any direct Chinese troop movements down the road the Chinese were building in Laos toward Cambodia or Thailand. They were also putting pressure on the easily malleable communist government in Vientiane to adopt a pro-Vietnamese position vis-a-vis Chinese interests. This diplomatic manoeuvre, along with the growing tensions along the Sino-Vietnamese border, was particularly unsettling for the Chinese, who were at the time deeply involved in their own domestic political problems.

Decision-making for War

There is still no concrete documentation of when and how Beijing made the decision for military action against Vietnam and to "teach Vietnam a lesson" for its "ungrateful and arrogant" behaviour as a move "to weaken the Soviet position in the "Third World". By most knowledgeable accounts it was taken at a Politburo weekly meeting in early July 1978. It is also apparent that contemplation of a military response to the crisis between China and Vietnam was a slow and deliberate process. Moreover, the action was initially considered as a localised inter-state conflict rather than as part of China's global anti-hegemonic strategy. During the initial years of the post-Mao era, Beijing employed a consensual leadership style that usually involved a prolonged process of informal consultations among senior leaders and subordinates, including lower-level governmental and military officers responsible for the matter, before a final decision.

The initial focus was on the border conflict, which had been perceived as a major source of the current escalation of tension between the two countries since 1976. A tentative proposal recommended a small-scale operation against one Vietnamese regional regiment at Trung Khanh, a border county adjacent to Guangxi province. However, following a review of updated intelligence advising of a forthcoming Vietnamese invasion of Cambodia, the majority of the participants argued that any military action to be taken must have a significant impact on Hanoi and the situation in South-East Asia. They recommended a strike on a regular Vietnamese army unit in a larger geographic area. Although the meeting ended without any specific decision, it set the tone of China's eventual war plan against Hanoi, and possibly was the first evidence of an association of military action on Vietnam's northern border with its aggression in South-East Asia.

Nevertheless, a large-scale military operation against Vietnam risked repercussions for China's international image in the region and the world. Deng Xiaoping's scheduled official visit to Thailand, Malaysia and Singapore in early November provided the opportunity to seek the support of these countries for China's Vietnam policy. During his trip, Deng impressed upon his hosts that China would use force against Vietnamese aggression, if Vietnam attacked Cambodia. At home, the media were full of editorials and commentaries condemning Vietnamese encroachment upon China's territory and warning of possible retaliation.

On 23 November1978, the General Staff convened another meeting at which a new scheme of war was deliberated. Taking into consideration the earlier recommendations, the General Staff broadened the scope and duration of operations. The plans made all major Vietnamese military positions and cities across the Guangxi and Yunnan borders targets for attacks, anticipating that this would deter Vietnamese aggression. Again, some felt that these operations did not go far enough as they were still limited to a remote area and posed no immediate threat to Hanoi. However they voiced no dissent, assuming the central leadership had given the matter meticulous consideration. The meeting designated the campaign to be carried out by the Guangzhou and Kunming Military Regions. It also recommended the transfer of the PLA's strategic reserves, a total of four armies and one division, from the Wuhan and Chengdu Military Regions to reinforce the Guangxi and Yunnan fronts.

On 7 December 1978 the Central Military Commission (CMC) convened a meeting, which allegedly lasted four to five hours, and decided to launch a limited war on China's southern border to hit back at Vietnam. The next day it issued an order commending the Guangzhou and Kunming Military Regions to conduct the military campaign with all troops to be ready for action by 10 January 1979. The instructions specified that the war would be strictly limited, conducted within 50 kilometres from the border and lasting two weeks. It then emphasised the core tenets of the PLA's traditional operation doctrine requiring the two regional commands to concentrate a superior force to envelope the enemy forces from flanks, to destroy the enemy forces one by one with quick-decision battles of annihilation, and then to withdraw immediately. The timing of this order suggests that China was responding to the forthcoming Vietnamese invasion of Cambodia, but by mounting a major military campaign even before Vietnamese forces crossed the Mekong was also reacting to several years of exasperation caused by Vietnam's ungrateful behaviour.

The important personalities in the 11th Politburo of the People's Republic of China, who were part of the decision-making process, were as follows:

1. **Deng Xiaoping**
   Vice Premier of the People's Republic of China
   The most powerful member of the 11th Politburo, and the person who declared war against Vietnam.
2. **Wei Guoqing**
   Director of the People's Liberation Army's General Political Department
   With plenty of military experience, Wei Guoqing served in the Chinese Red Army, was a battalion commander in the Seventh Army, served in the 344th Brigade, and was the commander of the 4th Division of the New Fourth Army, along with many other credentials. In 1950 he was sent to Vietnam as head of the Chinese Military Advisory Group to help Ho Chi Minh.
3. **Ye Jianying**
   Chairman of the Standing Committee of the National People's Congress
   He became influential after the overthrow of Lin Biao in 1971, and was appointed Defence Minister in his place in 1975.

4. **Liu Bocheng**
Vice-Chairman of the Standing Committee of the National People's Congress
Although a subordinate to Ye Jianying, Liu Bocheng had been elected as a member of the Politburos of the 8th through 11th National Congress, as well as holding the position of Vice-Chairman of the Military Committee. He was a long-time supporter of Deng Xiaoping.
5. **Xu Shiyou**
General in the People's Liberation Army
Moving quickly up the ranks of the Chinese military, Xu Shiyou was a commander in the Fourth Front Army, and by the age of 29, commanded the Red 9th Corps. He has served as Commander of the Nanjing Military Region for ten years with Zhang Chunqiao, earning the recognition as obtaining the single longest tenure of any MR commander. Under Deng Xiaoping he was rotated to Guanzhou MR as commander.
6. **Li Xiannian**
Vice Chairman of the Communist Party of China
Starting as a political commissar for the Chinese Red Army, he went on to be appointed China's Minister of Finance in 1954 as well as Vice Premier. He played a pertinent role in eliminating the Gang of Four, and following the death of Mao Zedong, became Hua Guofeng's chief economic advisor. Had Deng Xiaoping not risen to power as "Paramount Leader", Xiannian would have succeeded Guofeng.
7. **Li Desheng**
Member of the CCP Military Commission
He served as a general in the People's Liberation Army and was mentored by Chen Xilian. He was appointed Chairman of the Revolutionary Committee in 1968 and served in that position for 7 years. 1973 proved to be an influential year for him when he was elected a full member of the Politburo, a member of the Politburo Standing Committee and Vice-Chairman of the CPC Central Committee.
8. **Chen Yun**
Vice Chairman of the Communist Party of China
A very influential figure, Chen Yun was one of the Big Five (Mao Zedong, Liu Shaoqi, Zhou Enlai, Zhu De) of the Chinese Civil War. He was responsible for the fiscal aspects of China's policies, and in 1949, was named head of the Central Finance and Economic

Commission. He advocated for a more liberalised economy with a supply-and-demand-system rather than having the government mandate all fiscal policy. He is a subdued critic of Mao Zedong's "Great Leap Forward" and an advocate for Deng Xiaoping's "reform and opening" programme.

9. **Hu Yaobang**
   His rise to power is accredited to Deng Xiaoping's rise to role of "paramount leader". Was known to have liberal political views, and was purged during the Cultural Revolution along with Xiaoping. After he was recalled, he became director of the CCP's organisational department as well as director of Party propaganda.
10. **Geng Biao**
    Secretary-General of Standing Committee of Central Military Commission
    He served as a general in the Red Army, and became chief of staff, deputy head and deputy commissar in the Second Sino-Japanese War. He served as ambassadors to various nations including Sweden, Pakistan, Myanmar and Albania. Was appointed vice-premier of the State Council, and the Secretary-General for the CMC.
11. **Nie Rongzhen**
    Vice Chairman of the Military Central Committee
    Joined the Communist party in 1923, and served his first few years following the completion of a degree at the Soviet Red Army Military College as a political officer in Whampoa's Political Department. Worked with Lin Biao in the 115th division of the Eighth Route Army, and lead the Northern China Military Region during the Chinese Civil War. In 1955, was made Marshal of the PLA and directed the Chinese nuclear weapons programme. He was purged during the Cultural Revolution and reinstated as Vice Chairman of the MCC.
12. **Xu Xiangqian**
    Minister of National Defense
    After the formation of the People's Republic of China, Xu Xianqian was appointed General Chief of Staff of the PLA. He helped protect Deng Xiaoping after he was purged during the Cultural Revolution, and was a military supporter of the coup against the Gang of Four.
13. **Wu De**
    Chairman of the Beijing Revolutionary Committee
    Was mayor of Beijing, notable for suspending class in Beijing universities

in order to concentrate efforts on the Cultural Revolution. He was an advocate for Hua Guofeng as "paramount leader", and is known to have called for the repression of protestors in Tiananmen Square in 1976.

Beijing and Hanoi Commit to Forward Strategies

Until 1978, the actions of both Vietnam and China were severely limited. Vietnam had attempted to avoid full-scale hostilities with Cambodia and China was circumspect in dealing with Vietnam. As the year began, both China and Vietnam shifted to more active policies, leading to increasing friction. A fatal interplay of forward policies began.

Vietnam was also embarking on a more active policy course. In February, Hanoi offered Phnom Penh a three-point peace proposal calling for: (1) an immediate cease-fire with international supervision; (2) a 10-kilometre demilitarised zone, each side pulling back five kilometres; and (3) a border agreement and a peace and friendship treaty. The Pol Pot regime rejected this proposal, insisting talks could not begin until Vietnam proved its good intentions by not firing a shot for seven months. Hanoi termed the response ridiculous.

Hanoi then decided to go ahead with the training of a Cambodian refugee "army" to overthrow the Pol Pot government. Other major decisions involved the economic integration and socialisation of the reunited south and a crackdown on "bourgeois trade" and "capitalist elements" primarily in the Chinese Cholon section of Ho Chi Minh City. The Central Committee seems to have also approved closer contracts with Moscow and the build-up of forces along the Chinese border. After the meeting, it was rumoured that General Giap flew to Vientiane to talk with visiting Soviet Deputy Defence Minister Pavlovsky. Le Duc Tho toured the Cambodian border commands, briefing them on Politburo decisions, as he had done before major offensives in 1968, 1972, and 1975. (Le Duc Tho is best known for his part in the cease-fire of 1973, when he served as special adviser to the North Vietnamese delegation to the Paris Peace Conferences in 1968–73. He he negotiated the cease-fire agreement that led to the withdrawal of the last American troops from South Vietnam. It was for this accomplishment that he was awarded the Nobel Peace Prize, which he declined).

The Sino-Vietnamese Dispute Becomes a Crisis

Relations between China and Vietnam deteriorated rapidly during the first months of 1978. In February Chinese and Vietnamese forces had clashed at Don Van and Mong Cai, with 30 Vietnamese reported killed at Mong Cai. The propaganda war heated up quickly, with both sides charging the other with border violations, which occurred with increasing frequency. Then on 24 March, Hanoi implemented a programme, decided on at the Central Committee meeting in February, cracking down on the "bourgeois trade" and "capitalist elements" in Cholon and Hanoi. The primary targets of this campaign were the ethnic (overseas) Chinese traders and merchants in Cholon, who controlled the wholesale rice trade and had continued to trade in gold and foreign currency after the fall of Saigon in 1975. This included Chinese engaged in both legitimate and illegitimate banking and commercial interests. Hanoi also cracked down on the traders and shopkeepers, mostly Chinese, who dominated that city's small private sector.

Within days a mass exodus of the Chinese living in Vietnam had begun and within weeks serious fighting was reported on the China-Vietnam border. China expressed concern over the increasing numbers of overseas Chinese trying to return to their homeland from Vietnam and promised them protection. In response, Hanoi charged that Chinese subversive groups were spreading horror stories in Vietnamese cities to aggravate tensions, and that the rumour-mongers were causing the exodus. By the end of May Beijing's propaganda machine dropped any semblance of restraint and began accusing Vietnam of atrocities against the overseas Chinese. The Chinese media reports suggested that Vietnam was carrying out "Moscow's designs," and becoming a "second Cuba," by giving the Soviets a base at Cam Ranh Bay. On 27 May, Vietnam called for an end to polemics and proposed early talks. On 9 June the Chinese Foreign Ministry rejected the call for talks and announced a major cutback on aid to Vietnam, claiming that money had to be diverted to settle the mass of Chinese refugees that had been robbed and brutalised by Vietnam.

As May came to a close, Beijing dispatched two ships from Guangzhou (Canton) to pick up Chinese "victims" of Vietnamese "persecution" at Haiphong and Ho Chi Minh City. Hanoi flatly refused to permit the ships to land, standing on its right to control emigration. After two months the ships finally returned to Gauangzhou without having picked up any refugees. On 16 June, China announced it was closing the Vietnamese consulates in Kunming, Nanning, and Guangzhou, ostensibly in retaliation for Hanoi's foot-dragging in responding to Beijing's requests for Chinese consulates in Ho Chi Minh City, Haiphong, and Da Nang. Although China professed concern about its rights to look after the sizeable Chinese populations in these areas, each capital was probably trying to prevent the other from observing significant military preparations along their common border.

Claiming that the Chinese were reinforcing their border, the Vietnamese strengthened their own border forces, reorganised the military command in the border area with more senior cadres, and purged pro-Chinese generals. In mid-June the newly reorganised Vietnamese army began a major military thrust into eastern Cambodia, seemingly aimed less at taking territory than at chewing up Cambodia's modest army. Heavy air strikes and artillery barrages were to continue all summer and fall. Despite solid resistance by the Cambodian forces, Vietnamese cannon-fodder tactics inexorable ate up Cambodian reserves. As the Cambodian army became hard pressed, a wave of an estimated 53,000 Cambodian refugees slipped through the cordon into Vietnam, trying to avoid the mayhem of war and Pol Pot's excesses. The émigré army in Vietnam grew steadily larger under the command of So Phim, who had been a Pol Pot army leader until he mutinied in May 1978 after an alleged coup attempt.

Vietnam, hard-pressed by the costs of its war with Cambodia and experiencing a catastrophic flooding of its rice lands, needed ever-increasing amounts of assistance. On 28 June, Hanoi announced it was joining the Soviet-controlled Council for Mutual Economic Assistance (CEMA), the Soviet bloc equivalent of Western Europe's Common Market. The move reflected Moscow's efforts to share the increasing financial burden of support to Vietnam with other CEMA members. The price of greater help by the Soviet Union was the abandonment of Hanoi's pretence of neutrality between its two communist benefactors. On 2 July, Beijing responded to this action by terminating the last of its 60-odd economic aid programmes to Vietnam. The CEMA countries picked up less than a dozen of these. Hanoi's efforts to seek US assistance and investments to bolster its economy were shied away from by the United States, which refused to normalise relations with Hanoi, even after Hanoi dropped its insistence on war reparations in July. Although there were no longer any bilateral impediments to the normalisation of relations between the United States and Vietnam once Hanoi dropped its demands for war reparations, the US State Department opposed normalisation because of the Vietnam refugee situation and Hanoi's belligerence toward Cambodia. Cut off from Chinese aid because of the ever-deteriorating relations between Hanoi and Beijing, and refused US assistance, Vietnam had turned again to Moscow. Unlike previous years, Hanoi would find it much more difficult to resist Moscow's pressure for base rights and similar concessions by playing Moscow and Beijing off against each other.

June and July were months of serious stocktaking in Beijing. Vietnam's offensive in Cambodia had undermined Beijing's earlier confidence that they could "bleed" Vietnam by a drawn-out struggle on foreign soil against a hostile population. It was becoming clear that the Cambodian army could not long survive the heightened level of conflict.

By late summer the economic burdens of settling and providing for 160,000 refuges, with more expected, were putting a heavy strain on the drought-stricken southern provinces. Deng was forced to pay greater attention to the growing crisis in the south. Vietnam had become a major domestic issue as well as a foreign policy problem.

Diplomatic Activity Further Strengthens China's Geo-Political Position

In May China agreed to reopen talks with Japan on a peace and friendship treaty. The talks, which had begun in 1972, had been stalled by Japan's reluctance to antagonise the Soviet Union by accepting an "anti-hegemony" clause in the treaty stating: "neither should seek hegemony in the Asia-Pacific region or in any other region of the world and each is opposed to efforts by any other country or group of countries to establish hegemony."

One of the motivating factors for Beijing to enter into the peace and friendship treaty at this time was to make it difficult for Tokyo to show neutrality toward Beijing's and Moscow's escalating competition for influence in Southeast Asia. Not only would more cordial and friendly relations between China and Japan enable China to obtain the technology and capital needed for the four modernisations, but the peace and friendship treaty might serve as a deterrent to increased Japanese-Vietnamese and Japanese-Soviet economic cooperation by forcing Japan eventually to choose between foregoing the benefits accruing from better relations with China or supporting Beijing's anti-hegemonist policies.

In October Beijing also shifted its position on India. Having castigated India for twenty years as a "bully to its neighbours" and having conducted two limited territorial wars against India, the Beijing press now began to praise the Desai administration in New Delhi, which had been steadily moving away from the close ties with Moscow established earlier. India's Foreign Minister Vajpayee, scheduled to visit Beijing on 27 October, postponed the trip due to "illness." (The trip would be made later, during February 1979).

Seeking Washington's Support

From Beijing's perspective, the establishment of diplomatic relations on 1 January 1979 with Washington had altered the global balance of power in China's favour.

On 28 January 1979, Deng Xiaoping left for Washington on a historic visit to the US. One of the major (if unstated) purposes of Deng's trip was to ally the US with China in countering the Soviet-Vietnamese alliance in East Asia. Deng's trump card was the Chinese military plan against Vietnam, for which he wanted to win US support. Deng proposed that the US dispatch its naval ships to the South China Sea to contain Soviet naval activities while helping China with intelligence about Vietnamese vessels. Chinese leaders felt that giving the US Navy access to the naval base at Yulin on Hainan Island "would be conducive to the stability of Southeast Asia."

In a special meeting with President Jimmy Carter to discuss the Vietnam issue, the Chinese leader spoke about China's decision to attack Vietnam. Deng informed the Americans that to counter Soviet expansion, China considers it necessary to put restraints on the wild ambitions of the Vietnamese and to give them an appropriate limited lesson. Without divulging specific details of China's plan, Deng outlined possible Soviet responses and the ways to counter them. He said that if the worst possibility were to happen, China would hold out and would simply ask for US moral support in the international arena. Carter did not offer an immediate response and instead asked Deng to be restrained in dealing with such a difficult situation.

President Carter argued that a limited punitive war would have no effect on Vietnam's occupation with Cambodia, and he warned that it might drag China into a quagmire. Carter also predicted than an invasion of Vietnam would stymie China's effort to foster a peace-loving image in the world and might cause Americans to worry that Chinese military action in the future would impair US interests in the region.

In another private meeting with Carter, Deng was determined and tough, insisting that China must punish Vietnam and that the PLA would limit its action to a short operation. He acknowledged that international reaction could be divided at the time, but he was confident that opinion would favour China in the long run. The potential international backlash would not deter the Chinese leader because he would yield to nothing once he had made up his mind.

Before leaving Washington, Deng was surprised to learn that the US was interested in a joint US-China listening base in China's Xinjiang area targeted against the Soviet Union. The proposed installation in China was intended to help the US verify Soviet compliance with the Strategic Arms Limitation Treaty. Deng showed great interest in the idea and agreed to consider the proposal.

The two sides reached a tacit understanding that the US would help China with intelligence monitoring of Soviet forces in the Far East. Thus the US informed China of intelligence showing that none of the 54 Soviet divisions on the Sino-Soviet border were at full strength. Deng sensed that a new strategic relationship between China and the US was developing on the basis of the two countries' shared interest in countering Soviet expansionism. On the issue of Vietnam, the US side had not rejected or directly criticised the Chinese plans and had instead called for future intelligence cooperation.

Deng Xiaoping Makes the Decision

Although the Chinese war machine was primed in early December, no definite date for strikes had yet been determined. At a CMC conference on New Year's Eve, Deng formally proposed a punitive war against Vietnam. All participants, including Hua Guofeng, chairman of the CCP, were reportedly in support of this proposal. At the meeting, Deng appointed Xu Shiyou to command operations from Guangxi in the east, and Yang Dezhi, commander of the Wuhan Military Region, to command operations from Yunnan in the west, sidestepping Wang Bicheng, commander of the Kunming Military Region.

Apparently concerned about the change of command on the eve of the war, Deng subsequently sent two of his deputy chiefs to Kunming to supervise the transition and war preparations. Without a centralised command, two military regions would carry out the war independently with almost no co-ordination or collaboration. The meeting also reiterated that the invasion must be swift and all troops must be pulled back after achieving the operational objectives.

As Deng Xiaoping was the chief architect of the scheme, it is unlikely that anyone would challenge his decision given his seniority and prestigious status in the Party. Deng's control of the General Staff provided him with a convenient channel to set China's military machine in motion before the central leadership had made a formal decision. Acting like Mao, Deng privately consulted trusted associates before making a decision, and only then took his decision for formal endorsement by the Politburo. There were several major concerns:

(a) whether the Soviet Union would respond with reprisal attacks from the north to force China to fight a two-front war;
(b) whether the United States would take the opportunity to profit from the situation;
(c) how world opinion would react; and
(d) whether war with Vietnam would impede China's new agenda for economic modernisation.

The most worrying concern was the possible Soviet reaction. According to intelligence analysis by the General Staff, Moscow would have three military options in response to the invasion:

(a) a massive armed incursion including a direct attack on Beijing;
(b) instigation of the armed ethnic minority personnel, who were exiled in the Soviet Union, to attack China's outposts in Xinjiang and Inner Mongolia;
(c) use of skirmishes to mount border tensions between the two countries.

However as the Soviet Union did not have adequate forces to conduct any large military operations against China immediately, Chinese leaders, particularly Deng, were convinced that a defensive, limited and brief military action against Vietnam would not provoke Moscow's intervention and an international outrage. The Chinese military calculated the Russians would take 14 days or even longer to make a military response; by then China would have achieved its war objectives. The two previous border conflicts, against India in 1962 and the Soviets in 1969, corroborated this calculation. Nevertheless, the Chinese leaders could not lower their guard, and simultaneously ordered troops in the northern and north-western military regions to step up combat readiness for possible Soviet strikes.

The New Year's Eve meeting deferred the timing of military action. Western analysts argue that Beijing was still constrained by concern about international reaction. Deng's scheduled trips to the United States and Japan were thus arranged to test the waters. However, those intimately associated with Deng suggest that potential international backlash would not deter him because he would yield to nothing once he had made up his mind. Chinese leaders were more worried about whether their forces had enough time to make adequate preparations for the invasion. Chinese soldiers had not engaged in any war for a long period, while many of them could not comprehend going to war against a traditional ally and a small neighbouring state. Shortly after the New Year's Eve meeting, Deng sent Yang Yong, deputy chief of the General Staff, and Zhang Zhen, director of the General Logistic Department, to Yunnan and Guangxi respectively to inspect troops' combat conditions. Appalled by their lack of readiness, Zhang immediately recommended the postponement of the war for a month. Accordingly, the CMC agreed to push back the counteroffensives until the middle of February.

Yang made his report, along with suggestions on the war plan, on 22 January in the presence of the chief leaders of the CMC. It is likely to have been at this gathering that the Chinese leadership reaffirmed the war decision and determined a time frame for D-day. The next day, the General Staff held a meeting at which the war plan was finalised and troops were ordered to be ready for action by 15 February. In order to prevent the situation becoming out of control, the central leadership specifically required Xu Shiyou to stop military operations and pull his troops back after the seizure of Lang Son and Cao Bang, two major Vietnamese cities on the border.

On 11 February 1979, two days after Deng Xiaoping returned to Beijing from his trip to the United States and Japan, an enlarged Politburo conference was convened. Deng articulated the basic rationale for the attack on Vietnam, and subsequently a go-ahead order to launch attacks on Vietnam on 17 February was issued to the local military commanders in Guangxi and Yunnan. The timing of the offensive might also have been closely related to weather factors: it would be unfavourable to conduct military operations in the rainy season, usually beginning in April, or to attack too early when the Soviet armed forces could cross the frozen rivers along the China-Soviet border. Deng and other Chinese leaders had already carefully calculated all possible ramifications once their troops crossed the Vietnam border. They limited the scope, time and space for the war and labelled it a "self defensive counterattack," attempting to reduce any negative reactions at home and abroad. Once the war started, however, Deng, while paying close attention to what was going on, gave few specific instructions and orders (in contrast to Mao Zedong's leadership style).

Despite his power and prestige within the party, Deng still needed to convince his colleagues why China should use force against Vietnam. He offered three reasons.

(a) First, the current international anti-hegemony struggle against the Soviet Union was weakening because the United States, Japan, and Europe were afraid of starting a war. In light of Vietnam's invasion of Cambodia and provocations along China's border, the PRC itself must take the leading role in the struggle. The self-defence counterattack, Deng argued, was aimed not at a mere border dispute but at the wider situation in Southeast Asia and even the entire world.

(b) Second, Deng insisted that China needed a safe, reliable environment for its four modernisations. The PRC could not allow itself to be menaced by the Soviet Union from the north and Vietnam from the south, which would "wedge us in." China, he believed, should expose the hollowness of Vietnam's boast of being "the world's third strongest military power" and of "being ever victorious." If China failed to act, Deng claimed, it would simply fuel Vietnam's aggression and might encourage the Soviet Union to move in from the north. China's counterattack would thus also send a warning to the Soviet Union.

(c) Third, Deng argued that because the PLA had not fought a war in thirty years, Chinese leaders could not be "sure that our military is still good enough." He agreed with the CMC's recent decision to increase troop training but believed that real combat would be even more beneficial. Deng worried about the PLA's reputation, which had suffered a great deal in recent years as a result of the Cultural Revolution. He was convinced that a successful war against Vietnam would help to restore the PLA's reputation and provide more officers with war experience.

In dealing with Vietnam, Deng and other Chinese leaders drew a historical analogy with the Sino-Indian War of 1962. They were familiar with the success China had in quickly conducting a war against India when it intruded one hundred kilometres into Indian territory within just a few days. This fact may have been particularly powerful in shaping Deng's response. Since the Chinese Civil War, Deng had served in the army as well as senior party and government posts. In the 1950s and 1960s, he participated in battles of quick decision in Central Asia and watched the PLA conduct the quick, decisive campaign against India. Though Deng was aware of the problems plaguing the PLA, he is likely to have thought that a successful quick, decisive attack on Vietnam remained within the capabilities of the PLA. Should the attack be less successful than desired, it would provide reason to push through the military reforms that he had long advocated.

The final step to war was taken after Deng returned to China from travelling to the US and Japan in late January and early February 1979. Deng timed the attack immediately after his trip, when he felt that he had sufficient international support. The ASEAN countries were afraid the Vietnamese-Cambodian War might spread to Thailand and had condemned Vietnam's aggression. The US also did not express any strong opposition to a possible Chinese attack. Planning the attack after normalisation of US-China relations strengthened the impression that Washington was tacitly supporting the attack.

Deng personally determined and oversaw the political, diplomatic, and military operations of the war. To contain the costs of the war, limit escalation, and diminish the likelihood of Soviet intervention, Deng stipulated that the war would not be longer than the 1962 war with India (33 days) and that it would be a ground war involving no aircraft. To hedge against Soviet involvement, China pulled back three hundred thousand Chinese civilians from its border with the Soviet Union and continued to position China's best troops along the Soviet border. China deployed only second-line troops to the Vietnamese front. To provide maximum troop exposure to combat as well as to combine the strengths of various armies, the war involved Chinese troops from ten of the country's eleven military regions.

Assessing China's Decision to Go to War

According to Chinese scholars, the PRC's decision to wage war against Vietnam was influenced by Chinese leaders' overreaction to the Soviet military threat, which caused them to pursue strategic cooperation with the US against the Soviet Union. Because this policy emphasised confrontation, Beijing's approach to the region became rigid and militant. Chinese policymakers believed that a punitive attack on Vietnam would deal a blow to the USSR's global expansion strategy. Nevertheless, it does not adequately explain why Chinese leaders exaggerated the Soviet threat or why Deng was eager to inform the Carter administration about the decision to attack Vietnam, something that normally would happen only between two closely allied countries. Although the Soviet factor was influential in Chinese decision-making, other factors, including domestic politics, also played a role.

The PRC's policy toward Vietnam was guided by manifold considerations, ranging from historical tradition to revolutionary ideology and national security. The Chinese leaders' sense of superiority dominated their perceptions of China's relationship with Vietnam. Although officials in Beijing repeatedly declared that Vietnam should be treated as an "equal," such rhetoric reflected their strong belief that they had occupied a position from which to dictate the values and codes of behaviour that would dominate their relations with their neighbours. The PRC claimed that it had never imposed political and economic conditions on its military aid to Hanoi over the previous two decades, but it demanded that Hanoi recognise China's leading role in supporting national liberation movements.

If teaching a lesson was China's main objective, the PLA should have struck hard to achieve significant military results. But Deng asserted later that he would not need military achievements. He explained that teaching Vietnam a lesson was not based on a consideration of what was happening between China and Vietnam or in Indochina, but based on a contemplation of the matter from the angle of Asia and the Pacific; in other words, from the high plane of global strategy. Ultimately, his calculus was dominated by two priorities: improving China's external security environment and reforming and opening up China's economy.

In view of all these factors, the objective of China's decision to use force to teach Vietnam a lesson and to go to war is hard to assess without a careful evaluation of the geopolitical circumstances and China's drive for economic reform—conditions that in 1979 were fundamentally different from those in 1950. Whatever the rationale for the war, Deng's dictatorial leadership style allowed him to dominate Beijing's decision-making, and therefore the wisdom of his decision to attack Vietnam is still debatable. Whatever the shortcomings of its execution, the Chinese campaign reflected a serious, long-term strategic analysis.

8

FORCE LEVELS

CHINA

The total manpower of the People's Liberation Army (PLA), at the time of the Sino-Vietnam war was about 4.3 million in the army, the navy, and the air force. The army, which is the main force of the PLA, had 3.6 million men in 175 divisions (121 infantry, 11 armoured, 3 airborne, and 40 artillery). These figures of the PLA's strength, including the weaponry and equipment are drawn from *The Military Balance 1978-1979* published by the London-based International Institute for Strategic Studies, 1978.

These forces were stationed in eleven first-class military regions (MR), with a heavy deployment in the Beijing and Shenyang areas (52-55 divisions and 4,700 tanks). These eleven military regions comprised Beijing, Shenyang, Lanzhou, Xinjiang, Jinan, Nanjing, Fuzhou, Guangzhou, Wuhan, Chengdu, and Kunming. The Dongjiang (eastern Xinjiang) Military Region, established immediately before the war, was a second-class region under the Xinjiang MR. Guangzhou and Kunming military regions had approximately 12-16 divisions.

Prior to the 1979 war, the army had 9,000-10,000 tanks (T-59) mostly outdated. Its anti-tank weapons, conventional 100-mm anti-tank guns and rocket launchers, were old. It possessed no advanced firing equipment and techniques, such as laser or infrared rays. Its artillery had 16,000-20,000 field guns and rocket launchers. Their effectiveness was limited by their low mobility and lack of sophisticated, sensitive, range-sighting devices. Some of the guns were Second World War leftovers. They were so old that if they were not used in Vietnam in 1979 they would have been discarded as waste material. Its transportation facilities were mostly outdated and the ratio of trucks to troops was low. In the war, logistics proved to be a serious problem.

Deng Xiaoping was the overall Commander. Xu Xiangqian and Nie Rongzhen were appointed Deputy Commanders. Geng Biao was the Chief of General Staff.

Two fronts were established—northern and southern. The Northern Front, which included the Shenyang, Beijing, Jinan, Lanzhou, and Xinjiang MR's, was placed under the command of Li Desheng (Commander of the Shenyang MR). Before the war began, the Chinese government had already evacuated 300,000 inhabitants from exposed border areas in Heilongjiang and Xinjiang, and put the entire Northern Front on maximum alert. It was a precaution against a possible Soviet strike. After one week of fighting in the south, the potential tension in the north eased off because a Soviet attack appeared unlikely.

Since the war was being fought in the south, the command arrangements for the Southern Front were more important and complicated. Xu Shiyou (Commander of the Guangzhou MR) was appointed the Commander; Yang Dezhi (new Commander of the Kunming MR), the Deputy-Commander; and Zhang Tingfa (Commander of the Air Force), the Chief of Staff. Also, the Southern Front was divided into Eastern and Western Wings. The Eastern Wing covered Guangxi and Guangdong provinces under the command of Xu Shiyou. The Western Wing was under Yang Dezhi, covering Yunnan. The Air Force was under Zhang Tingfa. The South Sea Fleet was deployed in the Zhanjiang-Hainan area.

Drawing the offensive force from several military regions, the Chinese assembled approximately 31 divisions (330,000 men, i.e. about 10 percent of the total ground forces) and 1,200 tanks on the border. In the Eastern Wing under Xu Shiyou, there were five armies and two divisions. In the Western Wing under Yang Dezhi, there were three armies and four divisions. Several divisions from Nanjing and Fujian (Fuzhou) were earmarked as reserve units. They had T-62 light tanks, T-59 tanks; 122mm, 152mm artillery pieces; 107mm and l40mm multi rocket-launchers; 37mm anti-aircraft guns; and SAM-2 missiles (probably never used). 948 aircraft were stationed in 15 air bases in Yunnan, Guangxi, Guangdong and Hainan during February-March 1979. The South Sea Fleet had deployed 2 destroyers (missile), 4 destroyer escorts (missile), 27 fast patrol boats (missile), 20 submarines, and 604 other boats.

The details of the force-level are as under:

Commander (Xu Shiyou—Commander of Front HQ of Guangzhou Military Region in Nanning)

Deputy Commander (Yang Dezhi)

Chief of Staff (Zhang Tingfa)

Eastern Wing (Xu Shiyou)

41 Army (Guangdong) (121st, 122nd & 123rd Infantry Divisions)
42 Army (Guangxi) (124th, 125th & 126th Infantry divisions)
55 Army (Guangdong) (163rd, 164th & 165th Infantry divisions)
1st Artillery Division (Guangdong)
70th Anti-aircraft Division (Hunan)

Reserve (Mostly from Wuhan Military Region)
20 Army (58th Infantry division)
43 Army (Henan) (127th, 128th & 129th Infantry divisions)
50 Army (Chengdu) (148th & 150th Infantry divisions)
54 Army (Henan) (160th, 161st & 162nd Infantry divisions)

Troops from Guangxi Military Region
1st, 2nd & 3rd Frontier Defence Regiments
70th Anti-Aircraft Artillery Division
The Independent Infantry Division of the Guangxi Region
The Independent Tank Regiment of the Guangzhou Military region

People's Liberation Army Air Force Guangxi Direction (East Front)
Air Force of the Guangzhou Military Region
7th Air Force Corps

13th Air Force Division
(Aero-Transport Group)

People's Liberation Army Navy Guangxi Direction (East Front)
217th Fleet of the South Sea Fleet
8th Navy Aviation Division
83rd & 84th Boat Regiments

Western Wing (Yang Dezhi) Commander of the Front HQ of Kunming Military Region in Kaiyuan

11 Army (Yunnan) (31st & 32nd Infantry Divisions)
13 Army (Chengdu) (37th, 38th & 39th Infantry Divisions)
14 Army (Yunnan) (40th, 41st & 42nd Infantry Divisions)
43rd Division (Yunnan)
149th Division (Yunnan)
4th Artillery Division (Yunnan)
65th Anti-aircraft Division (Fujian)
The Independent Tank Regiment of the Kunming Military Region

Yunnan Direction (West Front)
5th Air Force Corps (Zhang Tingfa)
28 MiG-21
560 MiG-19
98 MiG-17
120 F-9
142 other aircraft

Navy (South Sea Fleet)
Destroyer, 2 (missile)
Escort Destroyer 4 (missile)
Submarine, 20
Patrol Boat 27 (missile)
Other boats 604

In addition to the regular forces, regional and militia units were also employed for logistics and security duties in the front and the border area. On the Xisha Islands (the Paracels), a garrison of 1,000 men increased their anti-aircraft gun positions. So did the number of patrol boats around the Islands. The air force in Guangdong and Hainan kept a close watch on the area from Hainan to Xisha.

VIETNAM

The People's Army of Vietnam (PAVN), in early 1979, had manpower of approximately 600,000. When the war broke out, Hanoi had deployed its forces as under:

Kampuchea	-	about 150,000-200,000
Laos	-	100,000
In the south	-	100,000
In the north	-	200,000-250,000

In the Hanoi area, there were five regular divisions (3080, 3200, 3290, 3860, and 4310) and four brigades (45-artillery, 329-engineer, 202-armoured, and 241-anti-aircraft).

In the Vietnam-Chinese border area, there were 150,000 local troops and militia, including six regional divisions (325, 3320, 334, 3370, 3380, and 386) and one regiment (241). Two regular divisions (3 and 3460) were known to be deployed in the Lang Son area. The local forces were well-trained and well equipped. Their strength may have been superior to some of the Chinese regular units. The figures of manpower and weaponry of the Vietnamese armed forces are based on *The Military Balance 1978-79* (London).

The Vietnamese government claimed they had a force of about 70,000 only, including several army regular divisions in its northern area. However, the Chinese claimed to have encountered more than twice this number.

Vietnam had approximately 300 combat aircraft in early 1979, including 70 MiG-19's, 70 MiG-21's, and some American-made F-5's captured in 1975. But in 1979 Vietnam's MiG-21's were more advanced than China's because they had sophisticated electronic equipment. Chinese planes were vulnerable to Hanoi's large array of Soviet-built surface-to-air missiles and radar-guided anti-aircraft batteries. In response to the Chinese build-up at the border, Hanoi had transferred some of its MiG-21's from the south to the north.

Prior to February 1979, Vietnam's navy had two Soviet-built *Petya* destroyers (with anti-submarine missiles), 30 fast patrol boats (supplied by China), 32 other patrol boats, and some American-made vessels. Its quantity and firepower were lower than China's.

In comparison, the figures show that, prior to the war, the Chinese forces on the border area were quantitatively superior to their Vietnamese counterparts by 3 to 1. Undoubtedly, China had employed Mao's strategy that "*in every battle, concentrate an absolutely superior force*" against the enemy. Manpower was held as the "decisive" factor.

During the war, some Vietnamese forces also used American military equipment captured during the Second Indochina War.

Senior General Van Tien Dung was the head of the Vietnamese military. The details of the Vietnamese forces (50,000 regulars & 100,000 militia) in the area of operations are as under:

1st Military Region (Major General Dam Quang Trung)—responsible for defence of the Northeast region

Main forces

3rd Infantry Division (Golden Star Division)—located at Dong Dang, Van Dang, Cao Loc and Lang Son town of Lang Son Province.

- 2nd Infantry Regiment
- 12th Infantry Regiment
- 141st Infantry Regiment
- 68th Artillery Regiment

338th Infantry Division—located at Loc Binh and Dinh Lap of Lang Son Province

- 460th Infantry Regiment
- 461st Infantry Regiment
- 462nd Infantry Regiment
- 208th Artillery Regiment

346th Infantry Division (Lam Son Division)—located at Tra Linh, Ha Quang and Hoa An of Cao Bang Province

- 246th Infantry Regiment

677th Infantry Regiment
851st Infantry Regiment
188th Artillery Regiment

325th Infantry Division—located at Tien Yen and Binh Lieu of Quang Ninh Province.

8th Infantry Regiment
41st Infantry Regiment
288th Infantry Regiment
189th Artillery Regiment

242nd Infantry Brigade, located at the coastline and islands of Quang Ninh Province.

Local forces

Cao Bang Province
567th Infantry Regiment
one artillery battalion
one air defence artillery battalion
seven infantry battalions

Lang Son Province
123rd Infantry Regiment
199th Infantry Regiment
seven infantry battalions

Quang Ninh Province
43rd Infantry Regiment
244th Infantry Regiment
one artillery battalion
four air defence artillery battalions
5 infantry battalions

Armed police forces (Border guard)
12th Mobile Regiment at Lang Son
four battalions at Cao Bang and Quang Ninh
some companies and 24 border posts

2nd Military Region (Major General Vu Lap)—responsible for defence of the Northwest region

Main forces

316th Infantry Division (Bong Lau Division)—located at Binh Lu and Phong Tho of Lai Châu Province

- 98th Infantry Regiment
- 148th Infantry Regiment
- 147th Infantry Regiment
- 187th Artillery Regiment

345th Infantry Division—located at Bao Thang of Hoang Lien Son province

- 118th Infantry Regiment
- 121st Infantry Regiment
- 124th Infantry Regiment
- 190th Artillery Regiment

326th Infantry Division—located at Tuan Giao and Dien Bien of Lai Châu Province

Local forces

Ha Tuyen

- 22nd Infantry Regiment
- 191st Infantry Regiment
  - one artillery battalion
  - eight infantry battalions

Hoang Lien Son

- 191st Infantry Regiment
- 254th Infantry Regiment
  - one artillery battalion
  - eight infantry battalions

Lai Châu

- 193rd Infantry Regiment
- 741st Infantry Regiment
  - one artillery battalion
  - five infantry battalions

Armed police forces (Border guard)
  16th Mobile Regiment at Hoang Lien Son
    some companies and 39 border posts

In addition, Vietnamese forces were supported by about 50,000 militia, in each Military Region.

Air force

372 Air Division
  one Air Flight of ten F-5s (captured from US forces)
  one Air Flight of ten A-37s (captured from US forces)
  one Air Flight of seven UH-1s and three UH-7s (captured from US forces)
  Air Transport Regiment 919,[36] responsible for transporting troops
  Several C-130, C-119 and C-47 (captured from US forces)

371 Air Division
  916 Helicopter Regiment
    several Mi-6 and Mi-8
  918 Air Transport Regiment
  923 Fighter Regiment
    several MiG-17s and MiG-21

The Vietnam People's Air Force did not participate in the combat directly. However, they provided support to the ground troops, transported troops from Cambodia to northern Vietnam, as well as performed reconnaissance tasks.

Air Defence

Northern and North-western regions
  255 Air Defence Regiment
  257Air Defence Regiment
  267 Air Defence Regiment
  276 Air Defence Regiment
  285 Air Defence Regiment

North-eastern region
  274 Air Defence Regiment

The Soviet Union, although it did not take direct military action, provided intelligence and equipment support for Vietnam. A large airlift was established by the Soviet Union to mobilise Vietnamese troops stationed in Cambodia to Northern Vietnam. Moscow also provided a total of 400 tanks and armoured personnel carriers (APCs), 500 mortars, artillery and air defence artillery guns, 50 BM-21 rocket launchers, 400 portable surface-to-air missiles, 800 anti-tank missiles and 20 jet fighters. About 5,000 – 8,000 Soviet military advisers were present in Vietnam to train Vietnamese soldiers.

During the Sino-Vietnamese War, the Soviet Union deployed troops at the Sino-Soviet border and Mongolian-Chinese border as an act of showing support to Vietnam, as well as tying up Chinese troops. However, the Soviets refused to take any direct action to defend their ally.

The Soviet Pacific Fleet also deployed 15 ships off the Vietnamese coast to relay Chinese battlefield communications to Vietnamese forces.

9

THE MILITARY CAMPAIGN

Build-up

Border clashes between China and Vietnam intensified following the Kampuchean invasion and China began to increase its military presence in its border regions. Accusations of armed border provocations and civilian and military casualties flowed freely between the two protagonists. Vietnam accused China of abrogating the border agreement re-affirmed by the two communist governments, in 1957, in what was shaping up as a border dispute.

China has a reputation for using military force in border disputes and so it came as little surprise when China commenced a marked military build-up. Besides the eight local divisions in Kuangchou and Kunming military regions, China was reported to have moved two additional armies totalling a further 60,000 men from the strategic main force into the area. Total troop concentration in the two military regions was increased to 300,000. The deployment of additional armies included substantial increases in artillery, together with an increase in the mechanised force to 1200 tanks and APCs. Tactical air power within striking range of Vietnam was boosted to a total of over 700 aircraft. Over 15 squadrons of combat aircraft, including the indigenously designed F-9 ground attack fighter, MiG-17 and MiG-19 fighters and IL-28 medium bombers were deployed to the border region.

Vietnam, on the other hand, was heavily committed in Kampuchea where it allegedly had over 100,000 troops of its main battle divisions, together with armour, engaged in military operations. The border region was defended by up to 100,000 regional force troops and irregulars, including ill-trained militia. Only 300 armoured vehicles were estimated to be available. Combat aircraft capable of commitment included Soviet MiG-21 and US F-5 fighters, but numbered only 300. Despite the Chinese build-up, however, no force mobilisations or deployments were reported in the weeks preceding the invasion, possibly partly because the Vietnamese were largely unaware of the size of China's force. Hanoi's air defence was known to be extensive and the presence of a Soviet naval detachment, including a *Kresta* II guided-missile cruiser and a *Krivak* guided-missile destroyer in the South China Sea, probably offered Vietnam a sense of security against attack.

That China was poised to launch a strike was obvious, but some observers believed the blatancy had destroyed the necessary element of surprise, indicating no armed assault would occur. On 15 February, on the same day China announced formal termination of the Sino-Soviet Treaty of Friendship and Alliance, Deng openly declared that China planned to conduct a limited attack on Vietnam. The official reason given for the move was the poor treatment of ethnic Chinese living in Vietnam, and the Vietnamese military occupation of the Spratly Islands. The actual reason was the Vietnamese refusal to withdraw their forces from Cambodia.

Chinese Strategy, Objectives and Preparations

China's prime motive for attacking Vietnam was to check Vietnamese ambition and aggression in South-East Asia and their threat to Chinese national security, as well as to expose Soviet weakness. But poor political calculation meant that Chinese leaders had put themselves in the difficult position of creating a strategy to punish Vietnam and they never stood a chance of success. China's clearly stated desire to "teach Vietnam a lesson" conveyed its foremost war objective to be "an act of revenge." From the outset, Beijing limited the objectives and the conduct of the war not to go beyond a bilateral border conflict. The military leadership of Guangzhou and Kunming was required to come up with an operational strategy that would not only accomplish the objective of punishment, but also limit hostilities in time and space.

The real question for local Chinese military planners was to what extent the objective of teaching Vietnam a lesson could be achieved or measured. The conventional wisdom of the PLA always lays special stress on annihilation of enemy vital forces (*yousheng liliang*). One of the PLA's operational traditions is the employment of an absolute superior force to ensure victory. By mid-January 1979 more than one-quarter of the PLA's field armies were assembled near the China-Vietnam border, a total of more than 320,000 troops. Drawing from his own combat experience and based on the operational and tactic style the PLA had developed in the past, Xu Shiyou responded to the central leadership's war requirements with an approach known as *niudao shaji* (using a butcher's knife to kill a chicken). The conduct of this engagement encompassed three basic elements:

(a) strikes must concentrate on the vital parts of the enemy's defence, but not on the enemy's strong point;
(b) overwhelming force and firepower should be used to smash the enemy defence at the point of engagement;
(c) attacking troops must move as quickly as possible to go deep, and strike all the way into the heart of the enemy.

In this way, Xu expected his forces to cut the enemy defences into pieces, break opponent resistance, and then annihilate the opposition.

In the light of these principles, the Guangzhou and Kunming Military Regions developed their respective war plans with an emphasis on the destruction of Vietnamese regular divisions on the Chinese border. The war would be fought in two stages. During the first stage, a two-pronged offensive would be mounted against Cao Bang and Lao Cai, to encircle two Vietnamese divisions there and to destroy them, while launching a simultaneous attack on Dong Dang to confuse Hanoi about China's war objective. Then, the PLA forces in Guangxi would concentrate on attacking Lang Son, while their counterparts in Yunnan would attempt to engage one Vietnamese division in the Sa Pa area. A total of eight PLA armies would be involved immediately, with one kept in reserve.

Beijing had also laid out a strategy for when and how the air force should be employed. The PLA Air Force planned to commit 18 air regiments plus six additional flying groups to prepare to assist the ground operations. To avoid escalating the conflict, the CMC confined the use of airpower within China's own territory, while ordering the air force units to prepare support for ground operations "if necessary," though without giving a clear definition of what or when a "necessary" situation might be. The order stipulated that any operations outside China's airspace must be authorised by the CMC. Based on this principle, the strategy required all air units to stand in combat readiness for air defence and ground support, and meanwhile to fly as many sorties as possible over the border airspace when the ground assaults started in order to deter the Vietnamese air force from taking action against China. Air command and control personnel and tactical control parties were sent to the forward command posts of the Guangzhou and Kunming Military Regions, army headquarters and the ground force divisions that would assume the main attack missions.

From late December 1978 throughout January 1979, Chinese troops carried out combat training and exercises. Since many of them were new recruits who had been engaged in agricultural production for a long time, such a frantic last-minute effort was, though helpful, definitely insufficient. Training was largely concentrated on basic soldier skills such as shooting and grenade throwing, with few units able to carry out any meaningful tactical training or exercise at regiment and division levels. Many officers reported that they were unsure about the fighting capability of their troops. In the end, the PLA troops designated for invasion were poorly trained and inadequately prepared for a modern war against Vietnam's forces, whose combat experience earned in 25 years of war preceding this conflict appeared to have been overlooked. For example, the 13th Army, designated as the main striking force in Yunnan, had to fill 70 companies with 15,381 additional soldiers, of which 11,874 were new recruits.

Despite the urgent need for training, the PLA continued its time-tested military tradition, using political indoctrination to raise morale and improve combat efficiency. A propaganda machine was set in motion to persuade soldiers that the central leadership's decision for war was necessary and just. Themes adopted for indoctrination were that Vietnam had degenerated into the "Cuba of the East," the "hooligans of Asia" and the "running dogs of the Soviet Union," trying to pursue its expansionist ambitions. The political ideology of Marxism, although shared by the two countries, did not prevent China from launching self-defence actions against a neighbouring small state when paramount national interests were involved. Lectures, accusation meetings, and photographic and material evidence exhibits served to instil patriotism and hatred towards the enemy. At least they offered an apparently valid explanation for the ordinary and less-educated Chinese soldiers of why China should launch military attacks on Vietnam, a brotherly, comradely country for so long.

On 11 February, just six days before the attack, Beijing rejected overtures by the Vietnamese calling for a cease-fire along the border and a UN-supervised demilitarised zone on both sides of the border.

Terrain Analysis

The Vietnamese side of their border with China is divided into two geographic regions, north-western and north-eastern, by their distinct topographies. In the north-west the Vietnamese provinces of Lai Chau and Hoang Lien Son have mountainous and densely forested terrain. In the north-east, comprising the provinces of Ha Tuyen, Cao Bang, Lang Son and Quang Ninh and parts of Hoang Lien Son, the topography is one of low hills and significantly less forest.

The Vietnamese divided those areas into two military regions. Military Region One included the provinces of Lang Son and Cao Bang, while Military Region Two was made up of the provinces of Ha Tuyen, Hoang Lien Son and Lai Chau. Within that larger regional geography, the provincial capital of Lang Son was the most important border city and transport hub, at 150 kilometres distance from Hanoi.

The coastal province of Quang Ninh was designated a separate "special region." The reason for that status was the area's importance in defending the direct approach to the capital of Hanoi.

The terrain from Hanoi north into China affected the plans of both the PAVN and PLA (see Map 5). Hydrology, mountains and vegetation defined the avenues of approach to Hanoi from the north. To the west of Hanoi, the Black, Red and Clear River result in few major roads from Hanoi to the Chinese border. These rivers also limit cross mobility corridor movement. The terrain is more mountainous to the north-west of Hanoi and includes the tallest mountain in Vietnam, Fan Xi Pan at over 3,000 metres. The dense vegetation in the northwest also affects movement off roads. To the east of the Clear River, the elevation flattens and the vegetation is less dense. In addition, a depression runs from Cao Bang through Lang Son to the South China Sea that increases the number of mobility corridors and allows for greater cross mobility corridor movement. Three major avenues of approach exist from the Chinese border to Hanoi. The farthest west avenue of approach follows the Red River and is 295 kilometres to Hanoi. In the centre, the avenue of approach from Cao Bang to Hanoi is 276 kilometres, and meets with the east avenue of approach north of Hanoi and the Red River. The eastern avenue of approach is the shortest at 154 kilometres and is the historical invasion route from China into Vietnam.

The terrain similarly affected the PLA ability to sustain an attack from Chinese territory. Roads and railways in China from the major cities of Nanning and Guangzhou easily supplied the Cao Bang and Lang Son avenues of approach. Movement to the Lao Cai avenue of approach is more difficult and requires following an indirect route from Guangxi to Yunnan Province.

The Chinese Offensive

On 17 February, Chinese forces, over 100,000 strong, attacked Vietnam along the entire border area. The PLA's self-defensive counter-attacks were carried out in three phases:

(a) The first was from 17 to 25 February, during which the Chinese forces smashed the Vietnamese first line resistance and captured the provincial capitals of Cao Bang and Lao Cai, and the key border towns of Cam Duong and Dong Dang, the gateway to Lang Son. Dong Dang Railway Station and the town are several kilometres short of the Friendship Pass border crossing. It is one of three main border crossings with China.

(b) The second stage was a campaign against Lang Son and its surrounding areas in the east, and Sa Pa and Phong Tho in the north-west, from 26 February to 5 March.

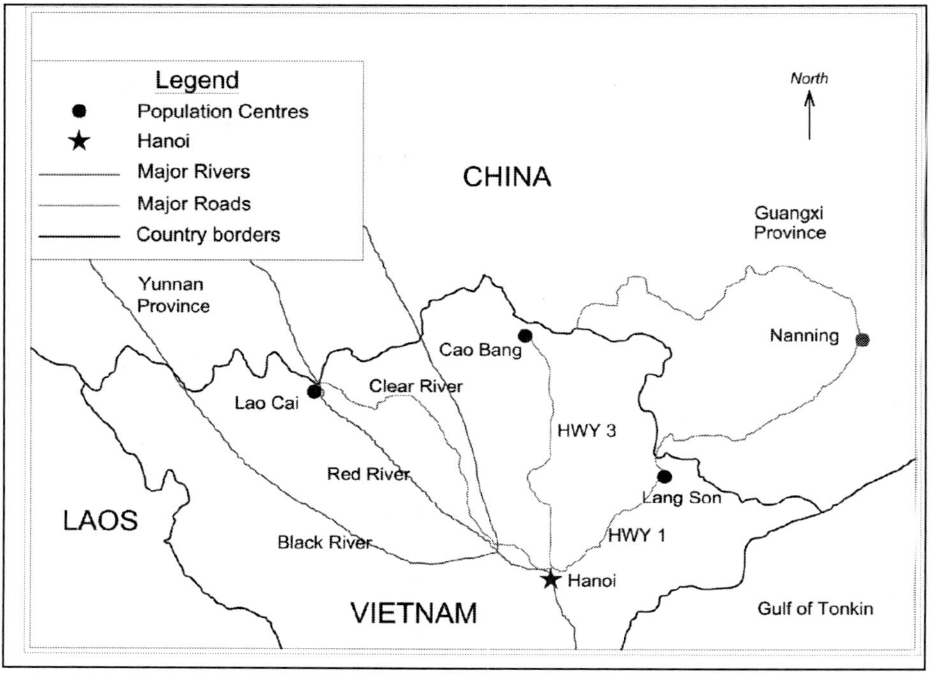

Map 5: Terrain of Northern Vietnam

(c) The final stage was a further effort to pacify the remnant enemy forces while demolishing military installations in the border region with China, prior to a complete withdrawal by 16 March.

The military operations were conducted inside Vietnamese territory along the border stretching for 900 kilometres from east to west. For 30 days, Chinese forces fought the bloodiest battles since the Korean War.

China's attack caught Hanoi off-guard, though some sources indicate that Hanoi anticipated the Chinese invasion, but not on such a large scale and in such force. Vietnamese intelligence apparently failed to get the Hanoi leadership to prepare for a Chinese invasion. Despite Beijing's sabre-rattling for several months, Vietnamese leaders could not believe a fraternal socialist country would ever attack it. When massive numbers of Chinese troops crossed the border, Prime Minister Pham Van Dong and Chief of the PAVN General Staff Van Tien Dung were visiting Phnom Penh. The broad manner of the PLA assaults also confused the Vietnamese high command from identifying the main axis of the invasion forces and the real objectives of the attack. The same day, Vietnamese Premier Pham Van Dong, who had arrived in Phnom Penh just hours before the invasion began, went ahead with the planned signing of a 25-year peace and friendship treaty with the new Vietnam-supported Cambodian government. Included in the treaty were commitments for mutual defence against "international reactionary forces," legitimising Vietnam's military presence in Cambodia.

FIRST PHASE: 17–26 FEBRUARY

At 0500 hours on 17 February 1979, the Chinese commenced their "counterattack" with extremely heavy artillery shelling, followed by tank units and waves of infantry troops. 130mm artillery batteries maintained a concentrated barrage of fire at points along the border as a prelude to the PLA assault. Following this bombardment, breaches were then made at 26 different points along the border. This tactic was obviously designed to confuse Vietnam as to the main axis of the attack. Where terrain permitted, hundreds of tanks poured across the border ahead of APCs and infantry. In particularly mountainous areas where access was limited, mounted cavalry and infantry provided the main thrusts. The Vietnamese claimed that throughout this advance, strike aircraft, including MiG-19s and F-9s, carried out forward attacks. Rather than provision of close air support, the strikes were aimed at strategic targets including communications centres, power plants, and radar and missile sites in a pre-emptive attempt to disrupt Vietnam's defence. There were no reports of aerial engagements and it would seem that the PLAAF achieved early air superiority.

In the East with the front-command post in Nanning, two main columns of forces advanced simultaneously. The first, led by 42 Army, advanced from Longzhou to Dong Dang, aiming at Lang Son. The second, led by 41 Army, moved from Jingxi and Longzhou to Cao Bang and Dong Khe. In addition, the 165th division of 55 Army advanced from Fangcheng to Mon Cai (on the coast). The main objective was Lang Son.

In the West, with the front-command post in Mengzi, three major columns attacked. Led by 13 Army and 11 Army, the first column advanced from Hokou to Lao Cai, on the rail line to Hanoi; the second from Wenshan to Ha Giang (east to Lao Cai); and the third (led by the 42nd Division of the 14 Army) from Jinping to Lai Chau (west to Lao Cai). The objective was Lao Cai.

Employing the Korean War tactic of human-wave attacks involving massive numbers of infantry, the PLA rapidly overran Vietnamese border positions. Within the first three days of the assault, the PLA controlled most of the border to a depth of up to 10 kilometres. By 19 February (Day 3), the wide front of attacks coalesced into two principal thrusts—down the Red River Valley to the provincial capital of Lao Cai, an important rail and road junction controlling access to Hanoi; and through the Friendship Pass toward the provincial capital of Lang Son, another strategic town with access to Hanoi. Heavy fighting for Lao Cai was reported on 19 February, and by 21 February the city fell to the Chinese. In pursuit of the second objective, the PLA had taken Dong Dang by 20 February, where the advance halted. During this initial attack phase, other major centres to fall were Muong Hong, Tra Linh, Cao Bang, and Mong Cai.

Understandably, the Chinese blitzkrieg was devised for maximum gain.

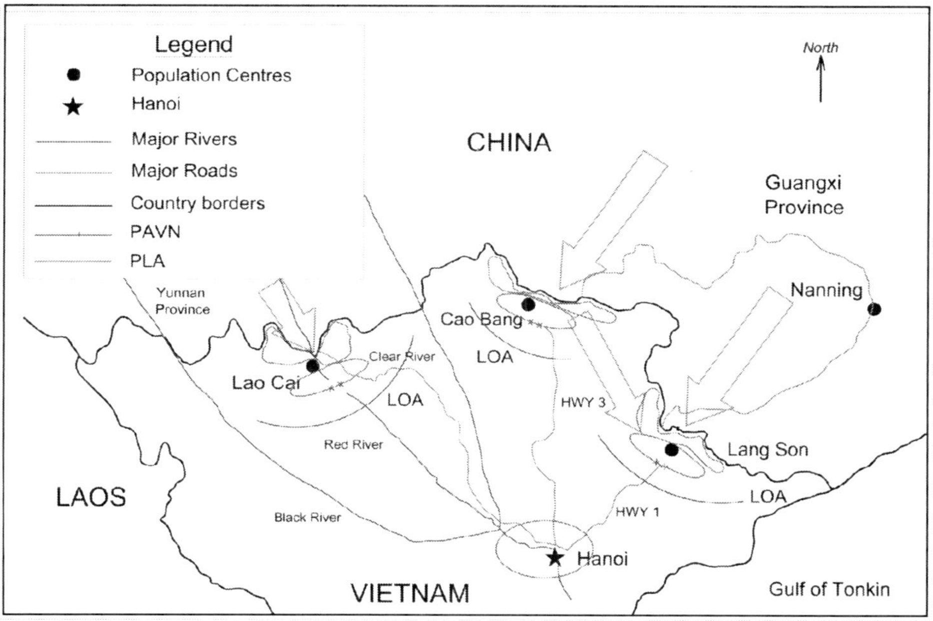

Map 6: Chinese Offensive Plan

But the Beijing authorities had never spelt it out. The analysis of the offensive around three objectives:

(a) Quick occupation of a strip along the border, about a few dozen kilometres in depth, which would include the towns of Cao Bang, Lang Son and Lao Cai. From this springboard, more assaults would be launched depending on the situation.
(b) Destruction of Vietnamese military forces and weakening of Vietnam's national defence capacity by eliminating the border guards, annihilating a major part of the regional troops, and mauling some of the regular units.
(c) Destruction of Vietnamese economic bases.

Advancing rapidly, the Chinese forces soon met with difficulties. The rugged terrain of the mountainous border area was substantially unfavourable to the movement of division-sized forces, trucks and other motor vehicles. The Chinese, lacking modern logistic equipment and being refrained from using air transportation, were forced to rely on old trucks, horses, donkeys and labourers for logistics. They were also compelled to divide and sub-divide their forces from the division to company and even platoon level. Their speed of advance was thus greatly reduced.

Despite the availability of over 700 combat aircraft, the PLAAF reportedly flew only 500 sorties in support of these thrusts, with little or no opposition from the Vietnamese Air Force. These air strikes were apparently effective, causing considerable disruption to communications and power supplies. Seven surface-to-air missile sites and a number of anti-aircraft artillery locations were claimed to have been destroyed or damaged. Chinese aircraft losses were not, however, disclosed.

By the end of 21 February, elements of the four PLA armies totalling 125,000 troops were estimated to be committed in Vietnam, and were concentrated on two major fronts: Eastern front (Friendship Pass) under command of Kuangchou Military Region and Western front (Lao Cai) from Kunming Military Region.

On the other hand, Vietnam's response had initially been minimal. Many of the border forces seem to have retreated ahead of the massive Chinese assaults, although Vietnam claimed to have inflicted over 5,000 casualties and destroyed 60 tanks by 21 February. Vietnamese artillery appeared incapable of suppressing the rate of advance of the PLA. No regular reinforcements were moved to the front and the Chinese encountered little concerted opposition in seizing territory. The Vietnamese Air Force was kept almost completely out of combat, either because of a desire not to escalate the conflict or because conditions for a counter-air war were not suitable.

Vietnamese Deployment and Actions

The Vietnamese had employed local troops and militia along the border area for the fighting while assembling their regular army in the plain south of Cao Bang and Lang Son. The purpose was twofold: to weaken the Chinese forces in the border fighting and to prepare for a major battle with the weakened Chinese in the plain. It would put the Chinese in an extremely disadvantageous position: they would have a long logistic line and would be out of their artillery cover range from the border.

The Vietnamese border defence was amazingly strong. The border provinces (Lang Son, Cao Bang, Hoang Lien Soh, Quang Ninh, Lai Chau and Hu Huyen) literally formed impregnable fortresses with tunnels, caves, and trenches manned by well-trained and well-armed militia all over the mountain range. They also employed various tactics and forms of warfare, such as tunnel warfare, jungle warfare, surprise attacks, booby-traps and land-mines, and bamboo "panji" stakes as part of the obstacle system. The PLA was lacking fighting experience. This weakness, coupled with the unfamiliarity of the rugged terrain, brought about enormous sufferings for the PLA.

Chinese Pattern of Attacks

Facing these mostly unexpected obstacles inside Vietnam, the Chinese forces, in addition to their breaking down their formations and units to the company and platoon level, adopted counter-tactics. They were reportedly under orders not to advance more than 50 kilometres into Vietnam so as to avoid the trap of a major battle on the plain. They had also held back more than half of their forces inside China as fresh units for replacement and renewal of attacks, when needed.

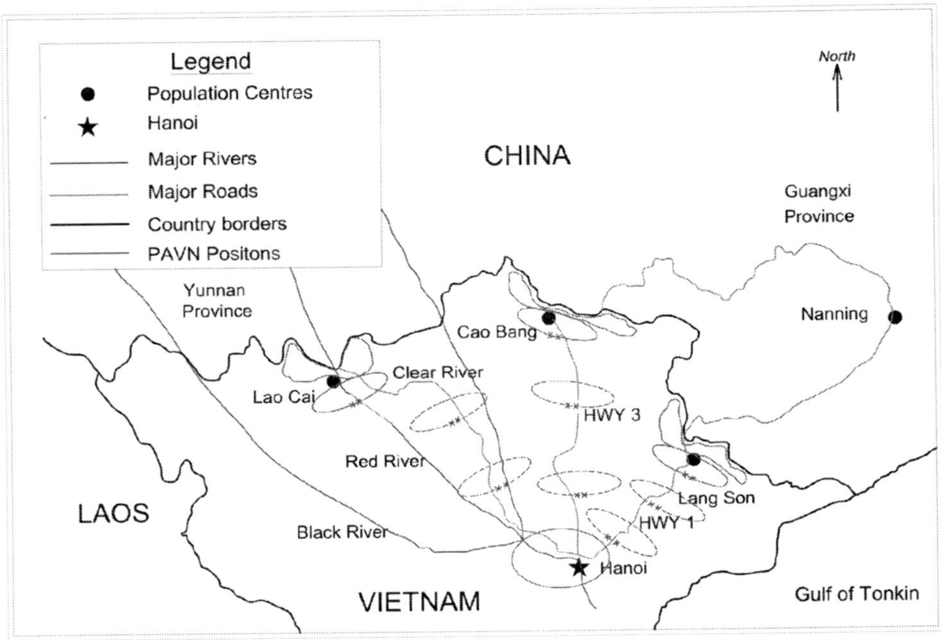

Map 7: Vietnam's Defensive Plan

The Chinese employed the tactics and methods of fire-wave and human-wave assault, while conducting tunnel searches and dynamite detonations, mine-explosions, surprise attacks, encirclements, and other forms of attack. In the first few days of the fighting, China imposed a news blackout on the war. Although Vietnam made some information on the war situation available, information was so scarce that even the Soviets were unable to analyse the progress of the fighting.

In brief, the Chinese attacks were a powerful and successful beginning. Fire wave and human wave tactics were coordinated well. The heaviest fighting was in the north-west border areas of Bat Xat, and Muong Khuong, and around the north-east frontier towns of Dong Dang, Huu Nghi, and Thong Nong. The Chinese advanced more than 15 kilometres into Vietnam and took several border towns. They had also crossed the Red River, pushing hard towards Lao Cai.

On the second and third days of the war (18-19 February), the intensity of fighting increased. The Vietnam resistance was incredibly strong. Although morale was high, the Chinese forces at the division level could hardly manoeuvre. Only small units could operate. The West Wing under Yang Dezhi fought more successfully than did the East Wing under Xu Shiyou. The Chinese forces were gingerly and painfully applying their revised tactics and methods, in conformity with the resistance, weaponry and obstacles being faced. After some losses because of booby-traps and mines, the Chinese used buffaloes to clear the way for the advancing forces. Advance was made tunnel by tunnel, hill by hill. Their slow progress necessitated a "pause" for reinforcements and/or withdrawal. Facing stiff resistance, the Chinese forces took Muong Khuong (Hoang Lien Son province), Trung Khanh (Cao Bang province) and Dong Dang (Lang Son province). The battle of Dong Dang was a fierce encounter in which the Chinese defeated the Vietnamese "Flying Tiger Regiment" (regular army). In the Mon Cai area (Quang Ninh province), the conflict became a see-saw struggle. Both sides suffered heavy losses.

While the battle continued during the week from 20 to 26 February, early and contradictory accounts of the war became available. On 20 February, Beijing reported for the first time that the Chinese had caused very heavy losses on Vietnamese forces since the beginning of the war.

They had advanced 15 kilometres into Vietnam, occupying 26 points. There were 10,000 killed and wounded on the Vietnamese side, only 2,000-3,000 on the Chinese side. In addition, seven Vietnamese missile bases were destroyed. But the Vietnamese gave a different account. After only three days of fighting, the Vietnamese had inflicted heavy casualties on the Chinese. In Cao Bang province alone (including Trung Khanh), four Chinese battalions were badly damaged and scores of tanks and armoured cars destroyed. As both sides made different claims, accounts of the fighting became contradictory.

By 20 February, Soviet advisers concluded that the Vietnamese uncoordinated and guerrilla-type defence would not be able to stop the Chinese forces from advancing. A recommendation was made to airlift an army (30,000 troops) immediately from Cambodia to reinforce the defence between Lang Son and Hanoi. Soviet sources indicate that their advisers made great efforts to find the Vietnamese leader and persuade him to act. Without understanding Beijing's war objectives, Hanoi appeared slow in response to the fast-changing situation in the battlefield.

The major development was China's capture of Lao Cai and Cao Bang, and they were poised to fight at Lang Son. On 21 February, the Chinese forces, reinforced with two divisions, resumed their attacks. After fierce, seesaw fighting, they captured the cities of Lao Cai and Cao Bang on the following day. As they continued to advance, they occupied more areas in the provinces of Ha Giang, Cao Bang, Lang Son, and Quang Ninh. New fighting also broke out in the Mon Cai (coastal town) area. It was reported that Vietnamese reinforcements (regular combat divisions, artillery and armour) had moved northward. The Chinese forces began fighting with the reinforced Vietnamese regulars on 22 February. By 26 February, more and more Chinese troops were assembled near Lang Son. While the fighting continued in the Lao Cai and Cao Bang areas, the battle of Lang Son began.

Statements/Reactions

The Chinese continued their message that the "punitive war" was a limited operation in time and in space and that the Chinese would withdraw from Vietnam immediately after the limited objectives had been obtained. The first statement was by Deng Xiaoping on 19 February. Geng Biao made a similar comment on 23 February, in Beijing, adding that the war would last "about another week, maybe a little more." A statement on 25 February by Wang Zhen, a deputy premier for industry, mentioned that China had no intention of moving into Hanoi. Undoubtedly, these public messages were disseminated for external as well as internal consumption. Externally, they served to dissuade the Soviet Union from intervening, a response to the US call for withdrawal, a tranquilizer to ease off several nations' anxiety about a much larger war, and to puzzle Hanoi.

A word on Soviet moves. In addition to a squadron of 11 Soviet naval vessels staying off the coast of Vietnam, the Soviet Union sent a cruiser of the *Sverdlov* class and a destroyer of the *Krivak* class to the South China Sea on 21 February. It was reported that the two ships would join the Soviet naval squadron off Vietnam. (The 16,000-ton *Sverdlovs* were the largest surface combatants in Soviet Navy. They were rearmed with launchers for surface-to-surface and surface-to-air missiles). Meanwhile, Soviet airlift of arms to Vietnam was reported to have begun. Two special Soviet and Bulgarian flights with military supplies flew to Hanoi via Calcutta. A military delegation from Moscow also departed for Hanoi.

In continuing to voice Moscow's support, Soviet military men spoke out. First Deputy Defence Minister Marshal S.L. Sokolov demanded in Moscow, on 22 February, that Peking take its "hands off Vietnam." On the same occasion in Hanoi, Colonel N.A. Trarkov, military attache of the Soviet Embassy, also demanded China's immediate withdrawal. Trarkov, in a militant mood, further stated that the Soviet Union would "carry out its obligations under the Soviet-Vietnam treaty." Apparently, Trarkov's message was more for Vietnamese, than for Chinese, consumption.

Despite these tough talks, a realistic and sober message was offered by Soviet officials to several Western and Asian diplomats in Moscow. It indicated that the Soviet Union would not intervene in the Sino-Vietnamese war as long as the scale of fighting remained limited. The Soviet government issued a statement citing its treaty obligations with Vietnam, urging China to "stop before it is too late" and demanding an "immediate withdrawal of Chinese troops from Vietnam."

As soon as the war broke out, the US made its official position clear.

While maintaining a neutral stand, it called for an "immediate withdrawal of Vietnamese troops from Kampuchea and Chinese troops from Vietnam".

In sum, at the end of the first period of the fighting (17-26 February), the development of the war became relatively clear: The Chinese had taken several border towns while maintaining no intention to advance to Hanoi; the war would continue for ten more days or so; and the Soviet Union would not intervene in the conflict. Meanwhile, casualties were extremely high.

Consolidation

By 22 February, the Chinese advance had largely halted, and there ensued a period of consolidation and reinforcement of occupied territory which now extended up to 20 kilometres inside Vietnam. No major new fronts were being established, although numerous skirmishes continued. A report that on 24 February the Vietnamese had driven a Chinese division from coastal Quang Ninh province was not substantiated, and subsequent reports indicated China still controlled the border region of this province.

Vietnamese counter-attacks against occupied positions were characteristic of this phase. The movement of Vietnamese heavy artillery to the Lao Cai and Lang Son areas had commenced by 23 February, although no regular infantry units were being deployed. Reports indicated some Vietnamese units were withdrawn from Kampuchea to assist in national defence. To halt deeper Chinese advances, an extensive defence ring was established north of Hanoi, including SAM and AAA sites to counter air attack, artillery, and, further beyond, entrenched regular infantry. A reported Chinese air-strike on the coastal port of Haiphong against Soviet merchant ships discharging military cargo on 23 February proved, not surprisingly, incorrect. The survivability of the PLAAF aircraft would have in any case been slim, and such a provocative action would have risked dangerous escalation.

Indeed, China's overall objectives in the conflict had become quite evident. The prime aim of the initial phase was to inflict heavy casualties and damage to Vietnam's border defence and regional centres to permit Chinese control of the area and limit further harassment. Seizure of provincial centres was intended to further demonstrate the capability of

China's military response and expose Vietnam's weakness. The conflict was also designed to force Vietnam to loosen its military hold in Kampuchea, hopefully to the extent whereby guerrillas of the deposed Pol Pot regime could escalate their activities. Other objectives were political in nature, attempting to regain lost stature and reinforce a claim for dominance in the region. China did not appear to be fighting for a large scale, prolonged war, and therefore limited both its objectives and actions. Vietnam also appeared content to maintain the conflict at a low level, minimising losses and controlling its response.

The lull in military activity during this intermediate phase permitted an intensification of the propaganda war. Predictably, there were vehement accusations flowing from both sides. The Soviet Union, through its treaty with Vietnam, attempted to exert considerable pressure on China, threatening punishment and 'grave consequences' if the invasion was not halted. The US played an even-handed role, calling on both parties to withdraw from their respective invasions in Kampuchea and Vietnam. Vietnam accused the US of tacitly approving the Chinese invasion, although it would appear the US position vis-a-vis China was far less sinister than the USSR's with Vietnam. The UN, a forum for much of the propaganda war, again proved its impotence, with the Security Council shackled by vetoes of the Soviet Union or China. Although Vietnam appeared to be winning the propaganda war, sympathy for the Chinese position was widespread.

It was soon apparent though that, despite the early military victories, the PRC had one further military objective. In the initial attack, Chinese forces apparently met with much stiffer resistance than they had anticipated and Hanoi failed to respond adequately. Thus, battlefield activity intensified once again on 22 February. In the heaviest fighting yet, Chinese forces launched fresh attacks on Highway 1 north of the Vietnamese provincial capital of Lang Son against Vietnamese units guarding the approaches to Hanoi. Chinese government officials announced that China's "punishment" of Vietnam was not yet finished. On 23 February, the PLA clashed for the first time with well-equipped regiments of the Vietnamese regular army that had been deployed in the Lang Son area over the preceding few days.

Despite the PLA's initial breakthrough, the terrain, particularly the lack of roads, and vicious resistance from Vietnamese regular forces, regional security units and militias, soon presented Chinese troops an unexpected combat situation, which unveiled many weaknesses and inefficiencies of the PLA in command, communication and logistics. Most of the problems were inherent in the PLA tradition. On several occasions, the Chinese front command urged direct air support when the ground assaults encountered intense opposition from the Vietnamese. The General Staff refused to grant such permission, instead ordering them to rely exclusively on artillery for fire support. The PLA and its generals were born out of an institutional tradition that was accustomed to fight infantry warfare with artillery firepower and numerical superiority. The spirit of the bayonet continued to prevail. As a result, the 1979 Sino-Vietnamese War was deadly and atrocious on the ground.

The success of the PLA's punitive invasion depended upon tactics of penetration, flank and envelopment of Cao Bang. The two deep-strike divisions, however, failed to reach their destinations within 24 hours. The mountainous terrain, with thick jungle and no roads, and ambushes by Vietnamese local forces and militias, created surprising difficulties for Chinese troops. Their delay forced Xu Shiyou to hold back an immediate attack on Cao Bang, even though one army under the command of a deputy, Wu Zhong, had already closed in on the city from east and south. However, an ongoing investigation of his political affiliation in the Cultural Revolution suspended Wu's commanding position in the midst of the campaign. In a cable on 20 February, Xu reiterated the earlier assignment that the campaign would continue under the command of his other deputy, even though the latter and his troops remained battling their way to Cao Bang from the north. Not until three days later did Xu and his staff officers come to realise that the city was defended only by a small number of Vietnamese troops screening their headquarters and the provincial government from retreat. He then ordered assaults on the city, which the Chinese forces took after several hours of fighting.

While making an urgent request for Moscow to fulfil its obligations according to the newly signed treaty of friendship and cooperation between their two countries, Hanoi's immediate response was to improvise, to throw up whatever resistance might delay the Chinese advance. The major battles were fought around the border towns of Soc Giang, Dong He, Dong Dang, Cao Bang, Lao Cai and Cam Duong, involving tunnel-by-tunnel and hill-by-hill fighting. Both sides demonstrated a willingness to press the attack and counterattack in spite of heavy casualties.

SECOND PHASE: 27 FEBRUARY – 4 MARCH

Despite the continuing fighting in the areas of Lao Cai, Cao Bang and Mon Cai, the war during this period was centred around Lang Son. Approximately 15 kilometres to the Friendship Pass and 135 kilometres to Hanoi, Lang Son faces a rugged region in the north and an open plain in the south. It is an objective that is hard for the northern forces to take but favourable to launch a major drive towards Hanoi. It is a strategically important city to Hanoi's defence.

Battle for Lang Son

By 26 February, Chinese reinforcements were reported moving down the highways from Cao Bang and Friendship Pass toward Dong Dang. Substantial numbers of infantry were accompanied by artillery and tanks, and it seemed the PLA was amassing a number of divisions for a major assault on Lang Son. The civilian population of the provincial capital was evacuated, and some 10,000 Vietnamese regular infantry were moved to the front, in addition to those irregular forces already in the area. Vietnamese artillery was moved in and emplaced on strategic mountain slopes. The heavy Vietnamese build-up and commitment of regular troops was the first during the conflict, and indicated the importance both sides obviously placed on the outcome of a fight for Lang Son. Artillery bombardment by each side had commenced on 27 February.

Air interdiction had not been employed by either party during this preparatory stage. Thus, each side was able to prepare for the battle with virtual impunity. The Chinese could have attacked the infantry and artillery columns moving toward Lang Son, but did not. Speculation followed that each side wished the battle to be a major encounter, involving regular forces, so that the outcome would be viewed as decisive for the victor. Ironically, in the midst of the massive build-up, China fired a psychological shot by accusing Vietnam of 'armed provocation' by refusing to 'negotiate' a settlement to the conflict.

The Chinese initiated their drive for Lang Son on 28 February. Again, artillery provided a heavy barrage before infantry attacks, shelling the city and mountains, as the Vietnamese returned the fire. Moving from three sides, the PLA divisions, estimated at 60,000 personnel, then surged forward employing human-wave tactics. Some PLAAF air strikes ahead of the Chinese attack were reported, and were probably flown against the artillery positions and other tactical targets. Air commitment however, was not extensive, and no Vietnamese air force retaliation was launched. Extremely heavy fighting was reported during the first two days of the assault, and Vietnam claimed to have inflicted heavy casualties. Vietnamese resistance was concentrated from within the city initially, but the forces gradually withdrew and bunkered into the surrounding hills as the enemy advanced.

The battle of Lang Son began on 27 February. China dispatched two more divisions from Dong Dang and Loc Binh (southeast of Lang Son) as reinforcements. New and fresh units also crossed into Vietnam. The stormy Chinese attacks met with fierce Vietnamese resistance on Hills 417, 473, 556, 568, 608, and 800. Heavy casualties were reported on both sides. Thousands of corpses scattered along Highway 1A (southwest of Lang Son to Hanoi). As the Chinese forces attacked, they also began systematically cutting off all the roads connecting with Lang Son. The PLA, albeit on a small scale, was employing Mao's strategy of "*the countryside surrounding the city*" to avoid a Vietnamese trap at Lang Son. It is important to note, while the battle of Lang Son was in progress, the Vietnamese forces attacked two Chinese border towns in Guangxi: Malipo and Ningrning. There was no significant damage, but it revealed some degree of vulnerability of the Chinese rear.

By 2 March, the PLA had generally surrounded Lang Son. It had gained control over most of the hills around that city except the strategically indispensable Khua Ma Son hill, a key position for launching attacks from and defending Lang Son.

The final assault was launched on 3 March preceded by the seizure of Hill 303. Tanks led the infantry in a head-long rush for ten minutes; then the hill was captured. Shortly after, the Vietnamese artillery on Khua Ma Son hill heavily bombarded the PLA. The Chinese tanks once again coordinated with the infantry and, after fierce exchanges of fire, and blowing-up of tunnels, the six Vietnamese firing positions on the mountain were destroyed. Finally rockets fired from the top of the feature signalled its capture. Soon after, Lang Son was taken. In this newly-captured strategic city, the Chinese forces found extensive tunnel works, including a road wide enough for several vehicles to drive abreast along it and an assembly hall for political meetings and entertainment.

The attack was escalated to a new phase when on 28 February, Chinese forces began a large scale attack on Lang Son with the intention of inflicting heavy damage on the Vietnamese regular forces defending the city. By 3 March, after an intense battle, Chinese forces drove back the Vietnamese and captured Lang Son. China immediately called for a cease-fire and announced that it was ready to withdraw from Vietnam. Although the attack was not an overwhelming victory for China, the PLA had inflicted sufficient damage on Vietnamese regular forces to strengthen their position vis-a-vis Hanoi and again demonstrate to the world that the PRC would take military action when it perceived its national security interests were threatened. Beijing was now ready to explore detente with Hanoi.

The belated takeover of Cao Bang upset the PLA's original campaign plan, which was designed to seek swift and decisive engagements. The Vietnamese forces dispersed into company and platoon-sized units, hiding in the mountains, forests and caves, and continuing to launch counterattacks. The relentless resistance by Vietnamese soldiers and militias forced the Chinese to revise their operational tactics, dividing troops into battalion and company-sized formations to engage in search and destroy operations in the Cao Bang, Tra Linh, Trung Khang and Guang Hoa areas. New tactics included roads blocks, combing hills, searching caves, torching the ground and tunnel explosions. Evidently unprepared for such operations, the PLA General Logistic Department flung flamethrowers into the battles in the midst of the war.

The day after the attack on Lang Son, on 1 March, China initiated detente measures intended to prevent the conflict from escalating further. The Chinese government sent a note to the Vietnamese Embassy in Beijing proposing talks as soon as possible to end the two-week old border war. Beijing proposed devising any constructive measures that ensure peace and tranquillity along the border and then proceed to settle their border disputes concerning the boundary and territory. Fierce engagements continued and hundreds of Vietnamese soldiers and civilians were killed.

It was not until 6 March that captured Vietnamese documents seemed to indicate that the PAVN division assigned to defend Cao Bang had been defeated. Without that, the PLA's heavy losses during the first stage would have meant that the operation looked much less successful.

Beijing became increasingly worried about the progress of the war, pressing the field commander in Guangxi to commence the decisive battle for Lang Son, a gateway shielding Hanoi from the north, as soon as possible. Apparently unsatisfied with what had happened at Cao Bang, Xu reorganised the operation plan and urged his troops to be more forceful against Lang Son. Six Chinese divisions were involved in this decisive battle, which began on 27 February, preceded by a massive bombardment. After fierce battles, Chinese forces first secured their control over most of the surrounding high ground and then captured the northern part of the city on 2 March, which was the scheduled date to halt the military operations. Because Hanoi's propaganda machine refused to acknowledge the Vietnamese defeat in Lang Son, Xu decided to continue the operation, pushing his troops across the Ky Cung River, which separates the city of Lang Son into northern and southern districts, taking the entire city, and then advancing further south to create a military posture to threat Hanoi. Although Beijing endorsed Xu's decision, on 5 March, Xinhua announced that China had begun withdrawing its troops from Vietnam, stating that the invasion force had been pulled out after achieving the goals assigned them after Chinese troops occupied the southern part of Lang Son. The PLA had achieved its final military objective, and at least some political prestige had been restored.

Minor fighting was also reported in other areas. According to Vietnamese sources, Dong Dang was completely levelled. The Chinese forces, for psychological warfare, offered rice to the Vietnamese people in Cao Bang and Cam Duong after they had taken or destroyed the areas. After Lang Son was reportedly taken, fighting was still in progress around

Lac Binh and Mong Cai. To secure their withdrawal, the Chinese forces blew up the bridge south of Lang Son. The Chinese also destroyed the Pac Bo historic museum complex dedicated to the memory of Ho Chi Minh and his years in the wilderness during the Second World War.

On 5 March, the Chinese government announced the withdrawal of the PLA from Vietnam. Ironically, the Vietnamese government called, on the same day, for a nation-wide general mobilisation for the war. A circular from the Central Committee of the CCP to all the party offices throughout the country gave some additional information about the war. It stated that the PLA had advanced 50 to 120 kilometres, taken the capitals of Lang Son, Cao Bang, and Lao Cai and 17 other counties and cities, and damaged severely four regular divisions and ten regiments of the enemy. The same day, the Chinese warned Hanoi against any attack on their withdrawing forces. In response, Hanoi announced on 7 March that to show Vietnam's "good will for peace," Vietnam would "allow" the invading Chinese army to withdraw.

On 15 March, Beijing announced that all Chinese PLA units had been withdrawn from Vietnamese territory.

In a possible diversionary tactic, Soviet naval vessels were supposedly deployed to the vicinity of the Paracel Islands. In response, the PLA Navy dispatched a number of vessels to avert any Vietnamese attempt to take the islands under a Soviet Navy smokescreen. No such action apparently eventuated and some doubt exists as to the veracity of the reports. Considering the presence of the two US Navy aircraft carriers *Midway* and *Constellation* in the South China Sea, any Soviet naval action against China could have been inflammatory.

Conclusion

The Chinese planned for a short war of no more than one month, with their main operation aimed at the capture of Lang Son, along with two subsidiary advances on Cao Bang and Lao Cai, in order to divide the Vietnamese defence. An important feature of their plan was to engage and destroy the regular PAVN divisions near the border so as to facilitate a possible follow-on advance to Hanoi.

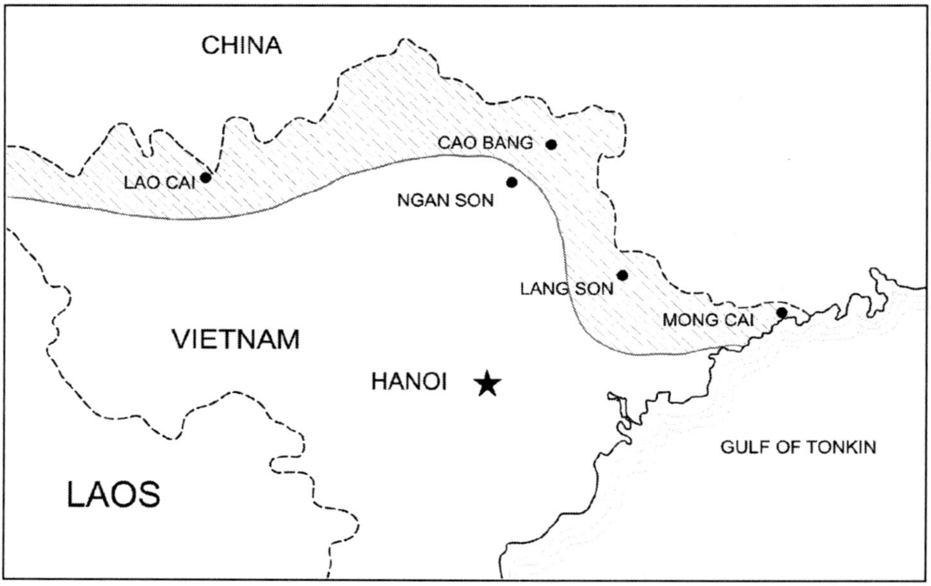

Map 8: Approximate Area Occupied by the Chinese at the End of the Conflict

Whether the Chinese planned to capture Hanoi remains open to debate. Their stated goal was, however, to "teach the Vietnamese a military lesson," and directly threatening their leadership before turning back across the border certainly could have been a part of that larger scheme. Such use of military force to teach lessons was not unusual for the Chinese. They had conducted a similarly-styled operation against India in 1962. On the other hand, the Vietnamese planned a defence with the primary aim of inflicting as much damage as possible on the invaders without at the same time suffering the loss of their own major units.

10

COMMENTS AND OBSERVATIONS

Border/Sea Disputes

Following the end of the war in Vietnam in late April 1975, and the formal unification of North and South Vietnam on 2 July 1976, relations between China and Vietnam went through dramatic changes, from seemingly normal relations in the mid-1970s to outright war in early 1979. The Sino-Vietnamese border disputes encompass both land and maritime issues. The major land dispute along the two countries 1,350 kilometre long border encompassed approximately 227 square kilometres of territory. (In 1999, the two countries agreed to split these areas. Vietnam receiving just under 113 square kilometres and the PRC just over 114 square kilometres).

The maritime disputes encompass or, where resolved, encompassed both maritime areas in the Gulf of Tonkin (Beibu Gulf to China and Bac Bo Gulf to Vietnam) and competing sovereignty claims over the Paracel and Spratly archipelagos. While an agreement dividing the Gulf of Tonkin was reached, the disputes related to the South China Sea proper remained unresolved.

Furthermore, China's claim within the, 'so-called', nine-dashed lines in the South China Sea overlap with Vietnam's. Coupled with the differences between the two countries along their mutual land border, the disputes in the Gulf of Tonkin and in the South China Sea caused tensions.

In particular, the disputes in the South China Sea and in the Gulf of Tonkin contributed to the deterioration of bilateral relations by adding yet another contentious issue to the growing rift between the two sides. In many ways these border conflicts reflected divergent policies with regard to other Cold War issues, such as their security connections with the USSR, and of the overall deterioration of Communist relations in the post-1975 period.

Relations between the PRC and unified Vietnam had been soured by China's 19 January 1974 attack against South Vietnamese forces stationed on the Paracel islands. Called a "counterattack" in Chinese sources, this date was in fact the 24th anniversary of Beijing's recognition of Hanoi. When Hanoi disputed China's claim to the Paracels, Beijing reminded them of a 14 September 1958 note from North Vietnamese Premier Pham Van Dong that appeared to support PRC sovereignty. The Sino-Vietnamese territorial dispute over the Paracels became increasingly bitter during the late 1970s, and helped push Hanoi closer to Moscow.

The overall deterioration of Sino-Vietnamese relations led to a militarised conflict that escalated into the PRC's attack on Vietnam in February-March 1979. China's announcement on 5 March 1979, the 26th anniversary of Stalin's death that it would withdraw from Vietnam was followed by attempts at negotiations between China and Vietnam from April 1979 through March 1980. However, the two parties could not reach an understanding. Bilateral relations remained tense during these talks and for most of the 1980s. Frictions were most visible along the common border, with mutual accusations about military incursions, claims to exclusive economic zone (EEZ) and continental shelf areas to the east of Vietnam's coastline.

Teaching a Lesson

As stated, on 17 February 1979, the People's Liberation Army (PLA) launched a large-scale ground attack across its southern border into Vietnam, crossing the border in twenty-six separate locations. China's intention was, in the words of Deng Xiaoping, to "teach Vietnam a lesson." The Vietnamese Army newspaper, Quan Doi Nhan Dan, the next day reported: "17 February 1979 will go down in history as a severe verdict of the 'Great Han' expansionists' crimes in trying to subdue and annex

Vietnam....Let us severely punish the barbarous aggressors and firmly defend our sacred national independence and sovereignty!"

And punish them the Vietnamese did. Estimates of Chinese losses vary, but analysis indicates that Vietnamese forces killed as many as 25,000 PLA soldiers, which means at least another 50,000 received serious wounds, for a total of 75,000 casualties out of an invasion force inside Vietnam that never exceeded 100,000 at any given time. After three weeks, ending in a climactic battle for Lang Son, Chinese forces withdrew across Vietnam's northern border.

There was no question that Vietnam had taught China a military lesson. Not only was the PLA badly bloodied, but it was bloodied mainly at the hands of Vietnamese militia, while regular Vietnamese units were held in reserve. This result should not have been a surprise. The Vietnamese Army was combat experienced, and fighting for its homeland. The PLA, on the other hand, had neither the motivation to fight nor the understanding of the terrain on the the Vietnamese side. It had not seen serious combat in many years, and had suffered during the Cultural Revolution. Thus when the Chinese force withdrew, Vietnam was legitimately able to claim a military victory.

On the other hand, there is no question that China taught Vietnam a political lesson—"You do not create a sphere of influence in Laos or and Cambodia; you do not attack Cambodia, a country friendly to China. You do not ally with the Soviet Union against us. You do not harass ethnic Chinese people in Vietnam. You do not make claims in the South China Sea that conflict with those of China. In a word, you are not fully independent to act as you wish in disregard of our interests. Remember, you are independent only because of Chinese help in your war of national liberation, so do not get out of line with your big neighbour".

The Chinese Offensive

Divergent Attacks. On 17 February 1979, the Chinese attacked on 26 points along the 800 kilometre border. Initial penetrations were effected at 20 points. Subsequently four major thrust lines were developed towards the provincial capitals of Lao Cai, Cao Bang, Dong Dang and Lang Son. After 17 days of very fierce fighting the Chinese managed to penetrate to a depth of 30 to 40 kilometres and capture the provincial capitals of the northern provinces. The aim of capturing these border towns was to draw out and destroy the Vietnamese regular army formations in a war of attrition. The Vietnamese however refused to rise to this bait. The well-armed and superbly trained Vietnamese Border Militia that slowed down the Chinese offensive to a crawl contested the Chinese advance almost entirely. The average rate of advance varied from two to three kilometres per day.

Battle of the Passes. The Chinese had initially adopted the technique of the divergent attack. This only describes the standard technique of trying to mask the main thrust lines by launching a large number of initial attacks along the entire front. From 26 initial points of attack the Chinese narrowed down to the four major thrust lines aimed at the provincial capitals. These main thrusts crystallised as under:

(a) Along the Red River Valley towards the town of Lao Cai.
(b) Towards National Highway Four aimed at the town of Ha Giang.
(c) From Jing Xi in Yunnan province towards the border town of Cao Bang.
(d) Along the traditional invasion route via the "Friendship Pass" towards Lang Son and Dong Dang. This was the shortest thrust line towards Hanoi along National Highway One. Hanoi was 135 kilometres to the south of Lang Son and had the Chinese decided to prosecute a full-scale war, this would probably have been their main thrust line.

Instead of adopting the Korean War pattern of infiltration and envelopment, the Chinese commander, Yang Teh Chi, launched massive frontal attacks spearheaded in most cases by tanks and supported by massive barrages of artillery. The Chinese use of tanks in the hilly terrain came as a surprise. These were used primarily for bunker bursting. The Chinese aim was to initially capture border passes before undertaking any outflanking movement. The Chinese infantry attacked in overwhelming strength supported by intense barrages of artillery fire. In many cases the Vietnamese launched skilful spoiling attacks and ambushes across the border to disrupt and disorganise the Chinese assaults. Radio intercepts had probably given them a clear indication of the Chinese D-Day. The

Vietnamese militia squads armed with anti-tank missiles were able to destroy a large number of Chinese tanks. To compound Chinese difficulties, the Vietnamese launched a number of cross-border raids on Chinese gun positions and were able to disrupt the fire support. The Chinese lacked APCs and casualty evacuation procedures failed to keep pace with the very heavy volume of initial casualties. Surprisingly the Chinese tanks and APCs used seemed to lack reliable radio communication and in many cases were seen using flag and hand signals. (This may also have been due to electronic jamming by the Russians). The Chinese initial attacks were badly disrupted and disorganised by Vietnamese spoiling attacks and counter attacks, mine fields, sharpened bamboo stakes and very heavy artillery concentrations.

Break out to Depth Objectives. After a week's intense fighting, the Chinese had a tactical-cum-logistics pause in their operations. The initial attacks had been badly mauled and disorganised. Yet the Chinese pressed on relentlessly. The initial 26 points of attack now converged on to 11thrusts. 17 infantry divisions supported by armour had launched the initial attacks. Eight fresh divisions were brought in and pressed through for subsequent phases. The Chinese had in most cases penetrated up to 15-20 kilometres but paid a very heavy price in personnel and equipment casualties. The tactical skill and finesse of the Korean War had been replaced by a steam roller advance spearheaded by tanks, preceded by intense artillery barrages and pressed home by waves after waves of Chinese infantry.

The Battle of the Provincial Capitals. After the pause, the Chinese resumed their offensive aimed at the major provincial capitals and key communication centres in the proximity of the border. Major battles developed at Cao Bang, Lang Son, Ha Giang, Lao Cai and Lai Chau. The aim of these attacks was to draw in the regular Vietnamese Army formations and inflict heavy attrition on them. There were fierce attacks and counter attacks. In Lang Son the Chinese launched 17 attacks to regain one objective. By late last week of February, the Vietnamese had still not committed any of their regular divisions which were being held back for the defence of Hanoi. It had also not pulled out any of its troops from Cambodia. In the provincial capital the Vietnamese withdrew from the towns into the adjoining hills. As the Chinese formations surged in they were engaged from all sides from the surrounding hills and quite severely mauled.

The Battle of Lang Son. The Chinese were quite surprised by the ferocity of the resistance at Lang Son. The Vietnamese had adopted their time-honoured defence of emptying the towns and occupying the surrounding hills. The Chinese now decided to call it a day and announced their unilateral withdrawal. However to cover this withdrawal they launched a massive offensive against Lang Son. The three-pronged attack was launched on 2 March 1979 even as most Chinese units in the rear had commenced withdrawal. Very fierce fighting erupted and the Vietnamese committed their Flying Tigers Regiment at Dong Dang. The 308th Infantry Division (an elite formation) was readied to intervene in the battle of Lang Son but had not moved, as the militia troops seemed to be handling the situation quite well. Having avoided a loss of face by "capturing" the provincial capitals, the Chinese announced that they had taught a lesson to Vietnam and staged their withdrawal. The Chinese had, on ground, captured four pockets of territory around the provincial capitals of Lao Cai, Cao Bang, Dong Dang and Lang Son. However (apart from one regiment) no Vietnamese regular forces had been lured into the battle. A number of Chinese divisions of the Third Field Army had been quite severely mauled.

Chinese Pattern of Operations

Gen Hsu Shih Yun (who had sheltered Vice Premier Deng Xiao Peng when he had been purged for the second time in 1976) was the overall commander of this operation. He was a "long marcher" and a member of the politburo and had been a vocal supporter of Deng. Gen Yang Teh Chih, Hsu's deputy, was in tactical control of the operations. He was also a "long marcher" and was the Deputy Commander of the Chinese forces during the Korean War. He had then developed the tactics of infiltration and envelopment followed by mass attacks. He was chosen to lead the attack due to the similarity of the terrain to Korea and assumed his appointment only in January 1979. Due to his exploits in the Long March he had earned the title of the "ever victorious General".

It was expected that Yang would follow the Korean pattern of offensive involving infiltration and envelopment followed by mass attacks. But in this case, perhaps keeping in view the Vietnamese skill at similar tactics, the Chinese followed a curiously direct and frontal approach. Here the Chinese infantry, supported by tanks and intense artillery barrages, launched mass attacks against the frontier passes in the first phase itself. The Chinese used the technique of attacking on a wide front with subsequent echelons converging on to their objectives in a series of multiple pincer hooks in subsequent operations.

The offensive was planned in three phases:

(a) Battle of the Passes.
(b) Break out to divisional objectives (approximately 15 kilometres in depth).
(c) Thrust to capture provincial capitals.

The Chinese offensive was based on a frontal and direct approach relying on the weight of numbers and fire power to push its way through. However, the limited Chinese objectives in terms of depth of penetration, suggested that the Chinese wanted to draw Vietnamese regular divisions into the conflict at an early stage. The possible avenues of thrust were:

(a) The Lang Son approach via the Friendship Pass is the traditional invasion route along Highway One. It is also the shortest route and the Chinese railhead of Pingxiang is very close to the border. As expected the main Chinese thrust took place along this route.
(b) The Coastal approach ran via Mong Cai along the coast and culminated at the Haiphong harbour.
(c) The Red River approach along National Highway Two led to the provincial capital of Lao Cai.
(d) The Black River approach led to Hanoi. The provincial capital of Laichu lay at its mouth. This was a very long and unlikely approach (unless the Chinese decided to attack via Laos)
(e) Subsidiary approaches led to the provincial capitals of Caobang and Hagiang and could serve to cut the lateral Highway Four which runs parallel to the border and links Highways One and Two.

These were the thrust lines available to the Chinese in case their aim was an all-out offensive aimed at the capture of Hanoi. However in actual fact, the Chinese aimed at a broad and shallow penetration all along the front which would take them till the line of the lateral Highway Four which ran parallel to the border. In so doing they hoped to draw into battle and destroy/decimate the regular Vietnamese divisions, who they felt would be compelled to react forward for the defence of the provincial capitals and important communications centres. This would result in major battles of attrition against the regular Vietnamese Army. They also calculated that this massive attack from the North would force Vietnam to withdraw troops from Cambodia and thereby remove the pressure on the guerrillas of Pol Pot.

Vietnamese Pattern of Operations

The Vietnamese saw through Chinese concept. Accordingly they decided to hold the frontier with their Border Militia (some 150,000 strong), while five to seven of their regular divisions took up crescent shaped defences along the avenues leading to Hanoi in two tiers. The first of these connected Tehbai on the Red River with Kuangteh on the East Coast. This deployment was viable even if the Chinese decided to capture Hanoi. Since the shape of North Vietnam is like a triangle (with the base along the border and the apex at Hanoi), such a defensive deployment in depth would enable the defender to correctly identify the main point of effort of the enemy and thereby permit the defender to suitably employ his reserves to block that thrust and launch counter attacks.

The border militia that fought the entire battle was not an ill-trained or second-rate force. It must also be noted that, at that point in time, the PAVN forces (regular or militia) were the most combat hardened in the world. The Vietnamese soldier is an excellent marksman, an expert at camouflage and concealment and has a great capacity for digging defensive positions. He is fleet footed and a very mobile and tenacious fighter.

Hanoi's strategy therefore was to defend the border with a screen of 100,000 local militia troops employing guerrilla tactics in the hilly and densely wooded terrain that was admirably suited for such operations. The Main Force (regular) Vietnamese Divisions were held well back for the defence of the Hanoi plains. The densest missile defence in history defended Hanoi and Hai Phong itself. (It was the density of this missile defence that probably prompted the Chinese to keep out their Air Force).

The Soviets moved in a Naval Flotilla to the South China Sea. Admiral Vladimir Maslov, the Commander of the Soviet Pacific fleet was himself located on the Flagship of this fleet, (which was crammed with sophisticated electronic gear for interception of signal communications and Electronic Warfare). Soviet reconnaissance aircraft were on constant patrol. However their effectiveness was curtailed due to dense cloud cover. The Soviets were closely monitoring the Chinese build up and military activity and keeping a close watch to see if the Chinese over stepped their stated brief of a limited war to teach a lesson. The legendary Vo Nguen Giap was the nominal commander of the Vietnamese forces at that time. However it was rumoured that he was then suffering from Hodgkin's disease and was too sick to be in charge of day to day operations. These were controlled by his protégé General Van Tien Dung, the man who had captured Saigon in 1975.

Capability of the PLA

Although the intention of demonstrating the PLA's superiority over Vietnam's forces may have been realised, it was certainly with reservations. Vietnam evaded, until the battle for Lang Son, a major confrontation with China, so the PLA was not fully extended as a fighting force. Even so, weaknesses were exposed.

An obvious realisation was the PLA's lack of sophistication as a modern fighting force, with much of its strength continuing to lie in a numerical rather than technological advantage.

In terms of commitment, this was the largest conflict involving the PLA since the Korean War, yet many of the tactics demonstrated little improvement. The continued reliance on human-wave infantry assaults illustrates the inflexibility of the PLA to cope with different warfare environments, such as urban, jungle or mountain. Technological shortcomings further restricted the PLA.

Communications hampered the Chinese conduct of military operations. The widespread dispersal of fronts and the number of different

PLA fighting elements involved, together with segregated control between two military regions, frustrated command and control aspects of operations. Field commanders were further hindered through inadequate communications, being unable to effectively co-ordinate artillery, armour and infantry. Air-ground communications also restricted application of air support to ground operations. By contrast, for example, the Soviet Union deployed a command and control ship to co-ordinate their naval and air elements in the area. The *Sverdlov* Class cruiser, *Admiral Senyavin*, also acted to co-ordinate intelligence collection activities. The Chinese certainly demonstrated no equivalent capability.

Besides the limitations imposed by political considerations, the PLAAF also suffered from technological obsolescence. Terrain and weather hampered air strikes in the initial phase, as aircraft such as the MiG-19 and F-9 lacked an all-weather capability and effective terrain avoidance radar to permit low level operations under adverse conditions. Thus, the PLAAF could not provide support at all times when required. Air support further suffered through poor communications. Although numerically immense tactical air power was potentially available, the air war was dramatically limited. However, if the various claims were correct the PLAAF would appear to have achieved and maintained air superiority for the duration of the conflict, although in the absence of a Vietnamese response this may be somewhat of a false indication of capability.

Operational Level Analysis

The Sino-Vietnamese War is relevant to the examination of Chinese and Vietnamese operational art because the strategic objectives for the two forces are identifiable. Both land component commanders were constrained to keep the war limited to the region and to Chinese and Vietnamese ground forces. The limited objectives of the war allow for a deeper understanding of the operational art employed by the adversaries. Although the war had limited objectives, it was still a significant campaign with multiple divisions engaged in combined arms operations in three distinct sectors. Finally, the capabilities of the PLA and the PAVN ground forces were similar and this parity required the use of operational art to achieve objectives.

In April 1975, two communist regimes took power and reshaped the strategic environment of Asia. The Khmer Rouge gained control of Cambodia on 17 April followed by North Vietnam reuniting Vietnam on 30 April. These two communist countries previously supported each other and the Chinese aided both during the Second Indochina War. However, after achieving their objectives in 1975, the consolidation of internal power took precedence over past support. For the new Socialist Republic of Vietnam, an appeal to their historical hegemony in Indochina became a rallying cry to unite a country fractured by civil war.

In December 1975, Vietnam aided a government overthrow in Laos and permanently garrisoned soldiers there to protect Vietnamese interests. In December 1978, Vietnam invaded Cambodia to replace the Khmer Rouge regime of Pol Pot with one amicable to Vietnamese regional hegemony. Also in 1978, the Soviet Union and Vietnam signed the "Treaty of Friendship and Cooperation" to counter Chinese influence and guarantee military and economic support for rebuilding Vietnam. Under this treaty, the Soviet Union provided military support, $700 million in 1978, for operations in Laos and Cambodia. The Vietnam-Soviet treaty went into effect prior to Vietnam's invasion of Cambodia and replaced a similar Sino-Soviet treaty that had expired on 14 February 1979. In this strategic environment, China was losing influence in the region to its historical "little brother"—Vietnam. China had to act to reassert its *Shih* in the region.

Western Intelligence sources have indicated that it took the Chinese 90 days to complete total mobilisation and deployment for this offensive. This indicated a high state of peacetime readiness.

While Chinese and Vietnamese diplomats postured on the world media stage throughout 1978, both sides were actually preparing for war. In November the Chinese began moving 30 divisions from their Kunming and Guangzhou Military Regions into positions close to the border. The Chinese tried to keep those deployments secret by moving the rail and road traffic at night, but the unavoidable disruption of civil traffic and commerce did not go unnoticed.

The Chinese People's Liberation Army Air Force (PLAAF) added to the congestion by redeploying about 1,000 aircraft along with some 20,000 personnel. The PLAAF built three airfields to accommodate those moves. The South Sea Fleet of the Chinese People's Liberation Army Navy (PLAN) prepared for battle by organising a special task force comprised of three frigates and several smaller escort vessels.

In mid-July the Vietnamese moved their 3rd Division to Lang Son, where it began to organise border defences and dig in. The local militia units were put on alert and were given extensive training. Fortifications, tunnels, depots and trenches were dug all across the border area, with special concentration in the Military Region One provinces.

In February the PAVN's 346th and 311th Divisions assembled in Cao Bang, where they were soon joined by the 567th and 852nd (separate) Regiments. By the end of 1978 the VPA 316th Division and the 254th (separate) Regiment were deployed to Lao Cai, where they were later joined by the 345th Division.

Vietnam's military objective was to retain Hanoi. The PAVN established an area defence to accomplish this objective. In 1979, the PAVN consisted of 600,000 soldiers. 200,000 soldiers were conducting operations in Cambodia against the Khmer Rouge, and 100,000 were securing Vietnamese interests in Laos leaving 300,000 soldiers for the defence of Vietnam. The deep, close, support operational framework best describes the PAVN defence. The support area was Hanoi. The PAVN established three non-contiguous defensive areas on the three main avenues of approach from China to Hanoi consisting of five total divisions. In the forward zone, militia forces conducted security operations close to the border. From west to east, two divisions defended Lao Cai and were tasked to delay PLA forces along the western avenue of approach along the Red River. The PAVN deployed these two divisions in December 1978 and had two months to prepare their defences.

Two divisions defending Cao Bang were tasked to delay PLA forces along the centre avenue of approach. The PAVN deployed these forces in early February 1979 and afforded them the least amount of time to prepare. The famed PAVN 3rd Division defended the eastern avenue of approach centred in Lang Son. (The 3rd Division was formed during the Second Indochina War to fight in South Vietnam against US forces. The Division then led the attack to seize Saigon in 1975). The PAVN reinforced the

3rd Division with tanks, an artillery regiment and air defence regiment, all tasked to delay the PLA along the most likely and fastest avenue of approach to Hanoi. The 3rd Division prepared their defence over seven months. The primary Vietnamese course of action was for the militia forces to provide early warning and disrupt the PLA attack as it crossed the border. The main battle area divisions would then delay the PLA attack and withdraw to subsequent battle positions along their avenues of approach until reaching final positions centred on Hanoi.

The military objective for the PLA was to defeat the forward PAVN divisions and seize the decisive terrain of Lang Son. The PLA employed 330,000 soldiers, organised into eleven armies to achieve this objective. The PLA divided their attack along the three avenues of approach to Hanoi. From west to east, three armies conducted a supporting attack along the western avenue of approach to defeat the PAVN defence and seize Lao Cai. The main effort with five armies attacked to defeat the PAVN defence, seize Cao Bang and isolate Lang Son along the centre avenue of approach. The east supporting effort with three armies attacked on the eastern avenue of approach to seize key terrain necessary to continue the attack on Lang Son. The plan for the attack consisted of three phases. The first phase required penetrating the PAVN depth areas, the defeat of the PAVN defences in the west and centre, and the seizure of Lao Cai and Cao Bang. The PLA plan was to seize the decisive terrain of Lang Son in the second phase. The third phase was the withdrawal of all forces north of the border. The plan set a limit of advance 50 kilometres into Vietnam for all ground forces.

The PLA attack began 17 February 1979. The PLA forces attacked simultaneously along all three avenues of approach. In the west, the PLA achieved its initial objective, the city of Lao Cai, by 19 February. The western PLA force then threatened further south by penetrating 40 kilometres by 1 March. In the centre, the PLA destroyed the PAVN defences and seized Cao Bang by 25 February. In the east, the PLA attacked across the border and seized key terrain around Lang Son, isolating the city from the north and south. The PLA achieved all first phase objectives by 25 February. On 27 February, the second phase began with the main effort attacking south to Lang Son. The PLA defeated the PAVN defence and seized the north side of Lang Son on 2 March. The PLA continued the attack until all of Lang Son was under Chinese control on 5 March. Within hours of seizing Lang Son, China announced their withdrawal and ended all attacks.

The PLA completed the withdrawal to Chinese territory on 16 March ending the campaign. After the Chinese withdraw, the Vietnamese government agreed to negotiations that began in Hanoi in May 1979.

Although each side claimed an overwhelming victory, closer examination is necessary to qualify the statements. Clearly, the conflict had been tightly limited, with objectives and actions designed to prevent escalation and protraction. Indeed, Vietnam may have intentionally withheld large scale commitment of regular forces and air power, knowing China's aims were limited and did not involve anything more than a punitive strike. Any large-scale counteraction by Vietnam could have prolonged the conflict and forced further action by China in pursuit of its objectives, whilst inflicting unnecessary casualties. Because of Vietnamese restraint, for whatever reason, China more readily achieved its required threshold for withdrawal.

Casualty claims were widely divergent. Vietnam claimed to have killed or otherwise put out of action over 60,000 Chinese and destroyed over 280 tanks and APCs. China, however, disclosed that the PLA suffered 20,000 casualties whilst inflicting 50,000 casualties on Vietnam. The extent of China's admitted losses was considered extremely high considering the level of conflict. An undisclosed number of prisoners were taken by both sides.

Despite the Soviet Union's constant rhetoric and threats, China maintained its objectives, apparently undaunted. Soviet retaliation was potentially massive, including conflict on China's northern border, but China's perseverance suggests an understanding of international tolerance, provided the conflict did not escalate. The Soviet Union played no overt military role other than resupplying Vietnam with military stores.

China again demonstrated its resort to military action to protect its territorial (and political) integrity, as it had done previously in Korea and with Taiwan, India and South Vietnam. Political aspects aside, the military action was designed to secure and protect the border with Vietnam.

The Two-Front Conundrum

The examples of the Sino-Vietnam and Vietnam-Cambodia wars of 1979 exemplify the response of highly militarised states to a "two front" situation. In late 1978 and early 1979 both China and Vietnam felt themselves being pushed into a two-front situation. Vietnam felt it was being hemmed in by China in the North and an Pol Pot in Cambodia in the South. At home it had to deal with a large ethnic Chinese (Hoa) minority in South Vietnam. China in turn felt that the Soviet-Vietnam Treaty of Friendship was getting it encircled in a two-front situation. The response of both these militarised states was highly proactive and decisive. They lashed out militarily before the perceived encirclement became a fact. The Vietnamese invasion of Cambodia is a classic example of a high-risk operation with very tight time schedules but equally high pay offs. They carried out this blitzkrieg in January 1979 before China could complete its mobilisation in the North. The Chinese responded with their invasion in just a month's time. Many analysts aver that China's invasion of Vietnam in February 1979 was primarily a response to the Soviet-Vietnam Treaty of Friendship. China wanted to demonstrate that it could not be deterred from the pursuit of its regional interests by any extra-regional power and the Soviet treaty would be of no avail to Vietnam. In other words they wanted to call the Soviet bluff. Both these direct and forthright responses to the two-front situations merit detailed analysis. The Sino-Vietnam War is also significant in that a military campaign was fought against a quasi-nuclear backdrop.

The Soviet Position

The Soviet position during this conflict merits description. In harsh language, both Kosygin and Brezhnev criticised China's attack as a "cynical and barbarous act of international piracy," demanded an immediate end of the Chinese "war of aggression" and warned China of Soviet "loyalty to the [Soviet-Vietnamese] treaty." But there was little further Soviet action beyond these warnings except for the continuation of arms airlift and naval deployment off the Vietnam coast. Since the Soviet Union had not militarily involved itself in the war, a Soviet promise of post-war aid to Vietnam was obligatory and easy to pledge. Kosygin, in his visit to India on 10 March, made such a commitment to Hanoi.

Role of the UN

A dilemma developed in the UN. Originally requested by Norway, Portugal, Great Britain, and the US, a debate on the situation in Southeast Asia and its implications for international peace and security, the Security Council found itself irreconcilably divided after five meetings on 23, 24, 25, 27, and 28 February. The debate was serious and acrimonious. The ASEAN members disapproved the invasions by both China and Vietnam and urged them to pull back their forces. The American delegation favoured a resolution along the line of the ASEAN position, asking for the withdrawal of "foreign" troops; no nation was named. The USSR and PRC argued against each other. The Soviet delegation warned that the Soviet Union would not support a resolution that did not condemn China and call for the withdrawal of Chinese troops. It submitted (together with Czechoslovakia) a draft resolution, on 23 February, which condemned China for its invasion, demanded the withdrawal of all Chinese troops and a full reparation for Vietnam's war damages, and called for an arms embargo against China. The Chinese delegate, criticised the Soviet encouragement of Vietnam's attacks against China and its aggression against Kampuchea. The Chinese delegation submitted its draft resolution on 24 February, calling for the immediate withdrawal of all Vietnamese troops from Kampuchea.

As the war ran apace, disagreements on proposed resolutions dragged on. Both the Soviet and Chinese resolutions had no chance to pass. Even the most agreeable ASEAN draft resolution, which was submitted on 16 March, when the withdrawal of Chinese troops was completed, would also face a Soviet veto, fluttered around the diplomatic terms by using "parties to the conflicts" and asking "all the parties" to withdraw without condemning China. To the Chinese delegation, the ASEAN resolution was acceptable because it would cover China's invasion, and urge the Vietnamese to withdraw from Kampuchea. If the Security Council pushed to adopt the ASEAN resolution, it would not only invite a Soviet veto and a more serious Sino-Soviet quarrel that most Third World nations feared, but also appear to accept a one-sided "pro-China" resolution. Trying hard to remain neutral, most of the Council members backed off.

Consequently, the Security Council failed to come up with a resolution throughout the war. This experience ironically confirmed what a UN diplomat apocryphally said in the first week of the war: *When there is a dispute between small countries, the dispute disappears. When there is a dispute between a large country and a small country, the small country disappears. When there is a dispute between big countries (big powers), the United Nations disappears!*

Deng as Decision-maker

Overall, the war was an operational failure, but because it was limited in goal, scope, and duration, Deng was able to use the failure to his advantage. He used the war to consolidate domestic control over the military and the country by implementing military reform. The attack also provided larger and longer-term geopolitical benefits: It demonstrated China's strength and will to resist the Soviet Union and Vietnam; it destroyed the illusion of a strong Soviet-Vietnamese alliance and mitigated the threat of encirclement; and it eventually economically and militarily overstretched the Vietnamese, preventing Vietnam from dominating Indochina.

Several key aspects of Deng's decision-making are worthy of note:

(a) Deng was a rational, thorough, and sharp thinker who made decisions of war and peace not only on the foreign policy implications of war but also on the domestic implications. Deng, in both his foreign policy and domestic policy, often emphasised getting the big picture or big idea right. He was confident in his capabilities, but he was also open to alternative ideas and updating his views.

(b) Though Deng had to convince his colleagues of the benefits of an attack, he did not disregard information or silence alternative views. He had more confidence than warranted of the PLA, but he was not oblivious to the military's weaknesses and did see the war as a way to battle test the military. Deng's plan for a limited war with Vietnam was designed to alleviate concerns about attacking Vietnam and questions regarding the PLA's military capabilities to do so successfully.

(c) Deng was correct in assessing that a limited war would bring Beijing neither great loss nor great victory. The war was executed after months of careful geopolitical calculation and preparation to keep the Soviets out and to prevent China from being bogged down in a long conflict.

(d) Deng's prejudices against Vietnam and inaccurate assessment of military capabilities may have prevented him from fully mapping out potential Vietnamese military responses. While these errors were significant, they were not devastating for Deng because he was able to rationally assess new information as he waged the war, including information from the battlefield that China was not performing well militarily and had experienced massive losses.

(e) Deng did not let setbacks lead to mission creep and did not expand the conflict from limited war to protracted conflict or occupation. Even when his general on the ground, Xu, wanted to continue the battle to capture Hanoi and bring China more military success, Deng was not tempted. For him, the losses the PLA suffered did not mean that China should continue fighting to attempt to obtain greater military success. He thus pressured his general to end the war.

In sum, Deng's decision-making model to launch the Sino-Vietnamese War was largely correct, but it was flawed with regard to Vietnamese and Chinese military capabilities. Deng made his decision to launch an attack by carefully and rationally considering various options, consulting with his colleagues, and updating his views as new information arrived. He neither silenced alternative views nor surrounded himself with advisors who merely echoed his thoughts. He laid significant international and domestic groundwork to obtain support before launching an attack and correctly assessed that the larger geopolitical environment would not be unfavourable to a limited war. Nevertheless, Deng's prejudices about Vietnam may have contributed to his underestimation of the Vietnamese ability to adapt to an enemy attack (by mobilising soldiers locally instead of diverting them from the Cambodia war) and overestimation of the PLA's war-fighting capabilities. Yet he was correct in his big-picture assessment that a limited attack on Vietnam could not have extraordinary consequences, either negative or positive. By maintaining his position and waging a limited war, Deng mitigated the blunder that arose due to his underestimation of the Vietnamese.

11

ASSESSMENT AND LESSONS

Appraising China's War with Vietnam

China's war with Vietnam in 1979 was the largest military operation that the PLA had initiated since the Korean War. Based on Mao Zedong's strategy that "*in every battle, concentrate an absolute superior force against the enemy,*" Beijing deployed nine regular armies along with special and local units, amounting to more than 300,000 troops, to conduct a war of punishment against Vietnam for one month. Air Force fighter units flew 8,500 sorties in air patrol missions, while transport and helicopter units made 228 sorties in airlift missions; the Navy dispatched a task force (consisting of two missile frigates and three squadrons of missile and torpedo fast attack craft) to Xisha Islands (Paracels) to prepare for Soviet naval intervention. In addition, Guangxi and Yunnan provinces mobilised tens of thousands of militias and labourers to support these military operations. During the conflict, Chinese forces captured three Vietnamese provincial capitals and more than a dozen border cities and county towns, claiming to have killed and wounded 57,000 Vietnamese troops and severely damaged four regular divisions and ten other regiments along with the capture of a large amount of weaponry. Beijing asserted that the 1979 war against Vietnam ended with China's victory. The PLA's victory claims include the destruction of 340 pieces of artillery, 45 tanks and some 480 trucks, and the capture of 840 pieces of artillery and more than 11,000 pieces of small arms along with many other types of military equipment.

Most independent studies, however, note that Vietnam had indeed outperformed the Chinese forces on the battlefield because of the PLA's problems in operations and reported heavy casualties. Hanoi claimed that only militia and local forces were committed to the conflict, and employed no defensive tactics but attacked constantly against the Chinese invaders. They lost Lang Son and other cities only after inflicting enormous casualties on the Chinese forces. Hanoi Radio at the time announced that the Vietnamese had killed and wounded 42,000 Chinese troops. Vietnamese estimates of Chinese casualties are 25,000 killed and another 50,000 wounded. Few Vietnamese records have been available to researchers about their performance and losses in the conflict other than information posted by individuals in cyberspace, which contrarily indicate substantial involvement by PAVN regular forces and heavier casualties. A reassessment of China's war with Vietnam relying solely on Chinese sources is one-sided but can be illuminating.

One approach to the evaluation of China's gains and losses is to concentrate on casualties. Beijing initially acknowledged that 20,000 Chinese soldiers were either killed or wounded in the border conflict with Vietnam. Existing scholarship tends towards an estimate of as many as 25,000 PLA killed in action and another 37,000 wounded. Recently available Chinese sources categorise the PLA's losses as 6,900 dead and some 15,000 injured, giving a total of 21,900 casualties from an invasion force of more than 300,000. China's casualties in such a short war were significantly high in any case, continuing to indicate one of the enduring characteristics of PLA's tactical and operational style: a willingness to absorb heavy losses when deemed necessary. An internal record shows that 10,202 wounded soldiers received treatment in 17 hospitals in the Guangzhou Military Region. Several unofficial Chinese sources also reveal that the casualties were lighter in Yunnan with 2,812 killed and 5,074 wounded. Chinese leaders consider casualties to be a relatively unimportant criterion for weighing military success as long as they believe the overall strategic situation was in their grasp and control.

From a Chinese perspective, the 1979 war with Vietnam was a deliberately orchestrated military response to Vietnamese policy towards China and its expansion in South-East Asia as well as Soviet global aspirations. Although this campaign revealed the PLA's deficiencies in modern doctrine and tactics, from beginning to end, China held fast to the initiative and tempo of the conflict. Beijing surprised Hanoi not only by waging massive attacks, but also by its quick withdrawal without becoming bogged down in Vietnam. Its gauge of the Soviet response to the invasion also succeeded in exposing Moscow's inability or unwillingness to back Vietnam. Vietnam's reliance on the Soviet Union for security was clearly a disappointing experience. What eventually turned even more critical is that the 1979 war was the beginning of Beijing's policy of bleeding Vietnam in an effort to contain Hanoi's expansion in Southeast Asia. A Vietnamese withdrawal from Cambodia following China's attack was desirable for the Chinese leadership, but they never anticipated an immediate withdrawal. China still commanded a strategic option by maintaining military pressure on Vietnam that included the constant verbal threat of a second attack, and occasionally intensified artillery shelling and major border battles for almost an entire decade during the 1980s. In the decade after the war, there were at least six major border clashes between China and Vietnam (July 1980, May 1981, April 1983, April–July 1984, June 1985 and December 1986–January 1987).

The war did not produce significant international consequences for China. The use of military force against Vietnam raised the suspicions of Indonesia and Malaysia, who were always wary of China's influence in the region. The Vietnamese occupation of Cambodia, that threatened Thailand, enabled the continuing growth of the strong opposition coalition by ASEAN countries against Vietnam. Regarding the Sino-US relationship, China's punitive invasion appeared particularly successful. Whereas Washington had publicly condemned both Vietnam's invasion of Cambodia and China's invasion of Vietnam, it did share China's interest in containing Soviet influence in South-East Asia. Beijing's willingness to use force, regardless of whatever casualties it suffered, made China a valuable deterrent to Soviet-Vietnamese expansionism; Washington continued to seek a close relationship with China to counterbalance the Soviet Union.

The Vietnamese leadership never seemed to act in comprehension of China's strategy and war objectives, but persistently maintained the 1979 invasion to be a prelude of Beijing's long-term scheme of infringing on Vietnamese sovereignty and independence. After China's announcement of withdrawal on 5 March, Hanoi called for a nation-wide general mobilisation for the war while continuing the construction of defensive positions in and around Hanoi. By the end of May, the PLA had demobilised to normal status. Vietnam, however, continued to be on guard, maintaining large numbers of troops along its northern border facing China at a time when its economy was in a worse state than at any time since 1975. As a result, Hanoi's attempts to fight two wars simultaneously, one in Cambodia and one on its northern border apparently came at a high national economic and social cost, absorbing Hanoi's effort to modernise its economy, and, more importantly, undermining its geopolitical ambitions. The Vietnamese leadership, however, failed to grasp the gravity of the situation and continued the dependence of their country on the Soviet Union until its collapse in 1991. If there are any lessons that the Vietnamese should draw from the 1979 war with China, it is that Vietnam, as one Vietnamese general later remarked, "*must learn how to live with our big neighbour.*"

Regarding the question of why China was anxious to use calibrated force against Vietnam in 1979, the analysis here is consistent with the assertion by other studies that perceived threats to territorial integrity and sovereignty are particularly important to Beijing, enough to expand PLA responsibilities well beyond defence against attack. Territorial disputes and border tension were ostensibly triggering elements to prompt Beijing to consider use of force against its southern neighbour, while the upsurge of emotional nationalism tended to reinforce a Chinese mentality that some kind of punishment on a traitorous erstwhile ally that had turned against China was required. This sentiment also played a significant role in bringing a broad consensus among Chinese political and military leaders to support Deng, the central player in making the decisions to deploy the military against Vietnam. On the issues of territorial sovereignty, which always raises the emotions of the Chinese, the military view seemed to be the determining factor in decisions to initiate actual hostilities. The September staff meeting, from providing recommendations for the central leadership to deal with the deteriorating relations between China and Vietnam, was the starting point of a major military operation. The military's analysis of Soviet reaction also helped clear up any misgivings for risk-taking, if any existed. The military nevertheless subjected themselves to the desires of the central leadership. Once the decision was made to wage a punitive invasion of Vietnam, PLA generals were eager to undertake their missions with preference to employment of maximum force.

Lessons Learned

Notwithstanding China's strategic success, several critical questions remain to be addressed, such as how the PLA perceived its performance in Vietnam, what lessons it learned from the campaign, and to what degree this experience affected PLA thinking about its future. As part of the PLA's tradition, all troops involved in the conflict were ordered to write summaries of their combat experience. In retrospect, the PLA leadership found itself in a contradictory position. While claiming that China won the war, they had to acknowledge the high costs the PLA had paid. In the view of the PLA leadership, an impartial evaluation of PLA deficiencies was imperative. However, they worried about a propensity for over-assessing the Vietnamese military capabilities and performance.

In due course, their national pride and cultural prejudice inevitably prevented them from making candid conclusions of the PLA's experience in the war, which can be synthesised into six themes:

(a) *The first focused on a traditional PLA maxim that any correct military decision and strategy must draw on a good grasp of the situation in all its aspects.* The 1979 war showed that the PLA paid scant attention to the combat doctrine and tactics of the PAVN before the war. As a result, the Chinese military underestimated the fighting ability of its opponents. Possible from fear of giving too much credit to the Vietnamese military, the PLA concluded that the enemy's regular forces lacked persistency in offence and defence and had few co-ordinated operations, but did concede that the Vietnamese guerrilla-type tactics, sappers and militias were surprisingly successful in keeping the Chinese forces off balance as they were anxiously seeking decisive battles with the main forces of the PAVN in a lightning war. A US officer once summarised the American experience in the Vietnam War, noting that it was impossible to penetrate, flank, or envelop the

Vietnamese fortified positions without taking extremely heavy casualties. The PLA's tactics of pushing its infantrymen into close massed combat with their opponents and its acceptance of high human losses may help explain why the Chinese made these assertions about the Vietnamese army's incompetence at defending its positions. Western analysts generally believe that these units of the PAVN, filled up with veterans of the long war in the south, proved to be battle-wise and highly skilled in guerrilla-war tactics. Recent Vietnamese sources indicate that they were recruits, and only joined the army in June 1978.

(b) *Unexpected difficulties in the operation led the Chinese to draw a second lesson from the conflict involving intelligence and planning.* Lack of information about a traditional ally presented a major challenge to Chinese war planning and operations. The PLA's assessment of the geography and terrain of northern Vietnam often relied on outdated maps and geographic information, while its reconnaissance capability was limited in the battlefield. The maps the PLA used were 1:100,000 scale, printed in 1965 based on the 1938 French edition, giving little detailed information. As a result, PLA forces often got lost during their march in North Vietnamese hill country. One major failure of the Chinese military was failing to consider the huge quantity of the militia forces in its calculation of Vietnamese military strength. The PLA experience showed that the Vietnamese militia put up more relentless resistance and made more surprise raids on the invading forces than the PAVN regulars. The PLA planners initially thought they had assembled an overwhelming force of 8:1 against the Vietnamese forces. There were 40,000 to 50,000 militias in the Cao Bang area alone, which significantly altered the force ratio to 2:1. During the campaign, the PLA never appeared able to maintain the force superiority to deliver a knock-out strike. The operation also demonstrates how difficult it is to carry out military operations in a foreign country if the local populace is mobilised to resist.

(c) *It was the first time that the PLA leadership conducted combined arms operations with tanks and artillery in support of infantry attacks, while assembling air and naval forces to provide cover.* Backwardness in doctrine and tactics prevented the Chinese forces from carrying out a real coordinated operation. While Beijing's political constraints and outdated military thinking proscribed the commitment of air forces to support operations, ground forces also demonstrated poor performance between infantry, tank and artillery units to carry out full combined arms tactics. A clear example was that the infantry had never trained with adequate knowledge of how to manoeuvre with tank units. Infantry soldiers, who fastened themselves to the top of tanks with ropes to prevent themselves from falling off on the march, were stuck when fired upon by the enemy. On the other hand, tank units, which often operated without infantry support and direct communication between the two parties, suffered many unexpected damages and losses. According to Chinese sources, PLA tank units experienced the most losses in the first four days of combat, accounting for 87% of total combat damages, but most were repairable. At the end of the war only 44 tanks and armed vehicles were total losses. The 1979 war experience taught the PLA valuable lessons in combined arms skills.

(d) *The issue of command and control derived largely from the PLA's traditions and culture.* Personal relationships between commanding officers and troops, which had been cultivated in the past, still mattered to the PLA. As interpersonal relationships were more important than institutional ones, it is not surprising that the leaders of the Guangzhou Military Region later acknowledged that they felt uncomfortable commanding the troops transferred from the Wuhan and Chengdu Military Regions during the campaign. These leaders also received many complaints from their rank-and-file about Xu's leadership style because he had not previously commanded them. The PLA's problems of command were compounded by lack of combat-experienced officers. Despite sending higher-ranking officers, who were war veterans, to lower-level troop units to help with command, PLA operations remained frustrated by the inability of lower-ranking officers to make independent judgements and coordinate operations at critical moments. Nevertheless, the 1979 war with Vietnam baptised a young generation of army cadres on the battlefield. One major problem, as the former chief of staff of the Guangzhou Military Region pointed out, was that some lower-ranking officers had a poor understanding of topography and map-reading and could only rely on instructions from their superiors.

(e) *The PLA lacked enough of a modern logistic supply system and structure to support a fast-moving, distant, offensive action.* The operational statistics suggest that the average daily consumption of ammunition and fuel was 700 tons in each category. Logistic operations were a major area for the PLA to draw lessons. Without adequate storage and transportation facilities, both the Guangzhou and Kunming Military Regions had to put together a supply system, which never functioned smoothly and efficiently. Considerable quantities of supplies were lost due either to poor management or to Vietnamese sabotage. As their forces advanced deeper into Vietnamese territory, logistic officers also found it hard to keep communication lines open without diverting a large number of forces to protect them. The PLA concluded that it is essential to create a transportation command to deal with the problems its troops encountered in the operations.

(f) *An interpretation of how the old doctrine of people's war applied to a conflict fought beyond China's borders.* One principle of the people's war doctrine is the mobilisation of the common people to support the war. The 1979 war experience showed that it was almost impossible for huge PLA forces to operate outside the country without whipping up popular support for the war at home. Beijing's propaganda machines aroused public patriotism and pride in Chinese soldiers. Strong expressions of patriotism helped the PLA get direct support for the operations from the people living in two border provinces. In Guangxi province alone, more than 215,000 local residents were mobilised to serve as stretcher-bearers, security guards and porters to carry supplies to the front; and over 26,000 militia members from the border region were actually involved in direct combat activities. The PLA at the time

> had a hodgepodge of a supply system that required every unit to be self-sufficient in "retail logistics," the supply system on the battlefield. PLA troops had to purchase daily supplies by themselves at local markets. Local governments made things easy for troops by simplifying requisition procedures, which helped them receive adequate material and fresh rations in the shortest possible time. Such an experience persuaded the PLA leadership that mobilisation of local governments and civilians to support a war was still the key to victory.

These lessons learned from the 1979 war with Vietnam may not be coherent, comprehensive and fully objective because the PLA does not evaluate its success in a military operation on the basis of the operational outcome but rather on the basis of the impact of the conflict on the overall situation. Deeply influenced by Mao's teaching that war is fundamentally a political undertaking, as long as China could claim to be successful in achieving its strategic and military objectives, the PLA would consider the problems resulting from tactical failures as secondary. This is also why these lessons vary significantly from those in Western studies. Study lessons learned by the PLA are based on only two sources: one is a *summary* of the role played by the students of the Guangzhou Military Region's infantry school in the war and the other is a *brief* analysis of the 1979 campaign by the researchers of the Military Science Academy. PLA studies consider the Cultural Revolution (1966–76) to be a detrimental factor that undermined the PLA's fine traditions, and as a result, the Chinese forces performed poorly in the war.

Lessons the PLA learned focus more on the tactical level of war with the emphasis on command and control, coordination between troops, force structure and weaponry rather than on the strategic and doctrinal philosophy. During its evaluation of the 1979 war experience, the PLA appeared to make no attempt to hide or overlook its own deficiencies and problems at the time; it nevertheless failed to take into account its own erroneous military thinking and traditions.

The PLA's Vietnam lessons and the continuing flare-ups on the China-Vietnam border throughout the 1980s might have helped the Chinese leadership to make the strategic transition from emphasis on preparation for fighting total war to preparation for limited and local war as the trend of the times. Few efforts were made during the transformation of the PLA into a modern force in the 1980s to correct its flawed military thinking, which always downplayed the role of airpower. As a result, if there is anything that the PLA still seems to be not honest about, it is the lessons of air superiority or close air support. PLA literature and textbooks continue to cite the Chinese air force's "deterrent capability" as the primary reason the Vietnamese Air Force did not become involved in the conflict. Marshal Ye Jianying even ridiculously commented that China's phony air operations in the war against Vietnam were an "ingenious way of employing the air force." Such a remark demonstrates the Chinese leadership's failure to appreciate the critical role of airpower in modern warfare.

Nevertheless, an overview of the PLA's experience in the 1979 war with Vietnam provides useful insights into how Chinese leaders approached matters of war and strategy. These were:

(a) Chinese leaders were deliberative and calculating on when and how military power was to be used, but did not hesitate from going to war once they had decided China's national interests were at risk or at stake.
(b) The PLA demonstrated a preference for the seizure and maintenance of operational initiative by deploying a superior force.
(c) The Chinese sense of military victory lay more in their evaluation of the geopolitical outcomes than in their judgement of operational performance on the battlefield.

Since the 1979 war with Vietnam, the PLA has undertaken sweeping revisions in defence doctrine, command and control, operational tactics, and force structure, while the world of military operations has transformed significantly since the 1979 war. Today, no one will expect the Chinese armed forces to repeat what they did in the border war with Vietnam. From a historical perspective, the distinct set of Chinese characteristics revealed in the 1979 war with Vietnam may remain relevant to the Chinese military institution and to understanding of the Chinese approach to employing military power not only in the past but also at present and in the future.

Evaluation

The PRC leaders held several discussions on the evaluation of the war. Different views and criticisms were voiced. In acknowledging a heavy loss on the Chinese side, both Deng Xiaoping and Chen Yun pushed aside any further arguments and thorough evaluation. Whereas Chen Yun implied that such a "no-win" war should not be repeated for financial reasons, Deng asserted a political victory of the war in spite of some military losses. Consequently, it was still a Chinese victory, Deng declared. Since Deng was the leader of the government, his views prevailed over those of Chen Yun.

During the 16-day fighting, the Western Wing under Yang Dezhi fought more successfully than the Eastern Wing did under Xu Shiyou. Casualties were also lighter in the West. Xu's less successful command in the war, which was criticised severely, coupled with his opposition to de-Maoization led to his removal from the post of the Commander of the Guangzhou Military Region in January 1980. On the contrary, Yang Dezhi was promoted to be the General Chief of Staff of the PLA in March 1980.

The PLA began to withdraw on 5 March. It was a leapfrogging process of withdrawal. In other words, as the front units withdrew, the units in the rear safeguarded the movement for an orderly retreat until the rear units appeared to be in the front; then the second run of retreat began. It was easy to manage because the retreat line was short and the Vietnamese were not pursuing. The withdrawal was complete on 16 March. Despite Deng Xiaoping's assertion that the PLA could have gone all the way to Hanoi if they wanted, the quick withdrawal was a right decision of Beijing for financial and military reasons. As Chen Yun pointed out at the Central Work Conference in April 1979, if the war continued six more months, the financial burden would be unbearably heavy. "After all," Chen argued, "what purpose will it serve even if we capture Hanoi".

As the war ended, there were several conflicting accounts on casualties. In a succinct form, a table of both sides' major losses is compiled as follows:

	Chinese	Vietnamese
Killed	26,000	30,000
Wounded	37,000	32,000
POWs	260	1,638
Tanks, armoured vehicles	420	185
Heavy mortars & guns	66	200
Missile stations	0	6

The Chinese treated the Vietnamese POWs well. Among the Vietnamese POWs, a colonel and a lieutenant colonel were reportedly to be the highest in ranking. There were at least 30,000 wounded Chinese soldiers in all major hospitals in Guangxi.

In other areas of the gain-and-loss balance sheet, the Chinese had gained perhaps 50-55 percent of their set limited objectives. Generally speaking, the PLA maintained its initiative in war, following closely its plans for advance and retreat. It operated considerably well, albeit slowly, in the unfamiliar, rugged terrain, including its anti-tunnel and anti-mine warfare. Due to a lack of modern logistic equipment, it made full use of the militia for logistic functions. The PRC was reportedly to have mobilised more than 50,000 militia men from Guangxi and 30,000 from Yunnan. They were organised in 102 battalions and several hundred companies, including mortar company, heavy machinegun company, anti-aircraft gun company, medi-care company, road-repairing company, transportation company, donkey-horse transportation units, and other logistic units. The militia system improved significantly after the National Militia Work Conference in July-August 1978. Its campaign slogan was "Every-man-is-a-soldier." It destroyed six missile stations, numerous bridges, roads, rail lines, and electric power poles.

The destruction in the region was rather thorough. Although no one can deny that the great majority of it was done by the Chinese, it may not have been done totally by them. It would be impossible to determine how much of the damage was caused by Chinese troops...and by Vietnamese troops as they attempted to regain Vietnamese territory. Regardless of a possible minor share of Vietnamese troops in the destruction, the immediate reaction of the Vietnamese people who suffered from the ruins was undoubtedly an intensive hatred for the Chinese.

Although the superior Chinese forces had partially damaged several Vietnamese regular divisions, such as the 3rd at Dong Dang, the 345th and 316th at Lao Cai and possibly the 346th at Lang Son, (345th and 316th divisions were reinforcements) they had not been able to destroy them substantially.

One of the biggest Chinese weaknesses was the outdated weaponry and logistics. The lack of modern weapons and logistic equipments, in comparison with Vietnam's, greatly disabled the Chinese forces to possess a superiority in firepower, troop mobility, attacks, and communications network. In addition, they underestimated Vietnamese military power. For instance, Deputy Defence Minister Su Yu reported to the 3rd Plenum of the CCP in late December 1978 that the PLA could take Hanoi in one week with only partial strength from the Guangzhou and Kunming Military Regions. In fact, it took the PLA 16 full days to capture Lang Son with a strength of 10 divisions drawing from six military regions-a strength almost as much as that of the Guangzhou and Kunming MR's combined.

Inexperience in war also contributed to the weakness of the Chinese forces. The Chinese leaders were aware of situation, but they probably had not expected specifically two subsequent developments. One was the inability of low-ranking officers to make independent judgments and coordinating operations at critical moments; the other was the morale problem which was not an isolated case of the military involved in the war.

In the Eastern Wing under Xu Shiyou, the morale of some units, albeit small in number, was so low that superior officers would have to force their men to advance. Low morale was also seen in the rear. According to the previously cited semi-secret document, several local leaders and cadres far away from the front nervously made arbitrary decisions, after the war broke out. Several cadres were even absent from duty. The Vietnamese mass media also publicized the Chinese morale problem as one of the three factors for China's "defeat".

In spite of the fact that both China and Vietnam had claimed a victory over the other, no one had achieved its major objectives. So far as China is concerned, its publicized "limited objectives" were only partially obtained. First of all, it had not destroyed some of Vietnam's strong divisions. Secondly, it was unable to pacify the border area free from armed conflicts. Thirdly, it had not forced the Vietnamese army to withdraw from Kampuchea. Fourthly, it failed to influence the Hanoi government to change its policy toward the Chinese residents in Vietnam. On the other side of the ledger, China had raised doubts for Hanoi about Soviet willingness to intervene with force against China. Moreover, the PRC had also obtained some support from the ASEAN for its attempt to stop Vietnam's further move in Southeast Asia. Furthermore, it had caused an immediate ill-effect on the Vietnamese economy.

Deng Xiaoping was right in saying that the punitive war would expose the weaknesses of the PLA for improvement. The military thinking of "people's war" was probably the most serious drawback. In launching this punitive war, China has taught both Vietnam and itself a lesson. Beijing's military authorities must have reached the conclusion that the PLA is incapable of fighting a modern war before it is modernised, in both weaponry and strategy.

Assessment

The faculty and students of the Guangzhou Military Region Infantry School had a unique perspective on the events of the 1979 Campaign. At the direction of the Military Region headquarters, the school assigned its faculty and students to the Chinese armies that deployed to Vietnam from Guangxi province. Cadre and troops from the school served with the 41st Army and the 42nd Army during the attack on Cao Bang, and they served with the 43rd and 55th Armies during the attacks on Lang Son. The temporarily assigned students knew the way the PLA was trained to fight, and they saw the way the PLA actually fought. Therefore, the record of their observations is extremely helpful in developing an understanding of the lessons the PLA drew from their experience in Vietnam. The problems the cadre and students from the infantry school found in the four armies were very basic.

They opined that the Chinese troops used very poor basic infantry tactics. Although the Chinese infantry were fit and capable of making enormous sacrifices, the massed infantry attacks, favoured by the Chinese, frequently failed. The Chinese soldiers were fine fighters. However, they had revealed defects—failure to adapt to modern warfare, to particular weakness in communications and transport. Moreover, large-formation warfare, using human wave tactics, was not suitable for operations in mountainous country. Owing to poor communications, some Chinese companies and platoons lost contact with the main forces and suffered heavy losses.

Chinese artillery was ineffective. Chinese gunners did not understand how to measure distances and calculate firing data. As a result, the Chinese artillery could not provide effective indirect fire. The Chinese artillery was limited to large-scale barrage firings on prominent terrain features or inaccurate fire on smaller targets. The Chinese apparently did not have a "call for fire" procedure.

Chinese combat engineering was crude. Although the Vietnamese were heavily outnumbered, they made up for their disadvantage, at least in part, by constructing strong bunker systems and surrounding them with mines. Attacking PLA troops were puzzled to see water buffalo hides hanging outside of Vietnamese homes in villages near the border. Then the troops realised that their own advance units had driven the cattle across minefields laid by the Vietnamese army, in order to explode the mines before the troops followed.

Land navigation was another problem for the PLA. It is very difficult to understand how a PLA unit that could not navigate its way to the objective could be considered ready for combat.

The Chinese logistics system failed. The Vietnamese had unexpected help in their defence against the Chinese attacks. Less than a week into the campaign when the fighting was most fierce, Chinese units began to report shortages of food and water. A 55th Army unit engaged in the attack on a vital hill near Lang Son, reported that its higher unit had not sent food for several days, and the troops had not eaten in two days. The Chinese logistics system, although its lines of support extended a mere four or five kilometres into Vietnam and less than 30 kilometres from its railhead at Pingxiang apparently failed.

The PLA's logistics problems were, at first glance, a matter of numbers. The Chinese force of 30 divisions required 500 tons of supplies every day for each division (15,000 tons). To move the 15,000 tons of supplies, the force needed trucks. The largest Chinese trucks (Zil-151, Zil-157, Ca-30) carried 4,500 kg. Therefore, the PLA invasion force needed 3,030 trucks to carry the supplies necessary to keep operating for one day. The Chinese divisions had trucks, but they were the prime movers for artillery and other heavy equipment. They were not supply trucks; further, the tactical formations did not have organic transportation regiments or battalions. An army that used prime mover trucks to move food, fuel, supplies and ammunition had no way to move its artillery, engineering materiel, or bridging equipment.

The PLA logistics troops had access to a few independent transportation regiments (702 transportation trucks each), commune trucks, packhorses, and coolies to make up the difference between the requirement and the transportation capacity of their units. But managing four modes of transportation had to be a nightmare. As a result, food, water, and ammunition frequently failed to get to the right place at the right time. These management problems were symptomatic of a failed logistics system.

The basic tactical lesson of the 1979 Campaign was that PLA tactics more closely resembled the massed infantry attacks of the past than the fire and movement/fire and manoeuvre tactics of a modern army.

The Results of the Conflict

Appropriately for such a complex conflict, the Sino-Vietnamese War ended ambiguously, with both sides possessing at least some claims to victory. The Vietnamese could claim they had defeated an invasion by a far more powerful neighbour without having to surrender territory or retreat from Cambodia, while the Chinese could claim they had shown the Vietnamese that they were willing to use military force to secure their interests. Is either side correct in their assessment? If neither side is fully correct, which is more correct?

One school of thought holds that China was unambiguously defeated in the war. China launched its attack in an effort to force Vietnam to withdraw from Cambodia. The Chinese withdrew from Vietnam on 16 March 1979, but the Vietnamese did not leave Cambodia until 1989. China's efforts only drew some Vietnamese troops away from Cambodia, as Chinese troops had only fought against Vietnamese border troops and militia, as opposed to regular units—thus, an invasion intended to teach Vietnam's leadership that it could not sustain its military deployments in Cambodia did the exact opposite. In the aftermath of the conflict, border tensions remained high, and Vietnam only increased its expulsion of Hoa. Under this interpretation, China's assault served only to demonstrate its own military limitations and accomplished none of its objectives.

Additionally, rather than weakening the Russo-Vietnamese relationship, China's invasion of Vietnam paradoxically had the opposite effect, strengthening the alliance between the two countries. Between April and July 1979, the Soviets refitted the 308th Division of the Vietnamese 1st Corps, along with other units, with new equipment, including 111 BMP-1 armoured personnel carriers—which were highly mobile and carried anti-tank guided missiles, and thus represented a substantial advance over the hardware hitherto available to either side. The Soviets also sent military advisors to the units that received the new hardware. The construction of Soviet naval and air facilities at Da Nang and Cam Ranh Bay were accelerated following the conflict, and contemporary observers felt that the USSR's military posture in East Asia was strengthened after the war. After the conflict, numerous pro-China elements within the Vietnamese government were either arrested or defected to China. By forcing Vietnam once again to turn to Russia for help, China's military offensive—which was aimed at upsetting the ongoing Russo-Vietnamese relationship—only achieved the opposite.

However, other perspectives take substantial issue with this conventional wisdom. The Vietnamese were forced to maintain a large contingent of troops on the border with China, which caused the Vietnamese government noticeable financial (and subsequently economic) difficulties. Additionally, some scholars—such as Henry Kissinger—write admiringly of the deterrent effect that Chinese action had on the Soviet Union and Vietnam, precisely because it showed Moscow that China was willing and able to oppose their plans by force—and further demonstrated that the USSR was unwilling to take military action to stop this. Lee Kuan Yew, the long-time Prime Minister of Singapore, stated that while "the Western press wrote off the Chinese punitive action as a failure…I believe it changed the history of East Asia."

12

CHINESE STRATEGIC AND OPERATIONAL DOCTRINE

Historically, Chinese military doctrine has been a very good indicator of the Chinese leadership's perception of the threats to China's security and their view of how the Chinese military should respond. The dilemma for the leadership has been that they have never had the wherewithal to carry out the doctrine's intent. China's military technology deficiencies have forced Chinese military planners to compensate with China's strategic attributes: a large army, large land mass, and nuclear weapons. However, the nature of modern, post-Cold War warfare—short, violent, often technical—and China's perceived security requirements diminish the utility of these compensating factors.

Past Doctrine

Chinese hegemony over their periphery increased or declined along with the strength of the dynasty in power. During weak dynasties, indigenous peoples rebelled, threw out the Chinese, and encroached on "China's gates." During strong dynasties, the Chinese reasserted their suzerainty and provided security from the "barbarians" by keeping them "outside the gates" of China proper. This method enabled China to double its land area by the middle of the eighteenth century and effectively ended the troubles with barbarians and fixed the borders with Russia and the Southeast Asian states. China was not always successful in keeping the barbarians out. The Mongols defeated the Chinese in 1323 and ruled China for eighty-six years. In fact, when China achieved its territorial apex in 1768, it was ruled by the Manchus who reigned until the fall of the Qing Dynasty in 1911.

China fought thousands of wars during its 5,000-year history to keep the country unified. In traditional China, warfare was considered an abnormal state of affairs. Confucius likened war to an insect that eats up resources. Armies were raised to confront situations requiring military force and were quickly disbanded when the situation was resolved. However, what China lacked in military culture, it made up for in applied strategy and doctrine. Sun Tzu was among the first, and still the most famous, ancient Chinese strategist. There were others and hundreds of titles of military writing from ancient China have survived and still enjoy a broad readership among military leaders.

Indeed, the teachings of the ancients have had a considerable influence on modern Chinese strategists, not least on Mao Zedong, who was perhaps the leading practitioner of the ancient precepts in the modern era. Two mainstays of ancient Chinese war-fighting doctrine are particularly evident: "*trading space for time*" and "*defeating a superior enemy with an inferior force*." The first refers to luring the enemy so deep that it is overextended and can be defeated at a time and place of one's choosing. The second has many variants, but in general terms the Chinese try to isolate small formations of the enemy, overwhelm them, and move on to others. The cumulative effect of several small victories is equal to or greater than defeating the enemy in one main battle, and defeat is usually avoided.

China's regional hegemony and its ability to prevail on the battlefield ended with its defeat at the hands of the British in the 1842 Opium War. After the war, China was virtually a semi-colonial country, so weakened by external exploitation and internal strife that it almost lost its 5,000-year-old national identity. The ultimate humiliation came at the hands of the Japanese, a former tribute state, who defeated China in 1895, and annexed Taiwan and Manchuria. Unlike China, Japan was able to master the industrial and technological attributes of modern warfare and adopt Western military doctrine as its own.

China's history of external exploitation ended after World War II. However, it took four years of applying the "trading space for time" and "defeating a superior enemy with an inferior force" doctrines before Mao Zedong could end China's internal strife by achieving victory over the Nationalists in China's civil war. On 1 October 1949, Mao proclaimed to China and the world that China had stood up and would never be humiliated by an external power or divided by internal disorder again.

People's War

Military policy is shaped by a variety of considerations, but it is the leadership's perception of threat that is paramount. The nature of the threat and the response to it are decisive in determining the doctrine of the armed forces and their development. In 1949, Mao clearly perceived the US and the West to be China's immediate threat and determined that "people's war" would be the military doctrine the PLA would employ to defend China. The approach was to gain victory after a long war of attrition by trading space for time. In the dark days of the war against Japan, the Chinese used to console themselves with a grim joke. One Chinese asks another about the results of the last battle against the Japanese:

> *'We lost 1,000,000 men,'* is the answer.
> *'How many did the Japanese lose?'* is the next question.
> *'One hundred,'* is the answer.
> *'Marvellous,'* is the retort. *'We'll soon have them on the run.*

In 1949 China had three strategic assets: a large population, a large land area; and an alliance with the Soviet Union. "People's war" was built around these assets. In Mao's model, the PLA and paramilitary forces, supported by the populace, would conduct protracted war against any invader. Initially, the PLA's main forces, using conventional tactics, would carry out a strategic retreat supported by guerrilla-type operations until the invading forces were overextended and dispersed. PLA forces would then be reconfigured and concentrated to annihilate the enemy in detail.

Ironically, though "people's war" was Chinese military doctrine for more than a decade, they rarely employed it; and when they did, it did not work very well. In Korea, save for early successes, when the use of deception enabled the PLA to move more than 300,000 troops into Korea undetected, Chinese units had a difficult time applying "people's war" principles because they could not take advantage of their numerical superiority and had no space to trade for time. The PLA's massed, unsupported (air or artillery) attacks against vastly superior American firepower did not work and in most cases led to disastrously high personnel and equipment losses. Korea was a wake-up call for the PLA and made its leaders painfully aware of the need to modernise weaponry, combat skills, and military doctrine before again engaging a modern military force.

People's War Under Modern Conditions

Two factors changed China's strategic thinking and military doctrine. In 1964 China acquired another strategic asset, nuclear weapons. However, they lost the Soviet Union as an ally and strategic partner; in fact, the Soviet Union replaced America as China's principal foe. Nuclear weapons gave the Chinese the capability to change their strategy and the Soviets gave them a reason.

For most of the 1960s and 1970s, Beijing's national military strategy was based primarily on defending China against a possible Soviet attack. During that period, the PLA compensated for its outdated capabilities by using concepts of operations based on protraction, attrition, and the threat of nuclear retaliation or—"people's war under modern conditions." Continental defence was still the core strategy, but it included the ability to conduct offensive operations short distances outside China's borders—fighting "outside the gates," as Mao would say. "People's war under modern conditions" differed from people's war in two ways. First, the intent of the new strategy was to defeat the adversary closer to China's borders, avoiding an endless retreat into the interior.

Second, cities would have to be defended because cities, and not the countryside, supported the logistical requirements of the Chinese armed forces. Nonetheless, the new strategy still relied on the PLA's massive size, and its ultimate defence was to fall back into China's interior and exhaust its adversary (the Soviets) through protracted war.

Although "people's war under modern conditions" was China's military doctrine for more than a decade, it was never used in conflict. PLA operations in the 1979 Sino-Vietnamese war were the most extensive and costly since the Korean War. But despite the new "people's war under modern conditions" strategy, Chinese equipment and combat performance had not improved since Korea. It was an ugly affair. One 180,000 of China's best troops fought 75,000-100,000 Vietnamese border and militia troops, and lost. Interestingly, despite the initial tactical surprise of a five-pronged advance, the PLA did not use its manpower advantage, trade space for time, or use deception techniques. The Sino-Vietnam War was largely a conventional affair, in which the two enemies engaged in largely set-piece frontal assaults on well dug-in positions, and the Chinese did not do very well.

The Chinese were shocked to discover that the traditions of the Long March, World War II and Korea were not enough to meet the Vietnamese, with their modern Soviet (and US) equipment and with the confidence gained at the expense of American forces. The PLA lacked adequate communications, transport and logistics and were burdened with an elaborate and archaic command structure. Their maps were 75 years old. Runners were employed to relay orders because there were few radios (and those they had were not secure). The PLA suffered more than 60,000 casualties, including 26,000 killed. Thus, in heavy fighting in 1979, the Chinese had nearly half as many soldiers killed in action in Vietnam as the US lost in 10 years.

It would be unfair to imply that China's hierarchy did not know the PLA's limitations. In the mid-70s some Party and military elites voiced concern, somewhat hesitantly, over the PLA's ability to defend China in modern war. Deng Xiaoping was one of them and, in 1975, was purged for his efforts. Intra-party struggles precluded PLA modernisation until 1978, when Deng was rehabilitated for the third time and a new military modernisation programme was revealed as the fourth component of the "Four Modernisations Programme." However, because it was the fourth priority, the military modernisation did not receive much more than planning consideration until the debacle in Vietnam.

Local Limited War

After China's Vietnam war debacle, Deng Xiaoping made a scathing speech in 1979 to the CMC, China's highest military body, asserting that the PLA's weaknesses in education, training, organisation, doctrine, tactics, and management procedures meant that the PLA could not maintain or employ advanced hardware even if the nation could afford to supply it. For the next several years the PLA focused on the organisational, doctrinal, and human aspects of military modernisation, while waiting for modern equipment and advanced systems.

Over the same period, as the world situation changed, Beijing's analysts concluded that reduced superpower influence meant that there was increased probability of small-scale wars flaring up along China's periphery. This would especially be the case, the Chinese thought, where border and territorial disputes had been held in check by the dynamic of superpower confrontation. In addition, they felt that the increasing scarcity of natural resources as a result of economic development could lead to territorial disputes. Furthermore, the Chinese forecast correctly, and before other analysts, that ethnic conflict would result from a lessening of superpower tensions.

By 1983, the Chinese had basically obviated the Soviet threat. In part, this change was because of the US military build-up, which convinced the Chinese that the US would prevail in any contest with the Soviet Union. There was also an emerging perception among Chinese politicians and military leaders that the Soviet Union was a "paper tiger." If the Russians could not defeat a ragtag bunch of Afghanis, went their logic, why should they be feared? Based on this analysis, China's defence policy shifted from a strategy designed primarily to deter the USSR to a strategy that could win localised wars around China's borders and maritime territories. The distinguishing characteristic of the new strategy was its intent to avoid retreating into the interior by defeating the adversary close to China's borders, or "closer to the gate" in Mao parlance.

The operational requirements for limited war were far more demanding than in previous doctrines. Under the traditional approach to "people's war" and "people's war under modern conditions," warfighting strategy was divided into three phases: defensive, stalemate and counter-offensive.

In a modern limited war, mobilising the entire population for war was no longer feasible. Protraction and attrition were precluded; speed, mobility, and lethality were in. Weapons systems for the new strategy had to have greater range, accuracy, and be able to operate at night in all weather conditions. Military doctrine and capabilities, especially for the Navy and Air Force, had to adapt to a new defensive perimeter that extended 1,000 kilometres from China's shore.

Nevertheless, the modernisation programme has not kept pace with the expansive defence policy, and China's strategic advantages—a large land mass and population, and nuclear weapons. Historically advantageous operational tactics, such as the use of deception and the hit-and-run techniques that allowed the Chinese to "shape the battlefield," were supplanted by a willingness to engage the enemy in conventional battles at times and locations chosen by the enemy.

Characteristics of Chinese Thought and Strategic Culture

Does culture matter in the conduct of strategy and warfare? The very nature of war is consistent among all peoples and is best defined by Thucydides' three motivations of "fear, honour, and interest." However, the opposing view would argue that culture becomes important in how a people interpret and give meaning or value to those motivations.

What are the characteristics of Chinese thought that distinguish it? There are two central philosophical concepts which, when combined, interact to form Chinese dialectical thinking. The first is the concept of change, and the second is the concept of the whole. As a result of this view, the Chinese value experience over logic because, from their perspective, one cannot know the world solely by observing its parts; one must also actively shape it and interact with it.

China's *Seven Military Classics* provide evidence of two Chinese strategic cultures: the first is offensive in nature and emphasizes the use of violence to resolve security conflicts; and, the second is more diplomatic and emphasizes preferences of winning over one's opponent through virtuous actions. According to the Chinese philosophy of change, nothing is immutable and the weak have an opportunity to become strong just as the strong may become weak. In this respect, one could argue that ancient

Chinese strategists exercised restraint in aggression in order to avoid the inevitable transformation from the aggressor to the victim. Therefore, ancient Chinese strategists preferred virtue over violence in order to maintain their legitimacy. However, one must remember that even though Confucianism abhors the use of violence, it permits warfare as a last resort to protect Confucian culture.

Culture matters in strategy and the PRC's political and military leadership both appreciate and understand the value of classical Chinese thought. Chinese thought and philosophy are integral elements of national identity, which for the CCP is the cornerstone for national unity.

The challenge that many Chinese strategists face is how to reconcile these intellectual and theoretical traditions with each other and with the PRC's ever-changing society. An example of the interplay between these traditions is the CCP's use of the Confucian concepts of harmony and virtue to push not only a domestic agenda of political order, but to also to influence the "soft" nature of its foreign policy.

Chinese Strategic Art

Chinese Strategic Art is the interaction of Chinese strategic culture with the PLA's *science of strategy* described in the Chinese Academy of Military Science's book, *The Science of Military Strategy*. It states that the science of strategy is "the military science to study the laws of war" which includes the laws which govern the conduct of war and those which govern "strategic evolution". This discipline studies a broad continuum of information that includes historical experience, current circumstances, and predicted future scenarios in order to develop sound strategic decisions and guidance.

According to *The Science of Military Strategy*, the science of strategy "commands operational art and tactics," as it is focused on the larger system as a whole while the operational and tactical levels only address a part of the overall system. Although the theoretical system seeks to derive general principles of war and strategy, it is important to note that these principles may change over time as experience and objective conditions change. The theoretical principles of the science of strategy then inform and provide the framework for the development of basic and applied strategic theory. There are six characteristics of the science of strategy: *practice, politics, comprehensiveness, antagonism, stratagem, and prediction.* In short, these principles describe the dynamic, iterative nature of the science of strategy which allows it to change as reality and current circumstances change. They emphasize the importance of combining practice or experience with the Chinese holistic and dialectic approaches to develop stratagems to defeat their adversary. However, the key characteristic of stratagem is "extraordinary energy from the national strength available and turn the passive to the active." Thus, "the science of strategy is a science of wisdom to sum up the laws of using stratagems."

The CCP leadership emphasizes the importance of "grasping" and "controlling" the "overall strategic situation."In 2002, Qiao Liang and Wang Xiangsui, the two PLA colonels who penned the book *Unrestricted Warfare*, shed light on the Chinese approach to the concepts of "grasping" and "controlling". They offer two metaphors to explain the Chinese strategic approach: the Chinese Box, and the Buddha's palm. The Chinese box approach, they explain is the practice of attacking "an issue with a framework larger than the issue itself." It is the practice of circumscribing the specific problem into a small mental box, then gradually placing it within boxes of increasing scale and context. In the end, they assert, "you come up with a framework of highest generality to harness the whole situation," and one's potential solutions are sufficiently comprehensive enough to allow the flexibility for manoeuvre as conditions change in the future.

The second metaphor is that of the Buddha's palm. In the legend of the Monkey King, the Buddha challenged the Monkey King to use his acrobatic skill to escape from the palm of his hand. As the story goes, no matter how hard or far the Monkey King jumped, he could not escape the end of the Buddha's palm. This metaphor encapsulates the desire of Chinese strategists to emulate the Buddha's ability to control the superior technological capability of the US military—represented by the masterful and skilful Monkey King. Mao Zedong referenced the same analogy in his essay *On Protracted War* to describe a concept of encirclement at the strategic level. According to Mao's interpretation, strategic encirclement of one's enemy is an important condition for victory.

The example of the *weichi* game is another example that reiterates the

Chinese emphasis on "grasping" and "controlling" the strategic situation as mentioned above. In the opening stages of the game, each player positions his pieces to both set the conditions for his strategic plans while also trying to ascertain his opponent's strategy. The object of a *weichi* game is to control space on the board by positioning one's forces to encircle the opponent's forces.

Stratagem is the plan or strategy that a Chinese strategist will use to surprise and defeat his adversary. One could argue that the key to stratagem is deception. After all, Sun Tzu did declare at the end of Chapter One of *The Art of War* that, "All warfare is based on deception." While this idea has merit, it does not reflect exactly what Sun Tzu meant by deception. From a Western perspective, deception is the act of misleading another person or merely disguising appearances. Military deception implies actions to deliberately mislead the enemy in regards to own capabilities, intentions and operations. For the Chinese, deception has a more nuanced meaning in regards to controlling one's adversary. In the text that follows Sun Tzu's declaration, he lists various actions that one may take in relation to his opponent and given the existing conditions. Some examples of these actions are: *appearing incapable when capable; offering a bait to lure the enemy; feigning inferiority while encouraging the enemy's arrogance; angering the enemy commander if he is prone to anger; and, attacking the enemy where he least expects it.* The Chinese understanding and execution of stratagem is more fluid and often an emergent response to the constantly changing conditions of the overall strategic situation.

The idea of winning victory by stratagem has always been the main idea of traditional Chinese strategic thinking. The Chinese understanding and execution of stratagem is more fluid and often an emergent response to the constantly changing conditions of the overall strategic situation. In particular, stratagem emphasizes "use of *limited force* to achieve victory", The ideal goals of Chinese strategic thinking are to "*subdue the enemy without fighting*", to "[win] others over with awesomeness and virtue" and to defeat enemies with "wisdom and stratagem."

No discussion of stratagem is complete without a discussion of *shashoujian*, commonly translated as the "assassin's mace" or "trump card." It is so broad a term that one could say anything about it and possibly be correct. *Shashoujian* is a very common idiom in Chinese society. In general, the term refers to "*the means or ways by which one overcomes a seemingly insurmountable obstacle.*" *Shashoujian* should be considered both as a weapon or weapon system, and as a warfighting concept. In discussing the development of Chinese military strategy, it needs to be understood that, while technology will influence change in strategy, it will not change the fundamental principle that people are the decisive factor in the war, and weapons are but the manifestation of human knowledge. People are the most important force multiplier.

The Five Elements

The primary text that provides the intellectual and philosophical basis for Chinese Strategic Art is Sun Tzu's *Art of War*. Sun Tzu's principles of war informed and shaped the development Mao's theory of people's war.

In chapter three of *The Art of War*, Sun Tzu specifies five conditions that predict victory. These conditions are as follows: *he who knows when he can fight and when he cannot will be victorious; he who recognises how to use large and small forces will win; the army whose ranks are united in purpose will be victorious; he who prepares against the unprepared will win; and, he whose general receives no interference from the sovereign will win.*

In the present the Chinese enunciate five themes that have withstood the test of time. These themes, which reflect Sun Tzu's five conditions, are as follows: *stress "Dao (moral influence);" strive for invulnerability by making "the state prosperous and the army strong;" plan deliberately to achieve a complete victory through the "combination of civil and military means;" use stratagem and foreknowledge to attack the enemy where he is weak and catch him by surprise; pay attention to maintaining the army by valuing unity of command, morale and fighting skill.* While it is important to understand the concept behind each element, it is equally, if not more important to understand the relationships between elements and how they elaborate the relationship between the Chinese strategist and his opponent.

The game of *weichi* is useful for understanding how a Chinese strategist would apply the five elements of Chinese Strategic Art. In *weichi*, two players start with an empty board. Unlike chess, there are no predetermined positions for each player's pieces. How one decides to array one's forces is left to the experience, knowledge, imagination and creativity of the individual. As the players interact, campaigns and battle fronts emerge across the board. Unlike in chess, one cannot hope to capture the king nor always plan for swift and decisive victory. Also, whereas in chess different pieces have different values and functions, all the stones in *weichi* are equal, and gain or lose value by virtue of their disposition. One succeeds by carefully deploying forces and fighting only when necessary. As the players interact and deploy their stones, they attempt to deduce each other's strategy and intent. If the acme of chess is to win in as few moves as possible, then the acme of *weichi* is to control the board and one's opponent regardless of how little or long it takes.

Application of Chinese Strategic Art

A study of the PLA's military history from 1949 to the present provides only a limited number of case studies with which to apply the concept of Chinese Strategic Art. The major conflicts since the founding of the PRC are as follows: the Korean War, 1950; the Sino-Indian War, 1962; and, the Sino-Vietnamese war (also known as the Punitive War by the Chinese), 1979. In addition to these local wars, wars which occurred on China's periphery, there were a number of smaller conflicts involving the islands off of China's coast, to include the showdowns between China and Taiwan in 1958, and 1995-1996.

Of these conflicts, the Sino-Vietnamese conflict in 1979 is an interesting case because it illuminates the conditions under which China is willing to conduct a local war and how it perceives or measures strategic military success. Many analysts view the conflict as a Chinese failure. The war lasted only three weeks, and, although the PLA captured six provincial capitals, they suffered significant losses and left the Vietnamese military largely intact. Thus, the absence of a decisive victory and failure to demolish the enemy's military equated to military failure. From a Chinese perspective, the war was a strategic success in that it yielded positive results both domestically and internationally.

Domestically, the war helped spur the modernisation effort within China, and provided the impetus for military reform and modernisation. This military modernisation was a necessary step to securing China's long-term security in the region after the Cultural Revolution sapped the spirit of both the PLA and Chinese society as a whole.

Internationally, the war provided China with an opportunity to open up to the West and establish an amenable relationship with the US. The Sino-US relationship was an important condition in preventing what Deng Xiaoping perceived as a Soviet attempt to strategically encircle China. In 1975, PRC aid to Vietnam ceased, and the Soviet Union moved to improve Soviet-Vietnamese relations, resulting in the Soviet-Vietnamese Treaty of Friendship and Cooperation on 2 November1978. This new treaty caused the PRC leadership to fear possible Soviet encirclement, especially since the sixth clause in the treaty stated that the Soviet Union and Vietnam would consult and support each other in the event of an attack, or the threat of an attack. Chinese fears increased in 1978 when Soviet military support and arms shipments to Vietnam increased.

To counter the perceived Soviet threat of encirclement, China's leadership focused on improving its relationships with Japan and the US. The US made an initial overture to Beijing when President Ford visited China in 1975. On 1 January 1979, the Chinese moved to normalise relations with the US. In response to Chinese overtures to Japan and the US, the Soviets moved to improve their relations with the Southeast Asian countries along China's border.

On 17 February 1979, the PLA began its offensive, crossing the Sino-Vietnamese border at 14 different points. Their commanding officer was Yang Dezhi, a former deputy commander during the Korean War. During the campaign, the PLA performed poorly, due mostly to the overall lack of combat experience of its troops and the lack of logistics and modern equipment. In spite of its shortcomings, the PLA still managed to capture several border cities and provincial capitals, including Lang Son—a critical part of Hanoi's defence. Even though Deng declared early during the fighting that China had no intention of seizing Hanoi, the disposition of PLA forces in Lang Son sent a clear message to the Vietnamese leadership that China could threaten the capital. Almost immediately following the fall of Lang Son on 3 March 1979, the PLA began withdrawal from Vietnam. The PLA completed full withdrawal on 16 March.

The Soviets responded to the Chinese offensive by positioning several naval vessels off the coast of Vietnam. That, however, was the extent of Soviet military participation. The non-existent Soviet military intervention on behalf of the Vietnamese signalled victory to the Chinese leadership. By attacking Vietnam, Deng sought to deliver the Soviets a strategic defeat without resorting to a larger scale military conflict with the superpower.

In the Sino-Vietnamese war, one sees Deng's combination of the elements of Chinese strategic art to attain the overall strategic goal of modernisation. His stratagem was to use the punitive war to achieve more advantageous relationships with the two superpowers while assuring China's national security during its period of modernisation.

China's national policy for the war was strong and that they achieved all of their campaign objectives (quantified as capturing three provincial capitals, and occupying 21 counties or towns). Chinese analysts attributed the difficulties and problems encountered during the campaign to a number of issues to include: lack of combat experience; poor equipment and training; incorrect organisation; and the Cultural Revolution.

Operational Art in the Sino-Vietnam War

An investigation of the Chinese concept of operational art in the twentieth century reveals a tendency to attempt to satisfy maximal political ends with limited military means. Therefore, a traditional dichotomy has existed in Chinese doctrine which professes a lead-power status in Asia while emphasizing anti-professionalism in the military. This political-military relationship has limited the ability of the PLA to function effectively at the operational level of war in power projection campaigns required to preserve such status.

The Sino-Vietnam War provides another example of China's propensity to attempt to secure maximum political objectives with insufficient military means; means which had not been developed because of an overwhelming political control of the PLA in which the old soldiers in positions of power perpetuated the people's war doctrine which had been successfully applied in the Sino-Indian War. But, unlike in 1962 versus India, Vietnam was a technologically superior military opponent with substantial experience.

China's main objective in this war was to punish Vietnam for its invasion of Kampuchea and show the Asian community that Peking would retain the right to determine the nature of political arrangements in its backyard. To do so would require a successful strike against the PAVN to substantially weaken its resources and its reputation in Southeast Asia. A secondary objective was to deter Hanoi's extension of its power across the Chinese border itself. Finally, convinced that the Soviets were using Vietnam as a bridgehead to the South, Peking wanted also to punish the Soviet Union. By attacking Moscow's chief ally in Asia, China would demonstrate her own strength while displaying Soviet weakness to SE Asia. Although a razor-sharp military instrument was needed to ensure success, China's blunt sword failed to deliver its blow and none of China's political objectives was met.

The PLA "counter-offensive" launched on 17 February 1979 was designed and controlled by Peking through an ad hoc operational command structure. Troops, totalling as many as 300,000, were drawn in from ten different military regions across the country to launch this punitive operation. In its initial strike, the PLA was once again able to establish local superiority through the principle of mass against only 75,000 to 100,000 Vietnamese militia and border troops. The principle of surprise was also achieved by launching the offensive before a significant Soviet military presence could be deployed in Vietnam and while much of Vietnam's leadership was absent from Hanoi.

As the fighting wore on, it became evident that the PLA did not have the capabilities necessary to obtain the swift, overwhelming victory required to achieve Peking's objectives. The Vietnamese militia proved to be strong adversaries with a superiority in firepower versus the obsolete Chinese arsenal. Command, control, and communication problems were evidenced by the poorly trained and educated PLA commanders' inability to coordinate attacks with infantry, armour, and artillery units. Furthermore, PLA operational sustainment capacity was severely reduced by people's war logistics which quickly deteriorated as the distance between its deployed forces and its immobile civilian "support-the-front" groups increased. Finally, Peking's lack of operational planning was evidenced when the provincial capital Lang Son was not identified as the strategic objective *until one week into the war.*

As in the Korean and Sino-Indian wars, the PLA conducted an operational pause after its initial thrust. In the Sino-Vietnam war, though, there was no psychological advantage to exploit due to the stiff resistance from the Vietnamese militia. When fighting resumed a week later, Mao's operational doctrine proved unable to cope against a modem army engaged in positional warfare. By the time Lang Son was finally secured, only 20 kilometres from the Chinese border, the PLA had sustained unacceptably high casualties (20-30,000) by again reverting to "human wave" tactics. Despite Peking's claim to the contrary, very few of the PAVN units were engaged during this campaign, most having been committed to the defence of Hanoi. Rather than move beyond Lang Son to the Red River delta and risk a possible escalation which would certainly have exacerbated her operational liabilities, China claimed victory on 5 March and announced a unilateral withdrawal.

It became readily apparent that the broad political aims of Peking were undermined by the limited nature of this operation with its inherent political and military constraints. Although damage to its countryside created severe economic problems, Vietnam not only failed to halt policies which China had repudiated, but confirmed that they, rather than the PRC were the force to be reckoned with in Southeast Asia. In response to their lesson, the Soviets strengthened their relations with Vietnam and rapidly increased their military and economic presence in SE Asia.

China's Lessons Learned

China, instead, was on the receiving end of many lessons it had forgotten from the Korean War. Weaknesses in Mao's operational doctrine were as decisive in limiting the conflict in military terms as any Chinese propensity to self-restraint during the operation.

Why, then, had this "territorial defensive" doctrine been utilised to project offensives beyond China's borders? It seems that this legacy was more than just a pragmatic response to very limited economic means. Chinese leadership had "band-wagoned" the people's war doctrine to power and to deny its capability to meet the demands of modem warfare would have been politically perilous.

With this preponderance of the human element in the doctrine, and lack of a legitimate enemy to test it for almost thirty years, the party had minimised the need for "professionals" and maintained firm control of the PLA throughout the operational level of war.

After the Sino-Vietnam War, Peking determined that it would be more politically dangerous to maintain an antiquated force and the doctrine upon which it was built. They determined that effective modernisation could only be achieved by discarding revolutionary myth and synthesizing the people's war with "modern conditions." Deng Xiaoping induced a military training programme to produce professionals with skills to derive relevant operational concepts in which modern technology could be projected offensively as well as applied defensively. They were no longer prepared to put their faith primarily in the political attitudes of the soldiers.

As a result, operational concepts have been developed which question the application of Mao's operational principles, primarily in regard to logistical requirements for operational sustainment. A "five-combat potential" programme stressed joint operations, quick reaction, electronics confrontation, logistical needs, and field endurance to meet the dynamic nature of modern military operations. China's military researchers recently focused on providing a relevant operational framework for fighting a fast-paced war against the Vietnamese in the Nansha Islands. They derived the principles of *surprise, focused attacks* (concentration of force), *three-dimensional warfare* (joint operations), *enhanced rear services support* (logistics), and *rapid decision with strict controls* (unity of command).

We can make the following assumptions concerning Chinese tendencies and capabilities at the operational level of war, based on traditional Chinese military dogma, case studies, and more recent doctrinal changes. First, the traditional use of surprise, mass, intelligence, and manoeuvre will be stressed initially, to create a limited military, but psychologically demoralising, advantage. At this point, an operational pause will likely follow to capitalise on this psychological condition and induce negotiations. This operational sequence would be in keeping with China's propensity to strive for maximum ends with minimal means. That point in time may present a potential weakness for the operational commander to exploit. Because China envisions limited fast-strike operations beyond her borders, operational sustainment capabilities may continue to be a weakness in operational design.

Although the modem PLA is developing much greater professional and technological means for a substantially greater power projection potential than was evidenced in the past, the PRC will likely continue to pursue policy objectives without adequate concern for operational planning. This will make it difficult for the PLA to develop a relevant operational design to sustain campaigns in an extended conflict unless Peking severs its operational level political constraints.

An effective concept of operational art can only be designed and utilised by a well educated, professionally trained officer corps. As Sun-tzu wrote, "*He whose generals are able and not interfered with by the sovereign will be victorious*".

13

CONCLUSION

War, as is becoming realised in the modern world, is more than a mere clash of arms. The development of armies and of their organisation and the narratives of campaign strategy and of operational tactics, which were formerly the military historian's exclusive concern, can be understood only in relation to developments in the world at large, in relation to advances in technology, and in relation to changes in political and economic organisation.

Military history offers soldiers an opportunity to improve their professional qualifications. Indeed, in a world growing ever more complex and in a society which increasingly questions old methods and values, soldiers must study their profession continuously i£ they expect to meet the challenges which the unlimited liability clause in battle may chose at any time. No one field of study will guarantee success on the battlefield, but lacking actual experience in combat the thoughtful soldier will do well to turn to the study of past wars.

Careful reading of military history can supply a valuable perspective for the critical examination of contemporary problems. Historical perspective leads to a sense of proportion and encourages the long view: it contributes to an awareness that life moves in a channel of continuous change, thus helping to counter excessive optimism or pessimism about current developments. Moreover, it will help one reassess the values used to weigh achievements, methods, and decisions. Shielded from the heat and passion of partisan argument, for example, one can learn something of the wisdom as well as the practical difficulties in the subordination of military forces to civilian direction.

Historically, Vietnam and China have had close ties, whenever Vietnam has considered itself under the Chinese sphere of influence. This means that Vietnam looked to China for political, cultural and socio-economic influence, and recognised the leadership of Imperial China. In turn, China provided income revenue through increased trade, as well as a defence system against other expansionist nations. An example of this is China's declaration of war against France in August 1884 due to the French expansion into North Vietnam. Ho Chi Minh, the leader of Vietnam, asked China for commanders to lead at the regimental and battalion levels of the Vietnamese Army. Instead, China formed the Chinese Military Advisory Group (CMAG) in order to provide hands-off assistance to Vietnamese fighters. Along with military personnel, China provided weapons, as well as helped with logistics and planning.

Sino-Vietnamese relations at that time were amicable because of a common French enemy and similar ideological viewpoints. However, there was underlying tension within this diplomatic framework because of the Soviet Union's support of North Vietnam. Like China, the USSR was providing arms in an effort to sustain Communism within Southeast Asia. The death of Stalin increased Sino-Soviet tensions as Nikita Khrushchev, Stalin's successor, was seen by Mao Zedong as a Western puppet and unable to adhere to the true principles of Communist ideology. Following the Sino-Soviet schism, Vietnam chose to ally with the USSR, embittering Sino-Vietnamese relations and providing a catalyst for future conflict.

A unified Vietnam, in 1975, placed for the first time in history a successful military power on China's southern border, which was not only independent of China's influence but also had various conflicting goals with China. To contain China, the Soviet Union needed a strong and united Vietnam on the southern border of China. As for the Vietnamese, their options in dealing with their two largest partners were broadened with the end of the war; it was no longer imperative for Hanoi to maintain its neutral status between them. Naturally, Hanoi would rather have a powerful but distant Soviet Union to balance a much closer but historically hostile China. Furthermore, in pursuing its own national interests in the region, post-war Vietnam found a much more sympathetic ally in the Soviet Union than in China. Therefore, a pro-Soviet tendency was inescapable.

Although China repeatedly expressed its rising discontent to Vietnam over the changing status quo, it took no militant steps for more than a decade. Chinese restraint finally snapped at the end of 1978 when Vietnam joined the Soviets in a joint security alliance. The Chinese attack on Vietnam in February 1979, however, was inconsistent with rational deterrence models: it occurred at a point when the odds for a victory or even for a significant gain in the case of a loss were too low for any rational cost/benefit analysis to have justified it. A phenomenon noticeable throughout history is the pursuit by governments of policies contrary to their own interests. If ways can be found to improve the use of information by those who make strategic decisions—to confront power with truth—it could reduce the likelihood and severity of bad decisions.

The history of the Sino-Vietnam War offers important insights that can help us assess strategic options and alternatives. If the policymakers of today and tomorrow draw on those insights, they will be better equipped to chart a nation's course. While it is not feasible to make policy solely on the basis of history, it would be equally foolish to ignore what lessons history has to offer. In the words of the ancient Chinese strategist, Sun-tzu: *Having heard what can be gained from my assessments, shape a strategic advantage* (shih) *from them to strengthen our position. By "strategic advantage" I mean making the most of favourable conditions and tilt the scales in our favour.*

China's post-Mao approach to territorial claims is, in effect, a subset of its general strategic approach under a calculative strategy. China has pursued a generalised good-neighbour policy that has focused on strengthening its existing ties in Northeast and Southeast Asia; mending ties wherever possible in South and West Asia, and exploring new relationships in Central Asia. This omni-directional approach toward developing good regional relations is a concrete example of the pragmatic-calculative strategy in operation.

China has unsettled territorial disputes with many important states on its periphery (e.g., Russia, Japan, Vietnam, and India.) Most of these disputes derive from the colonial era. New boundaries were drawn in accordance with the then prevailing local balances of power as opposed to historic, ethnic, social factors. As a result, China often lost marginal portions of border or periphery territory (e.g., the British annexation of the northern tip of Burma in 1886). It is impossible to determine the actual extent of the territorial loss because Chinese control was not well established; that is, it was often weak, occasionally non-existent, and sometimes merely a function of the suzerain relationships between Chinese rulers and local rulers.

Many disputes remain unsettled because for most of the post-Second World War period China and its Asian competitors were relatively weak and the Cold War enforced a pacification of these disputes. What may be more important than the loss of territory is the perception of the Chinese security establishment that often refers to the much larger deprivation and humiliation suffered by China over the centuries.

China, for the most part, appears to have accepted the borders it inherited in 1949, and to pursue mostly marginal claims as opposed to seeking renewed control over the larger expanses of territory it may have controlled or occupied at one point or another in its history. At the present time, Chinese territorial interests are focused mainly on disputes involving Russia, along the Ussuri River and along the Sino-Russian border west of Mongolia; India, principally Aksai Chin and in the Indian Northeast with respect to the McMahon Line and the status of the Indian state of Arunachal Pradesh; the South China Sea, where China and several Southeast Asian states have claims on the Spratly Islands; Japan, over the Senkakus; and Taiwan. The Taiwan issue is probably the most complex dispute to resolve in that it involves both the political status of the island and the right to rule.

Some points need to be understood regarding Chinese security perceptions:

(a) The peripheral areas will remain highly important for security as they, relative to their own strengths, will no doubt pose challenges to Chinese power.

(b) China today remains incapable of altering the structure or the threat of force without further increases in relative Chinese power.
(c) Renewed contentions with key peripheral states could seriously impede China's prospects for a peaceful regional environment and, by implication, frustrate China's desire for increasing its Comprehensive National Power (CNP).

To secure Chinese interests regarding territorial disputes there has been a two-pronged approach in Beijing's calculative strategy. If the dispute is considered to be minor and marginal to China's larger interests, Beijing has sought to resolve it amicably to pursue its larger goals. An example of a territorial dispute considered to be minor or marginal to China's larger interest is the border issue with Russia where China's overarching interests in improving its political relationship with Moscow and securing access to Russian military technology has resulted in quick, hopefully permanent, solutions to the Ussuri River dispute. The border disputes with Kazakhstan and Kyrgystan are additional examples of this approach where Beijing moved quickly to resolve amicably its border issues, given Chinese interests both in preventing external support to the separatist movements in Chinese Central Asia and in ensuring access to the energy reserves of the trans-Caucasus. If the dispute is significant but cannot be resolved rapidly to China's advantage by peaceful means, Beijing has advocated an indefinite postponement of the basic issue. China has adopted this tactic in the case of the territorial disputes with India, Japan, and several of the ASEAN states. Using constrained maximisation, Beijing has successfully avoided conceding any Chinese claims and has simultaneously prevented the dispute from destabilising the peaceful environment that China needs to successfully complete its internal transformation.

The strategic advantages to this approach are that it creates a favourable world opinion in that China is viewed as a conciliatory state seeking to resolve all outstanding disputes peacefully; it gives China a strategic pause in that it affords the PRC a relatively peaceful environment to gain economic strength and to restructure and modernise its armed forces at a time when the PLA is being modernised; it prevents balancing coalitions such as the US and Japan from arising against China in the event Beijing pursued more coercive strategies; and lastly, it is flexible. Although it is not possible to predict whether future Chinese leadership operating from a strong state position would conclude that the benefits of usurping control or more coercive bargaining would exceed the cost, it does allow the Chinese leadership to strategically position itself to resolve these disputes at a time of its choosing or when it has the strategic advantage.

It is reasonable, therefore, to add some grounding to the argument that the Vietnamese invasion of Cambodia was the major cause for war between the PRC and the Socialist Republic of Vietnam (SRV). Vietnam's invasion of Cambodia was as a direct response to incessant and increased provocations on the border by Pol Pot's regime. Beginning on Christmas Day 1978, the battle hardened PAVN quickly uprooted the loosely organised Khmer Rouge, installing its own government in Phnom Penh. However, somewhat ironically, considering Vietnam's recent history, this conflict mutated into an insurgency that continued throughout the 1980's. Members of the PRC were quick to denounce the Vietnamese actions.

However, to attribute the Sino-Vietnamese War in its entirety to the Cambodian issue is fundamentally misguided. The invasion, rather than being a base cause of conflict for these two countries, merely reinforced the tensions and pressures playing upon the fragile Sino-Vietnamese relationship. To put it another way, it is arguable that had the SRV and PRC been on better terms then Beijing would have been much less concerned about a Vietnamese predominance of power on its southern flank. It was precisely because this hitherto ally was now seen as a threat rather than a friend that the Cambodian incursion was seen as a justification for war. Thus it can be argued that whilst the Vietnamese invasion of Cambodia was a major short term cause for the ensuing Sino-Vietnamese War, a more substantial and in-depth analysis of the other structural and underlying deficiencies in the wider Sino-Vietnamese relationship is a prescient prerequisite to gaining the best understanding of their subsequent hostilities.

Foremost amongst the factors affecting the Sino-Vietnamese relationship was the wider schism in the global communist movement between its two great powers of China and the USSR. This Sino-Soviet split—beginning in the early 1960's and increasing in importance throughout that decade—had a massive effect upon communism itself and the wider Cold War. The split was not amicable, and almost led to full-scale war between the two nations. This meant that for emergent Socialist countries, there was now a choice that was not only available but had to be made – to tilt towards either the Soviets or the Chinese for aid and favour.

The Sino-Vietnam war raises classical questions of grand strategy: How can war be avoided? If it cannot, what peace is desired at the end of the war? These questions are to be addressed by politicians. Questions of how to fight—by what means—are the prerogative of the military profession. The Clausewitzian dictum that "*the political object—the original motive for the war—will determine both the military objective to be reached and the amount of effort it requires*", is well explained in the conduct of the campaign. Nevertheless, as Clausewitz also elucidated: "*War is an act of force, and there is no logical limit to the application of that force. Each side...compels its opponent to follow suit; a reciprocal action is started which must lead, in theory, to extremes.*"

In Clausewitz's view, genius is something the good commander-in-chief must possess. This is so because "*war is the realm of uncertainty; three quarters of the factors on which action in war is based are wrapped in a fog of greater or lesser uncertainty.*" And again: "*War is the realm of chance.*" This means that: "*Since all information and assumptions are open to doubt, and with chance at work everywhere, the commander continually finds that things are not as he expected.... During an operation decisions have usually to be made at once: there may be no time to review the situation or even think it through*".

The war was, by definition, the extension of a policy. "It seemed like a good idea at the time" is the epitaph of human actions. However: "*If one has never personally experienced war, one cannot understand in what the difficulties constantly mentioned really consist.... Everything looks simple...once war has actually been seen the difficulties become clear.... Everything in war is very simple, but the simplest thing is difficult.... Friction is the only concept that more or less corresponds to the factors that distinguish real war from war on paper*".

In spite of the fact that both China and Vietnam had claimed a victory over the other, no one had achieved its major objectives. So far as China is concerned, its publicised limited objectives were only partially obtained, viz:

(a) It had not destroyed some of Vietnam's strong divisions.
(b) It was unable to pacify the border area free from armed conflicts.
(c) It had not forced the Vietnamese army to withdraw from Kampuchea; and
(d) It failed to influence the Hanoi government to change its policy toward the Chinese residents in Vietnam.

On the other side of the ledger, China had raised doubts for Hanoi about Soviet willingness to intervene with force against China. Moreover, the PRC had also obtained some support from the ASEAN for its attempt to stop Vietnam's further move in Southeast Asia. Furthermore, it had caused an immediate ill-effect on the Vietnamese economy. Despite Deng Xiaoping's assertion that the PLA could have gone all the way to Hanoi if they wanted, the quick withdrawal was a right decision of Beijing for financial and military reasons.

A study of the Sino-Vietnamese War affords an increased understanding of how the PLA of China and the PAVN conducted a land campaign to achieve their strategic objectives. The limited offensive in 1979 by the PLA fit the Chinese pattern of behaviour set by the Korean War, the Sino-Indian War in 1962, and the Sino-Soviet War of 1969. Each used limited military force to contest threats to Chinese sovereignty and increase regional *Shih*. Specifically, Chinese leadership viewed regional alliances as external vulnerabilities that demanded action.

China conducted operational art by arranging tactical actions to achieve their strategic objectives in the Sino-Vietnamese War. China used tempo, operational reach and simultaneity to achieve their strategic objectives. The hypothesis that, when depth is achieved then Vietnam and China achieve their strategic objectives was not supported by the evidence. Simultaneity was a necessary condition for tempo and operational reach was critical to achieve depth.

A relationship also exists between depth and a limited war approach. Extending operations in space, time and purpose threatens the destruction of the opposing side's military forces and therefore elevates limited war objectives towards total war. The Sino-Vietnamese War provides historical evidence for future operational planners to consider the adverse relationship of depth to limited objectives. Operations in depth can result in catastrophic success that threatens limited objectives by destroying an agressor's military power.

The Sino-Vietnamese War is significant to future military planners in the region because it establishes a pattern of behaviour for Chinese use of force and how the PLA arrange tactical actions to achieve strategic objectives. Regional alliances are a key indicator for the Chinese use of force. The study is significant to military planners in any region because it shows the importance of reframing strategic objectives after operations begin and the relationship of depth to achieve limited objectives. Another area for future study is to examine the modernisation that has occurred in the PLA recently and how this modernisation may result in possible changes in Chinese operational approaches.

Today, Vietnam's leaders say that they believe China to be a good neighbour and value its comprehensive cooperative relationship with the country the most. Historically or geopolitically, however, there is every possibility that Vietnamese fears or unsettled issues as mentioned above will intensify again with the changing of the times. It is anybody's guess as to how this situation will evolve from now on. But one thing is clear: under no circumstances will the Vietnamese yield to Chinese pressure, and they will stand equal to China.

BIBLIOGRAPHY

Books

Boorman, Scott A., *The Protracted Game: A Wei Chi Interpretation of Maoist Revolutionary Strategy* (New York, NY: Oxford University Press, 1969).

Chen, King C., *China's War with Vietnam, 1979: Issues, Decisions, and Implications* (Stanford, California: Hoover Institution Press, Stanford University, 1987).

Christman, Ron, "How Beijing Evaluates Military Campaigns: An Initial Assessment," *The*

Lessons of History: The Chinese People's Liberation Army at 75. Edited by Laurie Burkitt, Andrew Scobell, and Larry M. Wortzell (Carlisle, PA: Strategic Studies Institute, 2003).

Clausewitz, Carl von, *On War*. Translated by Michael Howard, Peter Paret, and Bernard Brodie. (Princeton, NJ: Princeton University Press, 1984).

Chang, Pao-min, *The Washington Papers: The Sino-Vietnamese Territorial Dispute* (New York: Praeger Publishers, 1986).

Corr, Gerard H., *The Chinese Red Army: Campaigns and Politics Since 1949* (New York: Schocken Books, 1974).

Duiker, William J., *China and Vietnam: The Roots of Conflict* (Berkeley: Institute of East Asian Studies, University of California, 1986).

Elleman, Bruce A., *Modern Chinese Warfare, 1795-1989* (London: Routledge, 2001).

George, Alexander L., *The Chinese Communist Army in Action* (New York: Columbia University Press, 1967).

Graff David A. and Higham Robin (eds.), *A Military History of China* (Boulder: Westview Press, 2002).

Hood, Steven J., *Dragons Entangled: Indochina and the China-Vietnam War* (Armonk, N.Y.: M.E. Sharpe, 1992).

Joffe, Ellis, *The Chinese Army After Mao (*Cambridge: Harvard University Press, 1987).

Karnow, Stanley, *Vietnam: A History* (New York: Penguin, 1984).

Kissinger, Henry, *On China*. Reprint Ed. (New York: Penguin Books, 2012).

Lai, David. *Learning from the Stones: A Go Approach to Mastering China's Strategic Concept, Shi*. (Carlisle, PA: Army War College, Strategic Studies Institute, 2004).

Lawson, Eugene K., *The Sino-Vietnamese Conflict* (New York: Praeger, 1964)

Li, Jijun, "Notes on Military Theory and Military Strategy," ed. Michael Pillsbury, *Chinese Views on Future Warfare* (Washington, DC: National Defence University Press, 1997).

Mott, William H., and Jae Chang Kim, *The Philosophy of Chinese Military Culture: Shih Vs. Li* (New York, N.Y.: Palgrave Macmillan, 2006).

Nguyen-Vo, Thu-Huong, *Khmer-Viet Relations and the Third Indochina Conflict* (Jefferson, N.C.: McFarland, 1992.

O'Dowd, Edward C., *Chinese Military Strategy in the Third Indochina War: The Last Maoist War* (London: Routledge, 2007).

Peng Guangqian and Yao Youzhi, (eds.) *The Science of Military Strategy*, English version (China: Military Science Publishing House, Academy of Military Science of the Chinese People's Liberation Army, 2005).

Qiao, Liang and Wang Xiangsui, *Unrestricted Warfare* (Washington, DC: Foreign Broadcast Information Service, 2000).

Ray, Hemen, *China's Vietnam War* (New Delhi: Radiant Publishers, 1983).

Ross, Robert S., *The Indochina Tangle: China's Vietnam Policy 1975-1979* (New York: Columbia University Press, 1988).

Ryan, Mark A., *Chinese Warfighting: the PLA experience since 1949* (Armonk, NY: M.E. Sharpe, 2003).

Scobell, Andrew, *China and Strategic Culture* (Carlisle, PA: Strategic Studies Institute, U.S. Army War College, 2002).

Segal, George, *Defending China* (London: Oxford University Press, 1985).

Sun Tzu, *The Art of War*. Translated by Samuel B. Griffith (Oxford: Oxford University Press, 1963).

Tse-Tung, Mao, *Selected Military Writings of Mao Tse-Tung* (Peking: Foreign Languages Press, 1972).

Journals

Buszynski, Les, Vietnam Confronts China." *Asian Survey*, Vol. 20 No.8, pp. 838-844.

Duke, M. L. "Military Doctrine in Red China." *Marine Corps Gazette*, February 1967, 18-22.

Jencks, Harlan W., "China's "Punitive" War on Vietnam: A Military Assessment." *Asian Survey* 19, no. 8 (August 1979): 801-15.

McGregor, Charles. The Sino-Vietnamese Relationship and the Soviet Union. *Adelphi Papers 232*. (London: The International Institute for Strategic Studies, 1988).

Pribbenow, Merle L. "A Tale of Five Generals: Vietnam's Invasion of Cambodia." *The Journal of Military History* 70, no. 2 (2006): 459-86.

Zhang, Xiaoming. "China's 1979 War with Vietnam: A Reassessment." *The China Quarterly* 184, No. 1 (December 2005): 851.

Nelson, Charles R. "The Sino-Viet War: Causes, Conduct, and Consequences." *Parameters*, Vol. 9 No.3, September 1979, pp. 23-30.

Petrov, Colonel Yuri. "Ideological Indoctrination of Chinese Servicemen." *Soviet Military Review*, January 1980, pp. 44-47.

Tow, William T., "Chinese Strategic Thought: Evolutions Toward Reality." *Asian Affairs*, March-April 1980, pp. 250-259.

Tretiak, Daniel, "China's Vietnam War and its Consequences" *The China Quarterly*, December 1979, pp. 750-759.

Yuan, Fang, "Can the Chinese Army Win the Next War?" *JPRS Report: China*, JPRS-CAR¬94-024-L. Washington: 5 May 1994.

INDEX